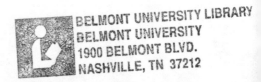

TECHNOS PRESS

FINAL EXAM
A Study of the Perpetual Scrutiny of American Education

Gerald W. Bracey

~

Historical Perspectives on Assessment,
Standards, Outcomes, and Criticism
of U.S. Public Schools

Published by TECHNOS Press
of the Agency for Instructional Technology
©1995

First Edition

ISBN 0-7842-0807-7
Library of Congress Catalog Card Number: 95-61639

02 01 99 98 97 96 95   5 4 3 2 1

Sukanya Dutta-White, Editor

David Strange, Compositor/Text Design

Printed by Metropolitan Printing Service, Inc.,
Bloomington, Indiana, USA

Contents

Prefatory Note

As the reader will soon discover, this book contends that much of the criticism of American public schools over the last century has been misguided and misinformed. To have included a chapter documenting that America's schools are doing a much better job than we have any right or reason to expect would have been easy. Indeed, such documentation constitutes the bulk of the currently five editions of the "Bracey Report on the Condition of Public Education," which appears each October in *Phi Delta Kappan* magazine. Readers seeking proof of my allegations are invited to seek out those reports or my earlier book, *Transforming America's Schools: An ℞ for Getting Past Blame* (1994), available through the American Association of School Administrators in Arlington, Virginia.

I decided to omit a chapter of current data pertaining to the condition of education in public schools because I did not want the analyses of this book to be seen in any way as dependent on, or even linked to, the data reviews in the various Bracey Reports. Those reports, at least the first two, were a quite accidental occurrence in my life. Quite literally, if the *Denver Post* had not in late 1990 reprinted a Richard Cohen column that had appeared two months earlier in the *Washington Post,* "Johnny's Miserable SATs," the Bracey Reports would not exist. Cohen's column piqued me to conduct my own analysis of SAT trends, taking into account the demographic changes over the years in who was taking the SAT. In contrast to the usual reports of large declines, that analysis showed only a small drop in the verbal score, none at all in math. That analysis, published in *Education Week* as "SATs: Miserable or Miraculous," led other people, most notably the Sandia engineers, to send me analyses of other indicators that corroborated what I had to say about SAT trends. Over a period of about three months, I amassed—by accident, I repeat—a mountain of data that *compelled* the conclusion that schools were not in the crisis that so many critics had alleged. This led to the first Bracey Report, published as "Why Can't They Be Like We Were?" the title itself an indication that I had no intention of any sequel but only wished to squash a certain mistaken nostalgia for "the good ol' days." But the appearance of that first article led to other people's sending me still other data, and the data have continued to roll in over the years. As they did, *Kappan* editors gave the report its name and indicated that they wanted them to be annual affairs as long as the data were sufficient to merit them.

As interesting as life has been since the Bracey Reports started appearing, that life is quite separate from this book, which is an intentional effort to look at and understand education reform and criticism seen from a historical perspective and through changes in our notions of assessments, standards, and outcomes.

As with any manuscript, the author owes much to many. Among those are Michael Sullivan, executive director of the Agency for Instructional Technology (AIT), and Carole Novak, manager of AIT's TECHNOS Press, who invited me to become their first Distinguished Fellow and to produce this book—or, at least, *a* book—as part of that fellowship. Thanks are due as well to Milbrey Jones and the staff at the U.S. Department of Education's National Library of Education. Without their assistance and their willingness to put up with my keeping books well past their due dates, my work would have been considerably more difficult. Thanks also to the Professional Library staff of Arlington Public Schools for similar considerations. Grant Wiggins, Archie Lapointe, and Charles Murray provided valuable commentary on part or all of the manuscript, but they are, of course, not responsible for its contentions. Finally, thanks to my wife, Aristea, who, in addition to providing her usual affection, support, and editing, said nothing (well, OK, very little) on the Saturday and Sunday mornings that I left the breakfast table for the computer rather than perusing the Arts and Leisure section of the paper for ways to spend leisure time.

Gerald W. Bracey, Ph.D.
AIT Distinguished Fellow
Alexandria, Virginia
September 1995

Prologue

From "An Aristocracy of Worth and Genius" to "All Children Can Learn": How Did We Get Here, Anyway?

Those who do not remember the past are condemned to relive it.
—George Santayana,
The Life of Reason (1905)

History is bunk.
—Henry Ford (1919)

It is likely that only an American philosopher could have fashioned Santayana's comment, for in no other country as this one do the citizens so often take Henry Ford's statement as gospel. It has been observed that our short national memory is sometimes a great asset. Only a nation with such amnesia could wage all-out war against two nations guilty of the worst kinds of mass atrocities, and then, only a few years later, include them among its strongest allies. This is in stark contrast to the mentality of, say, the former Yugoslavia, where the battle of Kosovo is discussed as if it occurred yesterday (it took place in 1389). This condition of memory produces new catastrophes today and, in all likelihood, tomorrow. On the other hand, our tendency to forget leads us constantly to reinventing wheels, or Sisyphus-like, constantly pushing the stone up the mountain one more time.

In researching this book, I found that in the history of American public education, we have gradually evolved from a focus on the "disciplined mind" attainable only by a few to a focus on observable outcomes, purportedly attainable by all.

In this evolution, there has been a pendular swing between two views of schools. One sees them as the great sorting machine, albeit one that contributes to social mobility. It is a more open, flexible sorting machine than that found historically in other nations. At other times, we have thought that all children can learn whatever we have to teach them, although this position has never been as explicitly stated in the past as it has in recent years.

We are currently in a period that adheres rabidly to the all-children-can-learn view. I have seen the sentence embossed in gold on at least one district's staff notebook covers. The embrace of this position is understandable given the savage inequalities in education in this country, but, like so many fads in education, the stance does not stand on any research base. The supposed pillar of support, mastery learning, cannot bear the weight. Few data, and none from well-designed research, have arrived from programs involving mastery learning's offspring, Outcomes Based Education (OBE). The stance is a philosophical, moral—almost religious—posture taken by a wide spectrum of educators and psychologists who ought to know better. I do not hold such a position and do not believe it has any meaning in terms of the "challenging curriculum" or "high but achievable standards" being bandied about in many quarters these days.

There are several strands of information that lead me to this conclusion. First, in the 1970s, we experienced a minor madness known as the minimum competency testing movement, a fad that invaded 35 of the 50 states. The competencies established by the various states were usually low, sometimes quite low. No one ever referred to them as "challenging." And, yet, some students never attained a passing score, itself often set low, even after four, six, sometimes ten attempts.

Related to this outcome is my second reason: to paraphrase the popular bumper sticker, variance happens. It happens even in Japan, a nation that worships homogeneity and makes every attempt to reduce the variance of many variables, including test scores, to zero. I have heard many times that by high school, 80 percent of the students cannot understand the difficult mathematics they are taught. A 1994 article, "Japanese Education— The Myths and the Realities," suggests that these stories have substance. The article is by Kazuo Ishizaka, a member of the Japanese National Institute of Educational Research, and a former principal and mathematics teacher. Ishizaka declares that in some Japanese high schools, the average on a national mathematics test where the highest score is 100 will be about 96 or 98. In his school it was 5. He wonders why his school was never asked to participate in international studies. (The same paper contains a scandalous revelation that for the 1987 Second International Mathematics Study in which Japan finished first, only schools that scored well above average on a Japanese-made test were selected.)

The schools of "competitor nations" (competition in the global economy has replaced "the red menace" as a scare phrase) are sometimes described as if they are monolithically good, but variance—enormous variance—happens in them. For instance, consider Taiwan, whose eighth graders finished first in math in the Second International Assessment of Educational Progress (IAEP) released in 1992. While the average score in Taiwan bested everyone else, the 95th percentile was *even higher*, relatively speaking, than other high-scoring nations. The 5th percentile, on the other hand, was *much lower* than the 5th percentile of numerous countries with only slightly lower averages. For example, Taiwan's average scaled score of 285 beat third place Hungary's by 8 points (285 versus 277). On the other hand, Taiwan's 95th percentile of 345 was 19 points above Hungary's at 326, but its 5th percentile of 222 was five points *lower* than Hungary's 227. While the distance from the lowest average, Jordan's, to the highest average, Taiwan's, was 39 scale points, the distance from the 5th percentile of Taiwan's distribution to the 95th was 125 scale points (National Center for Education Statistics, 1993). (All countries were scored with the scale used for the National Assessment of Educational Progress [NAEP].)

Does it even make sense, then, to speak of "Taiwanese schools" or "American schools" on the basis of average scores? I think not. Does it make sense, then, to say that in all countries some children will not learn? I think so.

If we were to use an image other than educational, we might more readily see the folly of our position: "All children can run." Obviously, this is not true. Some children have no useful legs nor can they propel a wheelchair in any way that might be considered a proxy for running. The great majority of students can "run," of course, but the difference in running speeds will be enormous. Anyone who thinks back on participation in school athletics will recall that running times varied enormously even among those sufficiently proficient to play on a varsity team. If the "high but achievable standard" was to have all children be able to run a mile, but to wait for the slowest to finish before moving beyond this point, it would be necessary for the faster children to spend a lot of time not running.

This is one of the major objections voiced by some to OBE programs, although the promoters of OBE deny that it is a necessary characteristic of the program. The alternative to holding the faster runners in check for some time is to allow them to keep on running. This, of course, increases their advantage over the slower runners in terms of distance traversed in a given amount of time. Despite the denials of OBE promoters, this happens in both mastery learning and in OBE programs, even in the programs described by OBE's leading sponsor, William Spady, founder of the High Success Network, Inc. Spady refers to "having the faster learners engage in challenging extension and enrichment activities" and "stimulating projects and exercises" while the slower students "master the initial material" (Spady, 1994). Such enrichment activities increase the initial advantage of the faster learners. Spady would prefer continuous progress programs, where each student moves as his or her progress permits, but in such programs the distance between fast learners and slow will be increased yet even more. Such programs would exacerbate the differences between the "cognitive elite" and the rest. In the 1970s, for example, most students passed a minimum competency test at first sitting and were free to move on. For some students, though, the material covered by the minimum competency tests *became* the curriculum.

One could object that our educational programs have never been designed to optimize the learning of all students and that maybe we now know enough to effect such optimization with the result that all children "learn." But when we look at some programs that would appear to enhance, if not optimize, such learning, we find enormous variance still. These results can be seen in data from Reading Recovery and Success For All, two compensatory programs that are probably the most effective in the nation. The programs differ somewhat, but both would be called "intensive," using as they do substantial amounts of one-on-one tutoring. They also seem to be based on sound theoretical principles and to reflect the good sense of practitioners as well. Under the tutelage of these programs, many students do indeed improve their reading scores substantially, a sufficient reason for both programs to enjoy expansion in the nation.

But some children do not improve much and some not at all. This is true even in Reading Recovery, where the criterion for treatment termination is often quite modest. Children are considered to have successfully completed the program when they attain the average reading score of their class. In some urban settings, this average itself is not very high, certainly nowhere near "grade level." In both programs, some students remain hard-core non-readers.

A third reason is that society will not—cannot—permit all children to learn. I outlined some reasons why in a short *Education Week* essay called, "What If Education Broke Out All Over?" (March 28, 1994). I argued there that if everyone learned, society would collapse, literally. I do not know if education so refines the senses or simply makes people allergic to sweat, but educated people will not collect garbage, unclog sewers, scour urinals, make up beds, bus tables, etc.

A current myth holds that the new jobs being created are all high skill, high tech. This is not true. While the implication of the myth is that schools must do more for more people, the Bureau of Labor Statistics' 1991 list of the 10 fastest growing jobs between 1990 and 2005 shows them to require some skills, but not to be necessarily high tech. Even the Hudson Institute's 1988 report *Workforce 2000*, considered by many to be the clarion call for a more highly skilled workforce, found that the to-be-created jobs only required eight more months of education than current jobs. Other estimates put the figure at four months. Either way, meeting these changing job demands poses no severe national challenge. The educational differentials between those entering the workforce and those retiring are sufficiently great to more than overcome the needed extra schooling. People retiring from the workforce in 1995 at age 65 (assuming that their pensions haven't disappeared) would have graduated from high school in 1948—when the chances were about 50-50 that they would have graduated at all. Currently, 83 percent of high school students receive an on-time diploma, another 4 percent return to obtain one, and another 4 percent attain a general equivalency diploma (GED).

In addition, the fastest growing jobs account for very few jobs, the new high-tech jobs for even fewer. On the other hand, the single top job in terms of numbers, retail sales, accounts for one-third more jobs than the top 10 fastest growing jobs combined, 4.5 million versus 3.2 million. Even U.S. Secretary of Labor Robert Reich, who has written glib pieces with glib titles such as "Workers of the World Get Smart," has admitted that no nation has solved the problem of creating both *more* jobs and *good* jobs. There is also mounting evidence that the good jobs are declining in number. In 1992, for instance, manufacturing lost 255,000 jobs. The restaurant industry alone added 249,000.

Not many were for executive chefs. Each month the Labor Department issues a cheerful announcement of how many jobs the Clinton recovery has generated but then has to note that the high-paying manufacturing sector is lopping off about 100,000 jobs a month.

Indeed, the call to "make work smart," perhaps the economic equivalent of "all children can learn," seems to have led us in a wrong direction. The arguments for making work smart were first described in the Center on Education and The Economy's 1990 treatise, *America's Choice: High Skills or Low Wages!* A 1992 follow-up book, *Thinking for a Living*, by the Center's director, Marc Tucker, and former Secretary of Labor Ray Marshall, expanded the notion of making work smart and at the same time expanded their claims for the wonders it would accomplish. Making work smart was a recipe not only for high wages but also for full employment. Look at Europe, they said.

Yes, look at Europe—and find 12 percent unemployment, 20 percent in some quarters, and 50 percent among some immigrant groups. Find Germany, already with the shortest work weeks and longest vacations in Europe, thinking about trimming the work week further. Find France tinkering with the notions of job sharing and cutting the minimum wage to get more people employed. An appropriate book to reflect the situation both here and abroad might be titled *America's Choice: High Skills and Low Wages.*[1]

In his 1992 book, *The Culture of Contentment*, Harvard economist John Kenneth Galbraith gave a name to the children who do not learn, to the low-paid, unskilled workers: "the functional underclass." According to Galbraith, we gloss over the dreary duties of the underclass by lumping all activities under the word "work" and then glorifying the word. But much work is intrinsically meaningless, repetitive, boring, even dangerous. Galbraith declares that the word "work" is used to cloak the fact that some people's jobs require activity that is "dreary, painful or socially demeaning and for others is enjoyable, socially reputable and economically rewarding."

The "working poor" will always be with us. They are not a social problem to eliminate, says Galbraith. "The poor in our economy are needed to do the work that the more fortunate do not do and would find distasteful, even distressing. And a continuing supply and resupply of such workers is always needed," since the children of such workers and the workers themselves seek to escape such demeaning conditions.

In theory, such as that promulgated by behaviorist B.F. Skinner, you could entice the cognitive elite to sweep streets by paying them more. In practice, it has never worked out that way. When a few countries have actually gotten to a point where too many people have learned, the solution to the shortage of dirty-work workers has been to import undereducated workers or workers from underdeveloped nations. Whether or not some groups of Americans have come to form a permanent underclass is a matter of some debate, but as a nation of immigrants, we are relieved of the solutions forced on other nations. Although our solution is functionally equivalent, the imported workers here do have the option of becoming citizens, something not afforded those—or their children—in most other countries.

But we refuse to see the sight that Galbraith insists that we look on:

> What is not accepted, and indeed is little mentioned [by the comfortable classes], is that the underclass is integrally a part of a larger economic process and, more importantly, that it serves the living standard and the comfort of the more favored community....The economically fortunate, not excluding those who speak with greatest regret of the existence of this class, are heavily dependent on its presence. (p. 31)

So it is that while we say everyone can learn and we want to educate everyone, the unyielding facts are that they *cannot* and *we do not.* This is not merely an unkind blow to our egalitarian impulse. Saying everyone can learn sets up educators for a great fall. By telling everyone that all children can learn, we set the stage for the next great round of educational failure when it is revealed that not everyone *has* learned, in spite of our sincere beliefs and improved practices. At this moment, articles being written about the schools include comments like the following from the April 17, 1995, issue of *Business Week*, whose cover asks, "Will Schools Ever Get Better?" The opening paragraph recounts in brief the usual litany of complaints, but in stronger terms than usual:

> Americans are fed up with their public schools. Businesses complain that too many job applicants can't read, write, or do simple arithmetic. Parents fear that the schools have become violent cesspools where gangs run amok and that teachers are more concerned with their

pensions than their classrooms. Economists fret that a weak school system is hurting the ability of the [United States] to compete in the global economy. And despite modest improvements in test scores, U.S. students rank far behind most of their international peers in science and math. (Mandel, p. 64)

None of these statements is true, but one can imagine what *Business Week* might write after another decade of "ineffectual" reform. Or even reform that showed improvement but not enough. After all, in 10 years it will be almost a quarter century since the appearance of *A Nation At Risk.*

Of course, one response to the above is that we will have a decade of *effectual* reform. I doubt it. Or rather, in spite of what I view as a century of almost continuous progress in public schooling, I doubt that we can effect the kinds of reforms that would satisfy critics. Indeed, I argue in Chapter Four that the well-intentioned standards movement itself will *increase* the disparities among the cognitive haves and have-nots.

Many other educational trends will produce, are producing, similar effects. For instance, the proportion of affluent students in preschool is much higher than the proportion of poor children in preschool. And the programs offered the rich tend to be developmental, even academic, while the poor often obtain only custodial care. This condition moves us farther from, not closer to, the first National Education Goal, that all children arrive at school ready to learn. At the same time, new technologies are increasingly being used for learning activities. And such machines are to be found much more commonly in the homes of the affluent.

Our notion that we constitute an egalitarian nation received a mighty shock in April 1995, when the *New York Times* reported on a new study showing that we are the most stratified nation in the western world. In England, a nation we often associate with a rigid class structure and centralized control of wealth, the top 1 percent of households control 19 percent of the wealth. In the United States, the top 1 percent controls 40 percent, up from 20 percent in 1980. The top 20 percent of U.S. households control 80 percent of the wealth. The bottom 20 percent of households earn only 5 percent of the income in this nation.

None of this is to say that many children could not learn much more than they presently do; they could. But if we predicate reform on unrealistic assumptions, not only do we set the stage for inevitable failure, we are prevented from seeing the present conditions as they really are.

The unremitting criticism of American public schools—abundant since their inception, but overwhelming since the end of World War II—has led to such misperceptions. For instance, in the Second IAEP of 1992, Taiwanese and Korean 13-year-olds had the highest scores in math. However, it was determined that Asian students in American schools outscored both countries. Hungary finished third among nations, and white students in U.S. schools tied Hungary (NCES, 1993). Thus a large majority of American students—the two groups constitute about 70 percent of the current K–12 population—perform at world-class levels, at least, if we define "world class" by the highest scoring nations.

In this same study, however, while Mississippi and Jordan tied for last place, black, Hispanic, and disadvantaged urban students all scored below them.[2] It is thus the case that many American students are "world class"—even in math, where we are such putative dolts—but some aren't even Third World. We are in a better state than thought overall, but, given the concentration of wealth noted above, are we likely to find that it is distributed to assist school systems which need it? Only if still more school finance systems are declared by state supreme courts to be unconstitutional or if more states show the progressive tendency of Minnesota and Michigan and look to voluntarily move toward shifting school funding away from the inevitable inequitable property tax base.

This book paints a picture of a system that has painted itself into a corner. There is a potential way out, but it involves taking a path that we have not been good at following in the past. John Gardner asked if we can be excellent and equal, too (1961). The answer is clearly "no," if by "equal" is meant "the same." Different students will emerge from school knowing different things as well as different amounts of the same things. But, we could ask, can we be *equitable* and excellent at the same time? If we look to another Gardner, Howard, we find a theory of multiple intelligences that *demands* that people be different (1983). Historically, we have not been good at saying that people are different but not unequal. To say that two outcomes are different has, historically, implied that one of them is inferior. About 60 percent of U.S. high school graduates go on to college although (historically) no more than 25 to 30 percent of them obtain college degrees. Thus, it would seem, almost half of our students need something other than a college preparatory curriculum. But when people propose, say, an apprenticeship system patterned after that found in Germany, many people recoil, knowing that such a system puts limits on the future (in fact, more and more German students are recoiling for the same reason).

At the same time as people recoil from differential outcomes, they shun any attempt at perceived standardization. One widespread criticism of OBE is that it denies individuality and tries to mass-produce students. Of course, acknowledging that the criticism is widespread does not necessarily imply that it is true. The confusion between standards and standardization is rife in American education, as it is in American life overall.

Getting out of the corner will not be easy, but I hold in this book that focusing on the outcomes of education requires us to try. As long as equal education is defined in terms of inputs and processes, inequalities of outcomes are tolerable. When the focus is on outcomes, inequalities become, at best, painful to see.

I hope that this book will provide a historical perspective from which policy and programs may be developed. It is my fervent belief that Santayana is right. Thus, in bringing some sense of history to the current enterprises, I hope to provide a useful context for future reform.

In addition, I hope these histories will debunk once and for all the notion existing in some quarters that there was once a Golden Age of American education from which state of grace we have fallen and must strive to return. Truly, this, to cite Mr. Ford, is "bunk." Chapter One provides a selective history of education in this nation, focusing on the always abundant criticism of public schools and the attempts to reform them, especially at the attempts made after the Committee of Ten's efforts a century ago.[3]

We are currently embroiled in many discussions about "authentic assessment," standards, and outcomes. These, too, are discussions lacking much in the way of historical setting. To understand what schools are and have been about, though, it seems to me that we should understand the history of outcomes and standards, and of how those outcomes and standards would be assessed. These histories all show evolving meanings of outcomes, standards, and assessments and constitute the other three major chapters of the book.

Some who have read these histories have commented that "we have played this song before," and indeed we have. This leaves the history of education with a sense of being unplanned and, in many ways, it has been. On a more narrow scale, Robert Slavin of Johns Hopkins University has observed that educational innovations arrive amidst much hoopla and no supporting data. They then exit as the data, usually disappointing in comparison to the claims, arrive. One might hope that, by developing a sense of what has and has not been thought about schools throughout our history, we might embark on a more planned journey into the future.

In addition, there are many in education now who have not lived through the modern era of reform, which I date from the end of World War II. Since then, schools have been seen as chronic failures, albeit for very different reasons across the decades. One sees that society has placed every important social problem on the schoolhouse doorstep and then reacted in anger and horror when the school's inhabitants have failed to, by themselves, solve the problem, whatever it might be. Again, for those who have not experienced the events of the last 50 years firsthand, I hope that this book will provide a useful context.

An examination of these histories might—but only might— provide a more realistic sense of both what schools have done and what schools can do. It is clear that one reason schools have failed is that they have not lived up to society's expectations, but my search through the history of schooling in this nation convinces me both that those expectations have often been unrealistic and that schools have come closer to meeting them than has been realized. We now all mouth the importance of high expectations for learning, but as we do so, we should recall from clinical practice the terrible anxieties and neuroses that can be generated by the imposition of unrealistic, perfectionistic expectations.

Why do we have such expectations of schools? Because they have emerged as our most important social institution aside from those that defend the land. All the more so at present. In addition to the schools' being the focal point for social problems, the church and the family are in decline. Many consider politics a cesspool of corruption and self-interest. Every day brings some astonishing new tale of fraud and malfeasance in business. Schools are refuges of integrity and fair play. Many critics tell schools to concentrate on academic matters and leave social problems to other institutions, but they fail to take into account the state of those other institutions and how that state affects the schools.

In addition to these reasons for assaults on schools, public schools are targets simply because they are public. And they are public in ways that no other institution in this nation is public. Businesses might have to answer to stockholders according to the bottom line (although this is largely myth; stockholders exercise very little power), but the information of how business and industry conduct their business is proprietary. Michael Moore's movie, *Roger and Me*, takes some liberties with historical accuracy, but still vividly shows the protection from inconvenient encounters that chief executive officers of large corporations enjoy. For months, Moore attempts to get an audience with Roger Smith, then president of General Motors, to ask him to explain how GM could inflict so much economic devastation on Moore's hometown of Flint, Michigan. He never succeeds. Some school principals can be forgiven for feeling pangs of envy at Smith's fortress-like security, security that prevails in spite of, as others have shown elsewhere, Smith's monumental incompetence.

I also hope that the histories presented here will provide convincing evidence that some of the reform efforts of the past were misguided, either because schools were *not* failing or because the reforms were based on unsound premises. We are currently in the throes of major reform activities aimed at certain goals and using certain standards. Are these also based on unsound premises? It is often said today in defense of goals and standards that if you don't know where you want to go, any road will take you there. The conclusion is that we need the goals and standards to show us the way. In the chapter on standards, I conclude that standards will take us *away* from where we want to be.

Finally, along with an acceptance of Santayana's maxim, I agree with a generalization taken from Jean Piaget. In studying epistemology, the nature of knowledge, Piaget concluded that to understand how knowledge manifests itself in adults, he had to learn how it developed in children. I believe that while knowing where you want to go is important in knowing how to get there, it is also crucial in human endeavors to know how you got where you are. Wherever you are on a map, you can set out for any other point. This is not true of human and social development, however. Learning some things permits the learning of others but forecloses the learning of still others. In the human trajectory, where you can go is to some extent constrained by where you've been and how you got where you are. I hope this book will help provide an account of the journey of public education in America.

This material is presented in four interlocking, overlapping chapters whose perspectives and emphases differ. The effect might be similar to that of Lawrence Durrell's tetrology, The Alexandria Quartet, *which depicts in each book the same events as experienced by four different people. No pretension is made that this book attains anything close to the artistry of Durrell's opus.*

—Gerald W. Bracey

Chapter One

As History Repeats Itself:
Goals, Critiques, and Social Farces

*Perhaps the greatest idea that America has given
the world is the idea of education for all. The
world is entitled to know whether this idea means
that everybody can be educated, or only that
everybody must go to school.*
—Robert M. Hutchins, *The Conflict in
Education in a Democratic Society* (1953)

*Only if the process succeeds and learning occurs
will we say that education happened.*
—Chester E. Finn, Jr., "The Biggest Reform of All," *Phi Delta Kappan* (April 1990)

Were Thomas Jefferson able to return to America
today, many aspects of contemporary society
would, doubtless, fascinate him. Surely this quintessential American tinkerer would be intrigued
by our gadget-oriented society. Given his taste for fine wine, he
would take delight in the growth of the American viticulture,
though, with his predilection, common in his day, for the sweet
white wines of Sauternes, it would take some time for his palate
to adjust to the dry chardonnays and the reds so in fashion now.
Given Jefferson's love of dialogue, one can imagine him spending long hours exchanging e-mail on the Internet.

America's education system, though, would confound Thomas Jefferson. On the one hand, he would be amazed; on the
other, appalled.

The level to which we educate so many people would stun
Jefferson. Many interpret his famous Declaration of Independence statement, "All men are created equal" as a moral stance,
a great moral insight. Certainly he had no leanings in that direction when it came to mental abilities, which he referred to as a

person's "genius." Jefferson viewed education as a sorting machine, the means by which to establish an "aristocracy of worth and genius"—as distinct from the aristocracy of birth and blood found in Europe.

He outlined his hopes for education in his 1782 "Plan for the More General Diffusion of Knowledge." He proposed dividing Virginia into five- or six-square-mile areas called "hundreds" and building a primary school in each within walking distance of all students. All citizens could send their children, boys and girls, to this school for three years. The costs for those unable to afford tuition would be borne by the state. Students could continue longer than three years at their families' expense. A "visitor" would be assigned oversight of a number of schools and each year would choose "the boy of best genius in the schools whose parents are too poor to give them further education, and to send him forward to one of the grammar schools, of which twenty are proposed...." Nothing in the treatise provided for the education of girls beyond the initial primary school; nothing provided for any schooling for slaves.

The selected students were to receive a one- or two-year trial period at the grammar school. The best of the lot would be educated for another six years and the rest discontinued. At the end of six years, half of those remaining would progress to three years of study at the College of William and Mary in Williamsburg.

In describing the impact of the first round of seining, Jefferson noted that "by this means twenty of the best geniuses will be raked from the rubbish annually...." *Raked from the rubbish?* Wow! Elsewhere in this section, Jefferson discusses the acquisition of skills in a fashion that imputes substantial importance to the nurture of human beings, but, clearly, for him, smart was something you are, not something you get. Schools are to function as a grand sorting machine. Confronted with our contemporary mantra, "all children can learn"—taken in most places these days to mean that all can learn a challenging curriculum at least to the level of the high school diploma—Jefferson would likely just shake his head, as does the man in the street.

THE GOALS AND PURPOSES OF EDUCATION

The tension between school as sorting machine and school as the great equalizer has pervaded American education with the pendulum swinging first toward one side, then the other. Currently, arguments rage over funding, ability grouping, and other methods for giving or not giving some groups advantages over others. At the same time, we have witnessed a steady growth in high school graduation rates from 3 percent in 1870 to 81 percent in 1991 to 83 percent currently (87 percent if those completing a general equivalency diploma, or GED, are included). More than 60 percent of these graduates attend some form of college although only half of those students obtain a bachelor's degree or better. This college "drop-out rate" is now seen by many as a source of concern, though previously it was viewed with pride by many institutions of higher education as evidence of high standards. The tension remains, though, because clearly not everyone is getting a good program of studies. The essential conflict of goals was summed up in the title of John W. Gardner's 1961 book: *Excellence: Can We Be Equal and Excellent Too?* Unfortunately, Gardner did not really answer the question in his book and the quasi-answers he did give now look naive and unduly optimistic. Perhaps the question should be rephrased: Can we have *equity* and excellence, too? We tend in this country to see "equal" in terms of standardization and sameness. In such a new phrasing outcomes could be different for different students—reflecting, say, Howard Gardner's notions of multiple intelligences (1983)—but still be equitable in terms of allowing the students to pursue higher education or obtain a good job.

Jefferson would likely show concern over such current trends as turning kindergartens into mini-first grades and at the general tendency towards accelerating everything. In the same treatise cited he wrote:

> There is a certain period of life, say from eight to fifteen or sixteen years of age, when the mind like the body is not yet firm enough for laborious and close operations. If applied to such, it falls an early victim of premature exertion; exhibiting, indeed at first, in these young and tender subjects, the flattering appearance of their being men while they are yet children, but ending in reducing them to be children when they should be men. (in Newman, 1978, p. 10)

Jefferson would be appalled at how the study of Latin and Greek has declined, but even more at the discussions of standards, achievements, and outcomes, and especially at the dreary conversation about how education is necessary to get a good job and to promote America's competitiveness among nations (there is some truth in the first contention, none in the second).

Jefferson did not see education as instrumental to vocation, nor did the rest of America until the second decade of this century. That was for Europe and her rigidly class-determined system. Let Europe educate her citizens for specific occupations that would maintain her ingrained stratifications of class. The primary purpose of education in America was to permit us to protect ourselves from our government. Indeed, Jefferson wrote:

> In every government on earth is some trace of human weakness, some germ of corruption and degeneracy which cunning will discover, and wickedness insensibly open, cultivate, and improve. Every government degenerates when trusted to the rulers over the people alone. The people themselves therefore are its only safe depositories. And to rend even them safe, their minds must be improved to a certain degree. (in Newman, 1978, p. 11)

Alleging that the government of England was corrupt because only one man in 10 had the right to vote, Jefferson proposed that "the influence over government must be shared among all the people." One (white) man, one vote. And, so that that "influence over government" be able to overcome the tendency toward degeneration and corruption, all must receive at least some education. Jefferson asserted that "if a nation expects to be ignorant and free in a state of civilization, it expects what never was and never will be." Jefferson would no doubt shudder at our terrible voter participation rates and the influence of special interests and political action committees.

Jefferson's view was not idiosyncratic. While his contemporary and fellow signer of the Declaration of Independence, Benjamin Rush, declared in 1798 that "manufactures of all kinds owe their perfection chiefly to learning," he did not mean that young men should study manufacturing. "The nations of Europe advance in manufactures, knowledge, and commerce, only in proportion as they cultivate the arts and sciences," Rush wrote. For him the only vocational education was a liberal arts education.

Jefferson's practical peer, Benjamin Franklin, had a more vocationally oriented view of education, but even he rejected the European approach to specific job training. For one thing, America suffered from a chronic labor shortage. This meant, in part, that Americans needed to learn many things. Looking to the future, one had difficulty in predicting what skills students would find essential. Franklin's proposal for the Philadelphia academy was for a school from which young men "will come out...fitted for learning any Business, calling or Profession." Today, of course, with job security rapidly eroding and much job-related knowledge becoming obsolete in a few years, some claim that the most important skill a person can learn in school is "flexibility." *Plus ça change.*

In two centuries, the perceived function of schools was transformed from protecting democracy from corrupting influences to securing individual and national economic well being. A complete history of this degenerative transformation is beyond the scope and purpose of this book. Let us note, though, that whenever faced with a large national problem, the United States has always turned to its schools. The rise of the cities after the Civil War led to compulsory education (prior to that time, only Massachusetts required attendance). Many businessmen opposed compulsory education because it would cost them their cheap child labor, but half of the motivation for compulsory education was precisely to protect children. The other half was to protect the nation from lawlessness. The rise of the cities, in part due to immigration, led to a rise in poverty and crime. The young hoodlums that became a part of the city scene in the 1870s should not be on the streets, argued social critics. In New York City, reformer Jacob Riis tried to mobilize people for a "battle against the slums" and contended that it "would be fought out, in, and around the public school."

Indeed, about this same time, the citizens were coming to see that in addition to imparting Jeffersonian civic virtues, the school was the means to achieve wealth. From the beginning, America was viewed as the land of opportunity, but the question remained: "How does one find that opportunity?" Some industrialization mythology saw the opportunity lying in personal characteristics. The myth of success held that anyone could get rich. But if anyone can get rich, being smart is not a requirement.[1] Thus, this industrialization myth held that the route to wealth was through certain personal characteristics. As educational historian Henry J. Perkinson put it:

> In addition to the magic virtues of industry, thrift, and perseverance, a young man needed to develop those qualities which most impressed employers. The lad who came to work on time always won rewards. Punctuality

counted, as did loyalty and obedience. The loyal and obedient employee caught the attention of the employer when he placed the employer's interest above his own. (Perkinson, 1991, p. 111)

Recent surveys, such as those reported in *America's Choice: High Skills or Low Wages!* (1990), indicate that employers currently are not so much concerned with a lack of skills in their employees, but with the lack of precisely these characteristics. In a 1993 article, Alan Wurtzel, the Chairman of the Board at Circuit City, a discount retail electronics house, put it this way:

> Circuit City is a large national company that seldom hires people right out of high school….in hiring new employees for our stores, warehouses, and offices, Circuit City is looking for people who are able to provide very high levels of customer service, who are honest, and who have a positive, enthusiastic, achievement-oriented work ethic. (p. A25)

Wurtzel did not mention that for all these qualities which he felt were largely lacking in high school graduates, Circuit City offered a starting wage of $4.25 an hour to its warehouse staff while the sales staff worked strictly on commission.

In the late 1800s, as secondary education began an enormous expansion, others saw through the kind of myth that the Wurtzels of the day were perpetuating. Although the fable was cultivated through McGuffey's readers and Horatio Alger's novels, most people realized that, *Ragged Dick* and *Mark, The Matchboy* notwithstanding, they would probably not grow wealthy merely by showing up to work on time and kowtowing to the boss.

Instead, a new notion began to take shape: namely, that the route to well-being passed largely through the schools. This idea had been popularized a great deal before the Civil War by Horace Mann who saw the school as "the great equalizer of the conditions of men…the balance wheel of the social machinery. Just see wherever we peer into the first tiny springs of the national life, how this true panacea for all the ills of the body politic bubbles forth—education, education, education" (quoted in Perkinson, 1991, p. 122).

Mann's theme was extended by, of all people, Andrew Carnegie. "The free common school system of the land is, probably after all, the greatest single power in the unifying powers which produce the American race. In these common schools, the children of Irishmen, Germans, Italians, Spaniards, and Swedes, side by side with native Americans…are transmuted into republican Americans and are made one in love for a country which provides equal rights and privileges for all her children." By "native Americans" Carnegie did not mean those who previously were called American Indians. Nor did he have anything to say about African Americans as part of America's "children."

To make the schools the source of economic opportunity, though, created another problem: there weren't many schools, nor were they articulated in any systematic fashion, nor did they offer anything remotely resembling a common curriculum. Historically, not only had schooling not been seen in terms of vocation, the universities had become rabidly anti-vocationalist after the publication of the "Yale Report" in 1828. According to David Coit Gilman, the first president of The Johns Hopkins University, the university's functions were "the acquisition, conservation, refinement, and distribution of knowledge." No job training, thank you. This view would hold sway for almost a century.

In 1890, Harvard president Charles W. Eliot spoke at the convention of the National Education Association (NEA) and complained that no state in the Union had a system of secondary education. Eliot noted that of 352 students admitted to Harvard in 1889, only 97 came from public high schools. Since most of these students came from Massachusetts and since Massachusetts was esteemed to have the best system in the nation, the low numbers reflected the disarray in secondary education in the nation. Indeed, it required decisions from the Supreme Court of Michigan in 1874 and of Illinois in 1878 and 1880 to establish the rights of those states (and, by implication, others) to levy taxes to support "the elements of a classical education" for high school students.

At the time Eliot spoke, the secondary school was almost as elite a gathering place as the university. In 1890, the United States was a nation of almost 63 million people. Of these, only 203,000 of age-eligible children were enrolled in secondary school while another 3 million were not. The colleges and universities contained 157,000 (Perkinson, 1969, p. 10). Throughout the 1890s the *School Review*, secondary education's principal journal, would be filled with articles asking questions such as these, which appeared in the 1897 volume: "What Should the Modern Secondary School Aim To Accomplish?"; "What Studies Should Predominate in Secondary School?"; "What Ought the Study of

Mathematics Contribute to the Education of the High School Pupil?"; "What is the Consensus of Opinion as to the Place of Science in the Preparatory Schools?"; "Can American History Be Put into All Courses in the High School?"

In 1892, Eliot stood before the NEA again, declaring that while the number of high schools was rapidly multiplying, nothing articulated these schools with the colleges. He disdained a single national curriculum and proposed the elective system he had recently set in place at Harvard. But he did call for one type of uniformity: Although all high schools should have more courses than any one student could take, the same course should be taught with the same curriculum and in the same way in all schools.

At this convention, the NEA decided to address the problem of the school-to-college transition with the Committee on Secondary School Studies, more commonly known as the Committee of Ten, the first of many "blue ribbon" committees to reform education. With Eliot serving as president, the Committee of Ten proposed that college entrance requirements be flexible, admitting students who had taken a program of studies in some combination of nine basic subjects. This recommendation led to the establishment of the Carnegie Unit for measuring attainment. The committee then used the prize of college admission as leverage to get high schools to *restrict* their offerings to these same nine subjects. At Eliot's suggestion, the College Entrance Examination Board (CEEB) was created to determine what courses their institutions would require for admission. In a further effort to bring some curricular commonality to the high schools, the board elected to administer standard examinations in these subjects, and chose at first to grade them as well. Universities objected to such grading by an outside source, though, and the process was soon stopped. The tests continued, however, and after World War I, the board became interested in using them to predict who would become successful in college, a venture that in 1926 produced the first assessment bearing the name, the Scholastic Aptitude Test (SAT).

Although different students could take different courses and still be admitted to the same college, the committee thought the same course should be taught in a uniform manner:

> every subject which is taught at all in a secondary school should be taught in the same way and to the same extent to every pupil so long as he pursues it, no matter

what the probable destination of the students may be, or at what point his education is to cease. (*Report of the Commission of Education, 1892–93,* p. 1423)

This recommendation came in spite of the committee's comment on the goal and purpose of secondary schools:

The secondary schools of the United States, taken as a whole, do not exist for the purpose of preparing boys and girls for colleges. Only an insignificant percentage of the graduates of these schools go to colleges or scientific schools. Their main function is to prepare for the duties of life that small proportion of all the children in the country—a proportion small in number, but very important to the welfare of the nation—who show themselves able to profit by an education prolonged to the eighteenth year.... (p. 1444)

This is an important position, if a curious one. The committee argued that even if not all children *could* learn—and it was assumed that most could not make it through high school—they should still be given an opportunity to learn the same curriculum as the small proportion that would obtain a diploma and the still smaller proportion that would go on to college. In today's terminology, the committee proposed equality of inputs while assuming inequality of outputs. Twenty-five years later, this policy would be attacked by the test developers as cruel.

As yet, however, the assessment community did not exist, and there was no psychology of individual differences. Dominant at the time was a "faculty psychology" holding that through the study of certain fields—mathematics, Latin, and Greek—one obtained a "disciplined mind." The Committee's report appeared fully 10 years before the French Ministry of Education asked clinical psychologist Alfred Binet to develop a means of identifying children who could not benefit from a normal education, a project that would lead Binet to invent the intelligence test. It was also five years before James Mayer Rice would issue his reports on spelling skills in which he would make the then-radical (and rejected) suggestion that education be judged in the concrete terms of outcomes rather than in terms of developing students' minds.

The Committee of Ten's report and the activities of the College Board served to expand secondary education and articulate high schools and colleges, but since most people would not go to college, it left the high school disjointed from the rest of the post-school world. Shortly into the 20th century, there arose a call for "commercial" high schools. These grew rapidly and trained many people for lower-level white-collar work. A decade later, there was also growth in "manual" high schools to provide blue-collar laborers.

Reading the Committee of Ten's report, one comes away wondering what people actually did all day in high schools. The committee contended that children entering secondary schools knew nothing of mathematics except arithmetic. They had no knowledge of algebra nor of the shapes of geometric forms. Students entering high school, said the report, had minds that were "blank" about the fields of botany, zoology, chemistry, and physics. The lack of experience with science, even in high school, imposed a terrible burden on university professors who had to teach not only these subjects but also all "new habits of observing, reflecting, and recording—habits which they should have acquired in early childhood." History teachers, said the committee, find that history "has never taken serious hold" on students graduating from secondary schools.

A glimmer of what a school day was like can be gained from the remembrance of Ralph Tyler in 1974 when he was a mere sprite of 72. Tyler refreshed his memory with reading and wrote:

> What I remember from my experiences as a pupil are the strictness of discipline, the catechistic type of recitation, the dullness of the textbooks, and the complete absence of any obvious connection between our classwork and the activities we carried on outside of school. John Dewey's two small volumes, *The School and Society*, and *Interest and Effort in Education*, had been published more than a decade before, but Dewey's profound influence on educational theory and practice was just beginning. The view held by most teachers and parents was that the school was quite separate from the other institutions in society and its tasks should be sufficiently distasteful to the pupils to require strong discipline to undertake them and carry them through. Furthermore, they believed that while in school children should not talk with one another; all communication should be between the teacher and the class as a whole or between the teacher and the individual pupil.

In this kind of setting, the innovation of the Socialized Recitation, which was introduced to us by our history teacher, seemed revolutionary indeed. It operated
as follows. For each major division of the history course,
we had the usual textbook study and class recitation.
After this phase of our work was completed, each student was required to select a topic (with the approval of
the teacher) which was germane to that division of the
course. The student then developed a report, using not
only the textbook but also other relevant sources of information. Finally, he presented his report orally to the
class and then responded to questions asked by his
classmates...

From the perspective of today, the Socialized Recitation may seem a very minor kind of innovation but it
had a real influence on the teachers who were being
introduced to Dewey's writings. It demonstrated that at
least some students would spend time and effort studying something in which they were interested. It showed
teachers that interest and effort in education were not
always antithetical. It indicated that some students could
take responsibility for questioning, and that discussion
and debate among students could contribute to learning. It also established the fact that a classroom could be
a learning society and need not be devoted solely to
drill and catechistic recitation. These conclusions are
now taken for granted, but in 1915 they were novel.
(Tyler, 1976, pp. 26–27)

It has been common in recent years for authors to claim that
technology has so revolutionized medicine that a doctor of a
century ago would be lost in a contemporary hospital, while a
teacher from the 1890s would feel quite at home. This *might* be
true for the physical setting. For other aspects, it is patently false.
What is taught and how are both radically different now from
then.[2] A nice post-Victorian teacher would last about five minutes with today's students. Even if she were able to manage the
class, she would be at a loss for instructional methods that the
students could comprehend, as Tyler's recollection clearly shows.

As we shall see, the innovation introduced by Tyler's history
teacher was still novel when the Progressive Education Association's Eight-Year Study began in 1932. For its part, the Committee of Ten recommended both opening up high schools to more

fields and starting many science, mathematics, and modern language studies in the elementary grades. In all areas, it offered "the course" as the fundamental measure of learning, a recommendation that would lead in a few years to the formulation of the Carnegie Unit by the Carnegie Foundation for the Advancement of Teaching. Although the Carnegie Foundation called it simply a "standard unit," the foundation's name was soon attached to it in common parlance. A Carnegie Unit was any major topic studied for at least 120 hours or the equivalent during a school year.

As a result of the various studies of secondary education, America moved toward connecting the schools with the worlds that followed them; but in so doing, it moved away from Franklin's notion that schools should prepare people for the unanticipated. It also moved away from Mann's idea of schools as the great equalizer and Carnegie's assertion that in American schools everyone received the same education. Life was getting more complicated. In 1908, Harvard's Eliot told an audience, "We must get rid of the notion that some of us were brought up on, that a Yankee can turn his hand to anything. He cannot in this modern world; he positively cannot" (quoted in Perkinson, 1991, p. 116). People began to speak of a person's "probable destiny," and schools returned to the function that Jefferson saw for them: sorting and selecting, although the purpose of the seining was now quite different, and the net was not quite so fine.

In response to the need for wise sorting for a much expanded student body, there arose a new occupation, that of professional selector, what is today called a guidance counselor. By 1910, there were enough selectors to hold a national convention, and in 1913 the National Guidance Foundation was born. By 1918, a reaction of sorts had set in. During that year the NEA's Commission on the Reorganization of Secondary Education promulgated its "Cardinal Principles of Education," which mentioned vocation as only one of seven functions of education and explicitly relegated it to a station subordinate to the traditional functions of education. The list of seven read thus: health, command of fundamental processes, worthy home membership, vocation, citizenship, worthy use of leisure time, and ethical character.

The school of Tyler's time—catechistic recitation and all—was seen as the ladder to success, but, in fact, there were several ladders. To the schools fell the awesome task of deciding which one, if any, a child should try to climb. No doubt, many in the schools realized that not all ladders were created equal. Studies beginning with sociologists Robert and Helen Lynd's 1929 *Middletown* found that the schools were, indeed, sorting children. Another sociologist, W.L. Warner, reported that while schools gave children a common experience and common literacy, he still found that "as early as ten or twelve, these children were all traveling different paths in life" (quoted in Perkinson, 1991, p. 191).

The choice of probable destiny was being abetted at this time by the rise of educational and psychological testing under the direction of scholars such as E.L. Thorndike, Lewis Terman, Robert Yerkes, Henry Goddard, Arthur Otis, and Carl Campbell Brigham, founders of the testing movement in this country. These men saw intelligence as a single, determinate entity; they thought people differed widely in how much of it they possessed. It was thus "obvious" (to them) that from the twin concerns of humanity and efficiency, people of different intelligence should receive different instruction, instruction matched to their abilities.

Education historian Henry Perkinson reports in *The Imperfect Panacea* (1991) that the schools received complaints during this period between the two World Wars from all of the school's clients: factories, offices, colleges. Certainly there was criticism, some of it contradictory. The *American Educational Digest* provided regular summaries and, occasionally, commentaries on such criticism. Here are a few excerpts from the 1922 volume:

> Large numbers of students are slipping through high school totally ignorant of the simple facts of English grammar, according to Professor E.R. Barrett, head of the English department in the Kansas Normal School at Emporia, says the *Newsletter*. A noun test given to freshmen in that school revealed figures upon which professor Barrett bases his criticism. Out of 335 test papers involving 159 ordinary nouns, only one word was not missed on any paper; five words were missed by one; the noun "use" was missed 229 times; the word athletic was called a noun 170 times; the noun "gentlemen" failed of a mark 211 times, and of those examined, nine students missed over 200 nouns each. Since a freshman class is rather a selected group of high school graduates,

and since a noun test reveals the most elementary knowledge of sentence structure, it appears that students enter college without getting, somewhere along the line, the practical drill in technique for intelligent expression in correct English, Professor Barrett concludes.

The tendency in the educational world in the last few years, says the Sandusky, Ohio, *Journal,* has been very decidedly toward the practical. The *Journal* goes on to say that school courses have been revised, always with the idea of fitting the student for some practical work in life. There has been a modification of requirements and manual training, domestic science and commercial courses have been substituted for language and higher mathematics. The cry has been that our schools have turned out boys and girls unfitted for any practical work in life. "Of what use is Latin or algebra to a boy or girl who expects to work in an office or store or factory?" is a question that has been asked repeatedly. The answer has been a great reduction of time given to these studies. It must be said, from actual experience, that this modification of studies has not resulted in any material improvement in the writing and use of our own language. High school students spell and write no better than they did years ago—probably there has been deterioration—and it seems that a smattering of the "practical" is not sufficient to qualify a youth for work.

Commenting upon the fact that while a public school was burning in New York City, some five hundred pupils gathered nearby and danced with glee at the prospect of a long vacation, Richard Spillane declares that such an incident is a powerful indictment of the public school system of some of our cities. Regardless of an inclination of the young to find interest, if not pleasure, in destruction, the writer sees in this a tragic lack of the school to appeal to the child. And he reminds us that in 1918, the latest year for which complete statistics are available, the appropriation for public education in the United States was $763,688,089. The wastage in the schools is great, the writer believes. For example, the average number of school days in the whole United States in a year is 160.7, and the average attendance, 119.8 days. Viewed as a business enterprise, it is questionable whether the public school is functioning properly. What is the trouble? The writer recalls the criticism regarding the rigidity of the school system, also the opinion that too little attention is given to essential branches of education and too much to nonessentials. A manufacturer turning out poor material would lose his market, "but the school goes on regardless of its output, without much attention from those who pay the bills or those most concerned." (Newman, 1969, pp. 33–42)

There was much, much more: the gifted received too much and too little attention; there was too much "new-fangled work" in the schools because the family was falling apart; education did, or did not, return value on the investment; arguments for and against the vocational and the practical in schools raged. Such perennial grievances and criticisms, which increased in number and harshness after World War II, led Lawrence Cremin to pen in his 1989 book, *Popular Education and Its Discontents*:

> Just about the time Adam first whispered to Eve that they were living through an age of transition, the Serpent doubtless issued the first complaint that academic standards were beginning to decline. (p. 89)

It was during the post-World War I period, and especially during the Great Depression, that high schools experienced tremendous growth. The reform efforts of 40 years earlier started the nation on a path toward universal secondary education. During the Depression, there was nowhere else to go.

Although ferment continued during the 1930s, perhaps the signal event of that decade was the commencement of the Eight-Year Study. While Eliot and the Committee of Ten had opened up college admissions by allowing electives, they had simultaneously narrowed them by insisting that courses be from a small group and by trying to obtain uniformity in instruction. As described by its director, Wilfrid Aikin, the Eight-Year Study grew out of a sense of both pride and frustration at the 1930 convention of the Progressive Education Association (PEA). Many at the meeting had seen the growth of secondary schools since 1900 from fewer than 1 million to more than 10 million students, or 70 percent of American youth. But they also knew that this growth had brought them a new student body with different needs. They knew that of six students who entered high school, three dropped out and only one went on to college. Yet the curriculum was geared to that one.

There were, in addition, many problems now surfacing in secondary education. As Aikin, reporting on the concerns of the study, described them, they have a contemporary ring:

> Secondary education *"did not have a clear purposes...it failed to give students a sincere appreciation of their heritage as American citizens....Our secondary schools did not prepare [students] adequately for the responsibilities of community life....The high school seldom challenged the student of first-rate ability to work up to the level of his intellectual powers....Schools neither knew their students well nor guided them wisely....Schools failed to create conditions necessary for effective learning.* In spite of greater understanding of the ways in which human beings learn, teachers persisted in the discredited practice of assigning tasks meaningless to most pupils and of listening to recitations....The classroom was formal and completely dominated by the teacher. Rarely did students and teacher work together upon problems of genuine significance.... *The creative energies of students were seldom released and developed.* Students were so busy "doing assignments," meeting demands imposed upon them, they were seldom challenged or permitted to carry on independent work involving individual initiative, fresh combination of thought, invention, construction or special pursuits.... *The conventional high school curriculum was far removed from the real concerns of youth....The traditional subjects of the curriculum had lost much of their vitality and significance....Most high school graduates were not competent in the use of the English language....Teachers were not well equipped for their responsibilities....Principals and teachers labored earnestly, often sacrificially, but usually without any comprehensive evaluation of the results of their work....The high school diploma meant only that the student had done whatever was necessary to accumulate the required number of units....Finally, the relation of school and college was unsatisfactory to both institutions.* (Aikin, 1942; reprinted in Raubinger et al., 1969, pp. 164–169)

In fact, the last concern dominated the day: Aikin reported that "in the course of the two-day discussion many proposals for the improvement of the work of our secondary schools were made and generally approved. But almost every suggestion was met with the question 'Yes, that should be done in our high schools, but it can't be done without risking students' chances of being admitted to college.'" The PEA established the Commission on the Relation of School and College to see if it could persuade colleges not to reject students while the secondary schools "attempt fundamental reconstruction."

Could the schools offer different curricula without jeopardizing their students' chances for college and their performance, once admitted? That was the big question the commission addressed. But, as can be seen from Aikin's list of ills, the goals of school reform were much more ambitious. The commission selected 30 schools and permitted them to develop programs they thought appropriate without regard to college admissions requirements. At the same time, the commission approached colleges, explained the study, and asked the colleges to cooperate. In the end, most colleges did waive their normal requirements for some 30 of what today some would call "break-the-mold" schools.

According to Aikin, the project was to be guided by two major principles:

> The first was that the general life of the school and methods of teaching should conform to what is now known about the ways in which human beings learn and grow. Until recent years learning in school has been thought of as an intellectual process of acquiring certain skills and of mastering prescribed subject matter. It has been assumed that physical and emotional reactions are not involved in the learning process, but if they are, they are not very important. The newer concept of learning holds that a human being develops through doing those things which have meaning to him; that the doing involves the whole person in all aspects of his being; and that growth takes place as each experience leads to greater understanding and more intelligent reaction to new situations.

The second principle was that the "high school in the United States should rediscover its reason for existence."

For each of the 1,475 students from the 30 schools, the study's research picked a group of students who presented the traditional high school record and who had about "the same intelligence rating, was of the same race, age, and sex, and represented the same type of family and economic background and the same size of community." Differences in grades attained in seven areas of study were small, but consistently favored those from the progressive schools. "The guinea pigs wrote more, talked more, took a livelier interest in politics and social problems, went to more dances, had more dates. Especially concerned with campus affairs were the graduates of the six most experimental schools. There were more dynamos than grinds among them" (Knight, 1952, pp. 114–115).

According to Ralph Tyler, who spearheaded the project, not only did the Eight-Year Study free the high schools from the rigid admissions requirements of colleges, it also led to the creation of the in-service workshop as a means of developing materials, programs, and the skills of teachers. More important for our purposes, it contributed greatly to the use of educational outcomes:

> Among the most significant outcomes [of the Eight-Year Study] were…wide acceptance of the concept of educational evaluation as a procedure for appraising the attainment of the several main objectives of an educational program. This concept largely superseded the narrower concept of testing in assessing educational programs and student progress….The recognition by educational practitioners of the value of defining educational objectives in terms of the behavioral patterns students are encouraged to acquire. This process was shown to be helpful in defining objectives that could be used to direct curriculum planning, to guide instruction, and to furnish specifications for evaluation. (Tyler, 1976, pp. 40–41)

Tyler lamented that the onset of World War II had limited the study's impact.

War or no, the expansion continued, and after the war it accelerated. But what might have been seen as an unmitigated triumph did not carry that aura. Lawrence Cremin observed:

> The popularization of American schools and colleges since the end of World War II has been nothing short of phenomenal, involving an unprecedented broadening of access, an unprecedented diversification of curricula, and an unprecedented extension of public control. In

1950, 34 percent of the American population twenty-five years of age or older had completed at least four years of high school, while 6 percent of that population had completed at least four years of college. By 1985, 74 percent of the American population twenty-five years old or older had completed at least four years of high school, while 19 percent had completed at least four years of college. During that same thirty-five-year period, school and college curricula broadened and diversified tremendously, in part because of the existential fact of more diverse students bodies with more diverse needs, interest, abilities, and styles of learning; in part because of the accelerating growth of knowledge and new fields of knowledge; in part because of the rapid development of the American economy and its demands on school systems; and in part because of the transformation of America's role in the world. (Cremin, 1969, pp. 40–41)

This comment leads Cremin to a puzzlement: "Yet [this expansion of schooling] seemed to bring with it a pervasive sense of failure. The question would have to be 'Why?'" That would, indeed, have to be the question.

Historian Perkinson and others provide an answer that focuses on the 1950s. Reviewing and interpreting the criticism leading up to World War II, Perkinson still concluded that

the schools, in most instances, did an adequate job of sorting and preparing youths for the factory, for the office or for a professional career. The selection was not perfect, the training not of the highest quality possible, but, on the whole, the schools did a fairly good job of selecting and training youths for their future careers. However, by the Fifties many realized that fairly good was not good enough. (Perkinson, 1991, p. 151)

The period from 1946 to 1960 fundamentally changed the American public school because society changed what it asked the school to do and why, and changed its basic attitude toward school. We have never recovered from either change. To this transformation we now turn.

SOCIETAL CHANGES AND THE "FAILURE" OF SCHOOLS

Prior to World War II, none of the critiques quoted (or others not cited) mentioned school performance in terms of national or international standards. A brief glimpse at the history of schools and the nation shows why.

Decentralized schooling was the rule. There were more than four times the number of school districts in 1930 as there are now. Although hearings before Congress regularly documented "savage inequalities" in schooling, it would be well into the Eisenhower era before any federal aid to K–12 education would be approved. Moreover, the high school was still an elite establishment. In 1930 the graduation rate was only about 30 percent. Although schooling had been seen as the solution to many national social problems, and although secondary education had grown a great deal, the universal high school was not yet a national institution.

As for the nation, recall that Presidents Woodrow Wilson and Franklin Roosevelt entered World Wars I and II, respectively, over much isolationist opposition. Oceans separated America from Europe and Asia. Americans have long been proud of pointing to the Canadian border, the longest border in the world, and noting its serenity. The minor incursions at the Mexican boundary were just that, minor. Trans-Atlantic tourism was for the wealthy few. Although American education philosophers had borrowed much from Europeans such as Herbart, Pestalozzi, and Froebel, not much of relevance or interest was happening abroad for most Americans attending school.

None of the historical documents from this period discusses the crucial technological transformation that permitted a national conversation. Starting in 1934, the amount of money spent on books, newspapers, and magazines increased each year, in constant dollars, until 1979 (Kaestle et al., 1991). Per person expenditures for people over age 18 showed a similar curve up to 1974. Beginning in 1946, the amount of money spent on electronic media began a steep and unbroken climb. The number of television sets in U.S. households increased from 10,000 in 1947 to 40 million in 1957 (Ravitch, 1983). This meant that a much larger proportion of the population likely would hear or read about any criticisms or discussion of school performance. Indeed, in his 1953 book, *Educational Wastelands*, Arthur Bestor observed that journalism, which he felt had no place as a college course of study, was being called something he derided as "mass communications." Bestor's disdain notwithstanding, the name change reflected reality. Nineteen fifty-two marked the first televised conventions to nominate presidents and the first installments of the situation comedy, "Ozzie and Harriet." The goal of educating all students had become popular in the early 1940s; after World War II, high school education became more of a universal phenomenon. At the same time it became possible to have a truly national discussion about education.

As it turned out, there were several national discussions. They came from different directions and pointed in different directions, but they had one message in common: our schools are not measuring up.

Attacking schools from the ivied walls of universities was a common pastime, but in the late 1940s, the crticisms became more common and more frenzied. Many of these assaults were against progressive education, and even the patriarch of the progressive movement, John Dewey, had warned earlier of Progressivism's excesses. As with later movements such as "open education" and "whole language," progressive education was difficult to describe precisely. According to Cremin, "throughout its history it meant different things to different people." Still, Cremin felt that all Progressivism shared common purposes:

> First, it meant broadening the program and function of the school to include direct concern for health, vocation, and the quality of family and community life. Second, it meant applying in the classroom the pedagogical principles derived from new scientific research in psychology and the social sciences. Third, it meant tailoring instruction more and more to the different kinds and classes of children who were brought within the purview of the school.... Finally, Progressivism implied the radical faith that culture could be democratized without being vulgarized, the faith that everyone could share not only in the benefits of the new sciences but in the pursuit of the arts as well. (Cremin, 1961, p. 88)

According to Cremin's protégé, Diane Ravitch, progressive schools generally shared these features:

> Active learning (experiences and projects) rather than passive learning (reading); cooperative planning of classroom activities by teachers and pupils; cooperation among pupils on group projects instead of competition for grades; the recognition of individual differences in students' abilities and interests; justifying the curriculum by its utility to the student or by the way it met identifiable needs and interests of students; the goal of "effec-

tive living" rather than the acquisition of knowledge; the value of relating the program of the school to the life of the community around it; the merging of traditional subjects into core curricula or functional problem areas related to family life, community problems, or student interests; the use of books, facts, or traditional learning only when needed as part of students' activities and experiences. (Ravitch, 1983, p. 44)

Although the Progressives described their education as "democracy in action," and while their educational activities certainly seem more interesting than the "catechistic recitations" described by Tyler, the above list contains many aspects that alarmed a number of constituencies. Many businessmen reacted sharply to the cooperative aspects of progressive education. Many people still cherished a simple ideal of the rugged individualist. To them, cooperative activities not only threatened to destroy that ideal, but smacked of socialism as well. Those who taught traditional subjects and saw their major function to be one of transmitting traditional bodies of knowledge were alarmed that such transmission received so little emphasis and, in many places, was actively discouraged. Alarming, too, to traditional educators was the emphasis by the Progressives on the present and the future at the expense of studying the past.

Also, many teachers were immediately threatened by the potential end of their occupation. The progressives had enthusiastically embraced recent experiments in psychology that appeared to repeal earlier laws holding that the study of certain subjects led to a general "mental discipline." That is, the research seemed to show that the study of geometry teaches geometry but does not discipline the mind or create more logical thinkers.

The works of the early Progressives have the power to startle even today. For instance, psychologist G. Stanley Hall reminded readers that

school means leisure, exemption from work, the perpetuation of the primaeval paradise created before the struggle for existence began. It stands for the prolongation of human infancy, and the no whit less important prolongation of adolescence. It is sacred to health, growth, and heredity, a pound of which is worth a ton of instruction.[3] The guardians of the young should strive first of all to keep out of nature's way, and to prevent harm....They should feel profoundly that childhood, as it comes fresh from the hand of God, is not corrupt, but illustrates the survival of the most consummate thing in the world; they should be convinced that there is nothing else so worthy of love, reverence, and service as the body and soul of the growing child...

Practically, this means that every invasion of this leisure, the provision of a right measure as our first duty to youth, has a certain presumption against it and must justify itself by conclusive reasons. (Hall, 1901, pp. 474–488)

Contrast this idea again against Ralph Tyler's report of his school experiences from 1915. Hall observed that until recently we were all, "even the mother of our Lord," illiterate and that we must now "overcome the fetichism of the alphabet, the multiplication table, of grammars, of scales, and of bibliolatry...."

Not only did Hall not argue that all children can learn, he contended that for some children, in fact, school was dangerous:

There are many who ought not to be educated, and who would be better in mind, body, and morals if they knew no school. What shall it profit a child to gain the world of knowledge and lose his own health? Cramming and over-schooling have impaired many a feeble mind, for which, as the proverb says, nothing is so dangerous as ideas too large for it. We are coming to understand the vanity of mere scholarship and erudition, and to know that even ignorance may be a wholesome poultice for weakly souls....

Hall then goes on to outline the permissible interventions at different stages of a child's life, based on what we know of those stages. From the perspective of contemporary thought, his writing is an interesting mélange of ignorance, naïveté and wisdom.

The spirit of the early Progressives was also caught well by Francis Wayland Parker. Parker was an admirer of Hall, but he wanted to take his "invasion of this leisure" beyond the walls of the school. In 1901, Parker contended that there were only two proper topics of study, nature and man. "Man, as a subject, is larger than history, comprehending, as he does, anthropology, ethnology, archaeology, philosophy, and a long series of sciences united in philosophy." He suggested that the study of man come from "physical contact with the great arteries of trade, with life all around of building and making—the paving of streets, the building of bridges, and all the vast and varied activities of a great city." History, if it need be studied at all, can readily be obtained from the "thrilling history that the newspaper brings us" (*Report of the U.S. Commissioner, 1901–02*, Vol. I, 257–264).

Given what Upton Sinclair had to say in novels such as *The Jungle* in 1906 about working conditions in various industries at this time, one must presume that Parker never actually took any children to a "great rolling mill" to develop their awe of work. Or if he did, he probably ensured that they saw a sanitized version of operations.

Following such leads as Hall and Parker, at times the rhetoric of the Progressives did seem rabidly anti-intellectual. In her book, *That All May Learn*, Purdue University professor of education B.L. Dodds argued that there was no reason to teach the classics, that very little time should be devoted to writing, and that social science should be devoted to the present since the "new fifty percent" of low-intelligence students then enrolling in high schools would not have their imagination fired by studying the past. Dodds also derided very bright people: "The academic person who can happily devote a lifetime to the pursuit of work dealing large with abstract symbols of experience as reported through writing could with far more justification be considered abnormal." She argued that the curriculum should be lifelike and meet students' needs; it should, therefore, focus on how to dress attractively, how to make friends with the opposite sex, and how to get a job (in Ravitch, 1983, p. 61).

The notion that the curriculum should be based on the "needs of youth" became a virtual catechism of the Progressives. One educator surveyed 2,000 teenagers about what they felt their needs really were. Naturally, they cast most of their needs in terms of the immediacy of their lives, not in terms of learning foreign languages or history. As a result, the educator recommended sweeping changes in the curriculum, including differences for boys and girls since boys wanted to study science and girls did not (Ravitch, p. 62).

As progressive education degenerated into "life adjustment" education, it provided a ripe target for caricature and parody. In addition, the Progressives became rigid and quasi-religious in their pronouncements. The result was an outpouring of criticism in the late 1940s and early 1950s.

In addition to all of these changes in the nature of educational theory and practice and their critics, post-war America was confronted with problems unlike any it had seen previously. We have seen earlier how America turns to its schools to solve its social problems. In the period after World War II, two enormous problems were laid at the feet of the schools: how to integrate society racially and how to win a nuclear arms race without obliterating the earth itself.

One of the most popular and influential attacks on schools in this period was Arthur Bestor's 1953 treatise, *Educational Wastelands: The Retreat from Learning in our Public Schools.* Bestor slammed the schools, especially "life adjustment" education, but he did not leave institutes of higher education unscathed.

Bestor's work is not without error, and some of his reasoning is specious. For instance, to document the decline of learning, he noted:

> the classical languages have virtually disappeared from the high schools, but the modern foreign languages have been buried alive with them in a common, unmarked grave. Fifty years ago, *half* of all student in public high schools were studying Latin; today less than a quarter are enrolled in courses in *all* foreign languages put together. (p. 57)

Bestor neglected to notice that 50 years prior to his book less than 50 percent of those eligible were enrolled in *any* school, and only about 7 percent received high school diplomas. At the time his book was published, enrollments were approaching 90 percent and graduation rates 60 percent.

In addition, Bestor argued, curiously for a historian, that schools needed to return to their historic function of intellectual training, of producing a disciplined mind. This ignored not only the purposes of education as outlined by Jefferson but also the more recent history of education in which schools had been seen as instruments of moral discipline and as instruments to solve a wide variety of *social* problems—schools would Americanize foreigners, end crime and poverty, teach people to cope with the industrial age.

But Bestor had considerable credentials as a professor of history at the University of Illinois. Beyond that, the book is beautifully crafted, an eloquent statement, and a wonderful read. It provides a rallying point for many concerned with the condition of public education.

Both life adjustment education and Bestor's attack on it reflect the dialectic between "an aristocracy of worth and genius" versus "all children can learn." For Bestor, there was also a moral imperative in providing a liberal education to all children. Citing unnamed Americans who committed the nation to universal education a century earlier, Bestor claimd:

> Liberal education, they believed, was not and should not be the exclusive prerogative of an aristocratic few. Even the humblest man, whatever his trade, was capable of a liberal education. In a democracy, he was entitled to it. (p. 38)

Life adjustment education had come into existence during a conference in Washington, D.C., when long-time vocational educator Charles Prosser proposed it for what might currently be termed the forgotten 60 percent. Said Prosser:

> It is the belief of this conference that, with the aid of this report in final form, the vocational school of a community will be able better to prepare 20 percent of the youth of secondary-school age for entrance upon desirable skilled occupations; and that the high school will continue to prepare another 20 percent for entrance to college. We do not believe the remaining 60 percent of our youth of secondary-school age will receive the life-adjustment training they need and to which they are entitled as American citizens unless and until the administrators of public education with the assistance of the vocational education leaders formulate a similar program for this group. (U.S. Office of Education, 1945, quoted in Bestor, 1953, p. 82)

Bestor was incensed:

> Consider for a moment the extraordinary implications of this statement. Sixty percent—three fifths—of the future citizens of the United States, it asserts without qualification, are incapable of being benefited by intellectual training or even training for skilled and desirable occupations. If this is true, it is a fact of the most shattering significance, for it declares invalid most of the assumptions that have underlain American democracy. It enthrones once again the ancient doctrine that a clear majority of the people are destined from birth to be hewers

of wood and drawers of water for a select and superior few. (p. 82)

This, too, is a curious statement from a professor of history who, presumably, would be familiar with Jefferson's plan and the influence of the psychometricians of more recent years who had introduced ability grouping as a "humane" gesture. But Bestor was adamant: for him, the only real education was a liberal education. Bestor's schools had no place for vocational training. Skill at an occupation, he believed, came from the disciplined mind created through liberal arts education, through the development of what psychologists would call generalization and transfer. If Bestor knew of the earlier psychological experiments purporting to deny the development of a general mental discipline, he didn't let on:

> The disciplined mind is what education at every level should strive to produce. It is important for the individual. It is even more important for society....The real evidence for the value of liberal education lies, where pedagogical experimenters and questionnaire-makers refuse to seek it, in history and in the biographies of men who have met the valid criteria of greatness. These support overwhelmingly the claim of liberal education that it can equip a man or woman with fundamental powers of decision and action, applicable not merely to huckstering and housekeeping, but to all great and varied concerns of human life—not least, those which are unforeseen...The West was not settled by men and women who had taken courses in "How to be a pioneer." (p. 64)

Bestor apparently did not notice that most such men and women had little or no education of any sort.

The problem, as he saw it, came from the wholly inappropriate roles then being played by schools of education. Every department of a university is a school of education, said Bestor. Professional "educationists" have a proper domain in pedagogy, the study of *how* to teach the disciplines. But he thought the pedagogues should leave the choice of *what* to teach to scholars in the disciplines. Professional educationists had overstepped their bounds and now proposed to determine the curriculum as well as how best to teach it. Bestor thought this intolerable. The result, he argued, had been that courses and even majors of no intellectual merit had crept into education through the system of electives:

> The free-elective system opened the door to courses in subjects that had no conceivable claim to scholarly or scientific standing. The university quickly became a bustling educational cafeteria, where every dish is plainly marked with its price in semester hours, and where a full-course dinner is defined (so far as the management is concerned) of any assortment costing 120 such credits, whether it consists of roast beef and vegetables or a tray full of candied ginger. (p. 62)

Bestor viewed these electives as squeezing out the essential courses in the disciplines. He pointed to declining enrollments in both mathematics and foreign languages: "It is a curiously ostrich-like way of meeting life needs to de-emphasize foreign languages during a period of world war and postwar global tension, and to de-emphasize mathematics at precisely the time when the nation's security has come to depend on Einstein's equation, $E = mc2$" (p. 58).

In addition, he contended, professors of education, administrators, and teachers now formed an "interlocking directorate of professional educationists" that was virtually impervious to influence outside itself. An apparent lover of allusion (the book's title, of course, invokes T.S. Eliot), Bestor resorted to paraphrasing Churchill's "Iron Curtain" speech to describe the workings of the interlocking directorate:

> Across the educational world today stretches an iron curtain which the professional educationists are busily fashioning. Behind it, in slave-labor camps, are the classroom teachers, whose only hope of rescue is from without. On the hither side lies the free world of science and learning, menaced but not yet conquered. A division into two educational worlds is the great danger that faces us today. American intellectual life is threatened because the first twelve years of formal schooling in the United States are falling more and more under the policy-making control of a new breed of educator who has no real place in—who does not respect and who is not respected by—the world of scientists, scholars, and professional men. (p. 121)

Finally, Bestor declared that the school was making a fatal

error in trying to address all needs of children, and he slammed the "needs-of-youth" approach to curriculum making. He cited one such list of needs compiled by the National Association of Secondary School Principals that stated: "all youth need to be able to use their leisure time well and to budget it wisely." Bestor wrung his hands:

> The idea that the school must undertake to meet every need that some other agency is failing to meet, regardless of the suitability of the schoolroom to the task, is a preposterous delusion that in the end can wreck the educational system without in any way contributing to the salvation of society. Much of the cant about education for "home and family living" is a disguised way of saying that the school must take responsibility for things that the family today is supposedly failing to do. If family life is in a parlous state, that is a national calamity. But it does not mean that we can or should reproduce its intimacies in the schoolroom. (p. 75)

He then made a brief argument against sex education. One wonders how he would look on the family and the school of today.

Bestor was at pains to establish that he was not an opponent of progressive education. Indeed, he had attended Lincoln School at Teachers College, the best known progressive school in the nation. He recalled its curriculum fondly, though he thought it a mistake to have abandoned Latin and Greek in favor of only modern languages. He believed the beginning of the end was in sight when the school introduced a course in "social studies" along with history. It marked the onset of a process that changed progressive education to what Bestor called "regressive education."

> The "social studies" purported to throw light on contemporary problems, but the course signally failed, for it offered no perspective on the issues it raised, no basis for careful analysis, no encouragement to ordered thinking. There was plenty of discussion, but it was hardly responsible discussion. Quick and superficial opinions, not balanced and critical judgment, were at a premium. Freedom to think was elbowed aside by freedom not to think, and undisguised indoctrination loomed ahead. I am surprised at how accurately we as students appraised

the course. I cannot now improve on the nickname we gave it at the time: "social stew." (p. 46)

In Bestor's eyes, many programs of "social stew" had turned progressive education into regressive education. Life adjustment education was regressive education run riot; a parody of education, Bestor called it. Clearly, it marked the closing of the American mind. Having analyzed and defined the problem to his satisfaction, Bestor turned to what to do about it. To start education reform back to its previous love of learning, Bestor proposed a Permanent Scientific and Scholarly Commission on Secondary Education:

> The commission should be established by the learned societies of the nation and by them alone. The reason for keeping the commission independent of all political and economic pressure groups, and hence of all non-professional associations, is obvious. The exclusion of educational associations is more controversial. (p. 125)

Bestor went on to explain that educationists and scholars of the time would disagree. As the educationists were well organized and the scholars were not, this placed the scholars at a disadvantage. But Bestor saw the commission as a means toward dialog between scholars and educators. Another agency, composed equally of educators, scholars, and parents at large would deal with matters of curriculum and "the general purposes of education." Bestor was unable to bring his learned society into being through the American Historical Association, which could not reach consensus on his proposal. Rebuffed, he founded the Council for Basic Education (CBE) in 1956.

The early work of the Council seems to have been devoted to attacking the hated "professional educator" on the one hand and "antidemocratic schools" on the other. Harry Fuller, CBE's first chairman of the board, referred to professors of education as "dreary intellectual sinks" (Fuller, 1951, p. 33). While some professors were first-rate, they were obscured by a "swirling dust, raised by the hot winds that emanate from the numerous educational opportunists and carpetbaggers who too often dominate our colleges of education and our public schools" (p. 34).

Fuller first made these comments at a meeting of the University of Illinois chapter of Phi Delta Kappa (PDK), an education leadership fraternity. Apparently, no one recorded how this audience of professional educators received his message.

Some of Bestor's and Council officers' arguments would resonate in certain quarters today. For instance, commissions that were nominally interested in workforce skills, such as the Secretary's Commission on Achieving Necessary Skills (SCANS) and the Committee for Economic Development, produced reports arguing essentially that a liberal arts education was the best vocational education. Arguments have been put forth in other quarters that ability grouping results in some children's receiving an inadequate, unchallenging education. Mortimer Smith, first executive director of the Council, found ability grouping insidious, saying it would lead the teacher "who finds Johnny or Mary a little dull-witted in the academic subjects to ease up on them on the basis of supposed lack of interest and ability and to shove them into more courses in manual training or industrial arts or home economics, where mechanical skill takes precedence over thinking" (Spring, 1976, p. 31).

Bestor felt the same way. He rejected both ability grouping and vocationalism. If something is worth teaching, he felt, it is worth teaching to everyone. And everyone could learn. The "dull-witted" just needed more time.

Bestor was hardly alone in voicing his sentiments, only the latest and most eloquent in a long line of critics from academia, nor would this line stop as education reforms of the 1950s proceeded. In the 1960s, the great Swedish sociologist, Gunnar Myrdal, observed that social scientists had abandoned their support of American public education (Myrdal, 1969). He also observed that social scientists in the United States tend to "move as a flock." Daniel Tanner of Rutgers University notes that many of them flocked towards specializing in attacks on schools (Tanner, 1993, p. 291).

Many commentators observe anecdotally that the faculties of the arts and sciences display at once an arrogance and a Piagetian egocentrism that places them at the center of the universe. Observing these qualities in academics in the 1960s, William F. Buckley, Jr., once stated that he had rather be governed by 100 names drawn at random from the Boston phone book than by the Harvard faculty.

The other great post-war force for school reform came from the events that followed hard on the heels of peace. While isolationist sentiments were still prevalent, they were dominated by the idea that the world was now inexorably interconnected and that America, not reeling from the physical destruction visited on the other Allies and the Axis powers, had to play a role. That role soon emerged as the counterweight to the perceived attempts of the Soviet Union to spread communism and dominate the world. In the view of some, the American public school was the perfect institution to subvert. Where Jefferson had seen education as the instrument to protect us from our own government, as the Cold War developed, critics, politicians, and the lay public increasingly saw it as the instrument to protect us from without. "The Commies Are After Your Kids" was the title of one widely circulated pamphlet. "Progressive Education Increases Juvenile Delinquency" was another.

The Communist threat was not the sole source of post-war critical looks at the schools. The National Education Association reported that from 1948 to 1951, there had been three times as many critical attacks on the schools as in the period prior to 1948. Diane Ravitch dates the mounting criticisms of progressive and life adjustment education from 1949 and observes they rose to a peak in 1953, the year of Bestor's book.

Ravitch's accounting is corroborated by other sources. Education historian Edward Knight, writing from the University of North Carolina in 1952, already saw the trend:

> It was pointed out above that as the first half of the twentieth century came to a close, criticisms of American education were perhaps more numerous and sharper than ever before, and that there was much confusion in the immense educational arrangements that the American people had established for themselves. (Knight, 1952, p. 462)

Gross and Chandler had a similar chronology in 1964 (Gross and Chandler, 1964, pp. 335–337).

Some of these attacks came from intellectuals who had been prominent in the Roosevelt "braintrust" and during World War II, but who had lost influence since the end of the war. The election of 1952, which pitted the intellectual, Adlai Stevenson, against General Dwight Eisenhower, was widely seen as a war between "eggheads" (a common epithet of the period) and common sense. Even Eisenhower increased the chasm by defining an intellectual as "a man who takes more words than are necessary to tell more than he knows."

In 1962, Richard Hofstadter looked back on the events of the Fifties as he chronicled what he saw as the rise of *Anti-*

Intellectualism in American Life. Where did it come from? The schools, of course, wrote Hofstadter, led at the university level by schools of education. The softness of the progressive and life adjustment curriculum amounted to spoon-feeding kids an intellectual pabulum that bred a disrespect for the life of the mind. With virtually everyone in school and most of them staying through the secondary years, all children were learning, but according to Hofstadter and the rest, what they were learning had been diminished in intellectual integrity.

We should note that then, as now, the political Left and the Right were able to agree that there were problems in the schools, but they split on solutions. Currently, the Right and the Left agree that schools are in crisis. Now, the Right sees the solution in terms of choice, privatization, and vouchers, while the Left calls for more resources. In the 1950s, the Left, at least as represented by academics, wanted intellectually disciplined curriculum and instruction that would instill respect for intellectualism. The Right wanted intellectually disciplined curriculum and instruction that would produce loyal Americans and defeat the spread of communism.

In this post-war era, a national need clashed with a philosophical principle. A combination of low birth rates during the Depression era and the demand of the military that it maintain a 3.7 million-man standing army conspired to produce shortages not only of scientists and engineers but also of public-school teachers and foreign-policy experts. European nations had long-standing means of controlling the pipeline to professions, but the United States had always told each child, in so many words, to "be all that you can be" (as a later slogan would phrase it). How does a democracy ensure that it has enough people in professions vital to national security?

The problem was most vexing in terms of requiring compulsory military service. Although the Supreme Court had issued two rulings that compulsory military service was constitutional even in peacetime, the thought of compelling people to join the military troubled many people, and many engaged in some conceptual judo with their reasoning on the issue. President Harry Truman managed to convince himself that military service would actually instill democratic values in youth. How such values could be instilled through totalitarian institutions apparently did not trouble him.

Others could accept compulsory service as long as it applied to everyone, but this argument lost its power when the service became selective. Still others saw compulsory military service as increasing the efficiency of the workforce: the military provided much better health care programs than many poorer sections of the civilian world, so fewer hours were lost to poor health in the martial sphere.

In addition to compulsory military service, some prominent figures argued that another means of solving the shortage of engineers would be to establish a National Science Foundation (NSF) as the focal point of planning and policy in all areas of science and engineering. Vannevar Bush, who had coordinated scientific policy during the war, spoke vehemently for both compulsory military service and the NSF. So did the Committee on the Present Danger, a group of 33 powerful leaders from business, industry, the military, and universities. According to the committee, "we need not only trained men but also the most modern weapons....This means we need both a reservoir of trained men and a continuing advance on every scientific and technical front" (Spring, 1976, p. 77). These arguments were made repeatedly.

Another prominent voice for both compulsory service and the development of scientific manpower was James B. Conant, scientist, former president of Harvard, diplomat, who, in a few years, would study the American high school. At this point, though, Conant was arguing for scholarships that would permit the development of scientists whose current financial status made college prohibitively expensive. "It is men that count," he said. "And today we do not have the scientific manpower requisite for the job that lies ahead" (Spring, 1976, p. 78).

Conant, an ardent advocate of ability grouping, felt that all children could learn what the nation and society needed. Conant's scientific aristocracy of worth and genius was greatly advanced in its efficiency over that envisioned by Jefferson. Nothing so subjective as a "visitor" would make the judgments of who had brains and who did not. The testing people had seen to that. The test developers, as certain that they were right as any group of researchers ever, vigorously promoted tests as means of identifying talent. Once identified, those found in possession of a wealth of genius were encouraged to pursue their educations. The promotion of tests increased when the idea of universal military service was abandoned in favor of the Selective Service System. Complaints had arisen that the system selected low-income youth for the military while the middle and upper classes selected themselves into college. Tests, on the other hand, would identify talent irrespective of social class. At least, that is what their developers hoped and touted. (See Chapter Two for an extended discussion of the rise of mental measurements.)

In 1951, the National Manpower Council was established. In the midst of gloomy reports about how Russia was outdistancing the United States in science and technology, the Council's first report confronted the problem that put America at a disadvantage: "A democratic society promises each individual the opportunity to develop his potentialities as fully as he can in accordance with his own desires" (Spring, 1976, p. 86). In other words, the Soviet Union, as a totalitarian state, can direct people to do what it wants and needs, but a democracy has to coax. The Council viewed its role to be one of making certain occupations desirable, for supporting certain programs of education financially.

In contrast to earlier reformers' interests in civics and the disciplined mind, the council saw the role of the secondary school unequivocally to be that of preparing students for work. Schools should teach reading, basic arithmetic, and communication. There was no mention of standards. As did Bestor, the council implicitly assumed that the university could establish these with ease.

In addition to preparing students directly for the marketplace, the council also saw the school as a socializing agency favorable toward work. In its report of 1957, the council stated that "the school environment exposes youngsters to conditions and experiences comparable, in a number of important ways, to those which they will encounter when they go to work. The school enforces a regular schedule by setting hours of arrival and attendance; assigns tasks that must be completed; rewards diligence, responsibility and ability; corrects carelessness and ineptness; encourages ambition" (quoted in Spring, 1976, p. 87).

Ironically, in the 1980s, many anecdotes spread about the lack of skills in American high school graduates. Systematic employer surveys, though, found employers faulting schools, not so much for not teaching skills, but for failing to instill this work ethic. Attitude was repeatedly the number one concern of those hiring (see, for example, *America's Choice: High Skills or Low Wages!*).

The council wrestled with the notion that the concept of manpower applied to the service of society was incompatible with that of a democracy. It resolved the dilemma by arguing that without the realization of individual potential, there would be a terrible wastage of manpower. The concepts of individual potential and wastage were both presented, however, in terms of the needs of society, not of the individual. There was no room here for a person with an IQ of 150 who opted to be a sales clerk.

Not all people were convinced that the council had resolved the dilemma. Economist-philosopher Kenneth E. Boulding told the council that "the manpower concept is basically, I suspect, an engineering concept....Society is conceived as a great machine, feeding Manpower in at one end and grinding maximum qualities of the Single Well-defined End at the other" (Spring, 1976, p. 90). This is fine for a slave society where people are treated as domestic animals, said Boulding, but not for a free society.

The year 1956 saw not only the founding of the Council of Basic Education but also the emergence of yet another vocal critic of public schools, Admiral Hyman G. Rickover. Rickover had his own perspective on America's manpower needs. Often referred to as the father of America's nuclear navy, Rickover told various audiences that he had interviewed people associated with nuclear power plants for 12 years and that he found many people who could not adapt rapidly to new situations, people who could not cope with modern technology. The cause of these problems, Rickover said, was the American public school, which failed both to identify and to develop talent.

At this time, the reform of schools meant mostly changing them to crank up the number of scientists and engineers available to help win the Cold War. Central Intelligence Agency head Allen Dulles provided Rickover with figures showing that the Soviet Union would produce 1.2 million scientists and engineers between 1950 and 1960, while the United States would produce but 900,000 in the same period. "Let us never forget," said Rickover, "that there can be no second place in a contest with Russia and that there will be no second chance if we lose" (Rickover, 1959, p. 45). Apocalyptic rhetoric was the order of the day.

Like Arthur Bestor, Rickover shunned life adjustment education and saw the professional educator, with his control over curricula and certification laws, to be the weakest link in America's military strategy. Unlike Bestor, though, Rickover didn't believe in teaching everything to everyone. He thought, erroneously, that the comprehensive high school was developed in the spirit of Jacksonian democracy at a time before differences in intellectual capacities were known and before IQ tests, which showed such differences, were invented. Rickover was interested in sifting for talent, recognizing it early, and developing it intensely. For him, boarding schools for the gifted seemed the best way to go.

People often think back on this era and date the surge in criticism and reform to 1957 and the Russian launch of the first man-made satellite, but this is not accurate. Ravitch dates the rise in criticism of schools from 1949, and Bestor's book appeared in 1953, while Rickover and the Council for Basic Education both saw light in 1956. By 1957, the need for greater numbers of scientifically trained people was being voiced in many quarters.

In 1956, a reaction to this need led to the startup of a major curriculum reform in physics. Jerrold Zaccharias, a physicist at the Massachusetts Institute of Technology (MIT), hit upon the notion of using teaching films and classroom equipment to improve physics instruction. The films would break with the traditional approach, which still stressed Newton and the laws of motion and force. The new physics would emphasize particles. The new physics was to be implemented through the Physical Science Study Committee (PSSC), of which Zaccharias was chair, and funded by the NSF. PSSC physics stressed pure physics, not applications, which were seen as reflecting the life adjustment school of thought. Science is ideas and methods of inquiry, the PSSC said, and their materials would reflect that.

There was, therefore, plenty of ferment percolating in education before the fall of 1957. But in October of that year, the Russians launched the satellite Sputnik. The airwaves in this country crackled with dire-sounding newscasts of what this meant, except when a report that the whole thing was a hoax occasionally surfaced. It was not a hoax, of course, and it was taken as proof that the school critics were right. Sputnik was unarmed, but many came to believe that it killed progressive education, nonetheless.

By March 1958, *Life* magazine rolled out an extensive four-part series comparing U.S. and Soviet education. For the opening salvo of the series, *Life* enlisted the aid not of any educator or education critic, but of Sloan Wilson, the best-selling author of *The Man in the Gray Flannel Suit.* Save for Wilson's obsession with Russia and a few giveaway terms and names, his essay had a completely contemporary tenor and cast the critique of schools in its modern terms:

The facts of the school crisis are all out and in plain sight—and pretty dreadful to look at. First of all, it has been shown that a surprisingly small percentage of high school students is studying what used to be considered basic subjects. Only 12 percent are taking any mathematics more advanced than algebra, and only 25 percent are studying physics. A foreign language is studied by fewer than 15 percent of the students. Ten million Russians are studying English, but only 8,000 Americans are studying Russian....

> People are complaining that the diploma has been devaluated to the point of meaninglessness....It would be difficult to deny that few diplomas stand for a fixed level of accomplishment, or that great numbers of students fail to pursue their studies with vigor. Studies show that brilliant children in this country are nowhere near as advanced in the sciences as their opposite numbers in Europe and Russia. Why? (p. 36)

Wilson answered that 50 years earlier, American schools were "carbon copies" of European schools, offering a rigorous education only to those who could afford it. In pursuit of our egalitarian goals, he argued, we changed all that with progressive and life-adjustment education:

> Instead of trying to find students to fit a rigid curriculum, the schools decided to try to hand-tailor a course of instruction for each child. If poor Johnny could not learn chemistry or mathematics, the schools would not throw him into the street. They would teach him woodworking, they would adjust him to life, they would make him a better citizen. And after he served his four years in high school, they would give him a diploma as fancily lettered as anyone else's. (p. 37)

Wilson admitted that "there was a basic humanity in these changes and common sense, too," but the silliness of the life adjusters had gotten out of hand. He decried the plethora of electives and that talented students interested in learning "have to play the role of 'queer duck.'"

Wilson pointed to the school band and baton-twirling majorettes and reasoned that high school must look like a carnival to a newly arrived student:

> It is hard to deny that America's schools, which were

supposed to reflect one of history's noblest dreams and to cultivate the nation's youthful minds, have degenerated into a system for coddling and entertaining the mediocre. (p. 37)

Wilson had spotted something that looked to him very much like a "rising tide of mediocrity" 25 years before *A Nation At Risk* articulated it. To get out of this mess, Wilson wrote, we needed to generate a genuine respect for learning. It was one thing, he said, for the rugged frontiersman to say, "'I'm as good as you are' to the whole world of bewigged and beribboned aristocracy, but it is quite another for a callow adolescent to slouch in his jeans and motorcycle jacket in smirking disrespect for a good and honest physics teacher....It goes without saying nowadays that the outcome of the arms race will depend eventually on our schools and those of the Russians" (p. 37). To effect a cure, he contended, we would have to "get tough" with our kids.

Wilson's essay framed the issues in essentially contemporary terms. First, the specter of mediocrity was raised along with the notion that there is a "crisis" in public education. Certainly Sputnik was a shock that made Americans feel vulnerable, but were the current schools to blame? A 30-year-old engineer in 1957 would have graduated from high school around 1945, the very year that Charles Prosser first proposed to establish "life adjustment" education. And, of course, Prosser had not proposed it for the college-bound in the first place.

"Standards" were not invoked in terms of absolute achievement but in terms of how we compared to other nations, especially Russia. International studies that administered the same test to students in different countries had not been invented yet; the "data" comparing U.S. schools to others came largely from content analyses of curriculum offerings. In the Soviet Union there were also schools that specialized in mathematics and science, and differential curricula for students of different abilities were the norm.

A very similar round of accusations occurred in the 1980s when America experienced a recession. Many versions of "lousy-schools-are-producing-a-lousy-workforce-which-is-killing-us-in-the-international-marketplace" argument echoed in many quarters. No one seemed to notice that the overwhelming majority of the workers who would be in the workplace in the year 2000 were already there. Nor did many at the time notice that the notion that the schools have much to do with the health of the economy is a truly nutty idea. The shout of "competition in the international marketplace" had come to replace "the Red Menace" of the Fifties as a scare tactic. In the 1990s, the critics kept up their bombardment, even as the economy recovered. In early 1994, a spate of articles appeared with titles like "The American Economy: Back on Top" (Nasar, 1994, p. 1), with the schools receiving no credit for the recovery. As Stanford University's Larry Cuban put it in a title of an article, the putative link between education and the economy was "The Great School Scam."

Earlier, Columbia University's educational historian, Lawrence Cremin, had made a similar argument more genteelly:

> American economic competitiveness with Japan and other nations is to a considerable degree and function of monetary, trade, and industrial policy, and of decisions made by the President and Congress, the Federal Reserve Board, and the Federal Departments of the Treasury, Commerce, and Labor. Therefore, to conclude that problems of international competitiveness can be solved by educational reform, especially educational reform defined solely as school reform, is not merely utopian and millennialist, it is at best a foolish and at worst a crass effort to direct attention away from those truly responsible for doing something about competitiveness and to lay the burden instead on the schools. It is a device that has been used repeatedly in the history of American education. (Cremin, 1989, p. 102–103)

The validity of Cremin's claim should have been apparent to anyone by the late fall of 1994. During the course of the year, the Federal Reserve Board raised interest rates seven times. In November of 1994 the U.S. Congress voted to approve the Uruguay Round of the General Agreement on Tariffs and Trade (GATT). In terms of impact, it does not matter whether the highly vocal advocates of the treaty or their equally vocal opponents turn out to be right. Either way, GATT will have the kind of enormous impact on U.S. competitiveness that education could never have. At this writing, the decline of the dollar against other currencies, especially the Japanese yen and the German mark are having profound effects on competitiveness, making U.S. goods much more readily purchased abroad and generally increasing the competitiveness of U.S. industries overseas. In addition, the United States and Japan just concluded an agreement on car imports that had a lot to do with competitiveness, nothing to do with schools.

In his *Life* essay, Sloan Wilson also appears to have assumed that the high school diploma had at one time represented a "fixed amount of achievement." This "fixed level of achievement" notion would return 20 years later with the rise of the minimum competency test (MCT) movement. The arguments for such tests were often cast in such terms. Today, once again, we hear arguments that achievement should be measured in terms of "absolute achievement."

Wilson's call to "get tough" with students was echoed in many subsequent reform efforts and continues to be repeated as one strategy to solve our schooling problems. The meaninglessness of the diploma continues to haunt educators, even though its presumed meaning in years past is illusory. Again, during the minimum competency fad, accusations abounded that diplomas were awarded on the basis of "social promotion" for students who had endured a certain amount of "seat time." They abound today, even as test scores in many cases reach record levels.

Finally, Wilson may have been playing fast and loose with the data, something common among school critics today (Bracey, 1995). How did he know that 10 million Russians were studying English? How did he know that brilliant students here lagged far behind their foreign contemporaries? No international comparisons that would provide such information existed.

Was there any actual evidence that students were learning more in school pre-Sputnik? We were not as obsessed in those days as we are today with data and with indicators of quality, and there are very few of either that bear on the question. The Scholastic Aptitude Test (SAT) average verbal score had fallen to 476 by 1951, a decline no one has examined, probably because no one can explain it. The era of "Ozzie and Harriet" family coziness would begin in 1952, and while some like Bestor complained about the decline of the family, the two-parent, two-child family was still the norm. Television was not yet a big presence. And drugs were largely monopolized by jazz musicians and a few small, marginalized groups. A student who graduated in 1951 would have been largely protected from the anti-intellectualism of life-adjustment education.

But from 1951 to 1957, the year of Sputnik, the number of students taking the SAT had increased more than 450 percent, from 81,200 to 376,000. Yet the verbal score showed no further decline from this deeper dig into the talent pool, hovering steadily around 475. It began its notorious decline only in 1963, when the number of examinees had risen to 1,163,900. The math section of the SAT showed no tendency to decline until 1968, five years after the verbal score begin its long slide. Much of the decline in these years was attributed to changes in the composition of those taking the SAT, as colleges opened their doors to women and minorities (Wirtz et al., 1977, p. 18).

In 1957, scores on the Iowa Tests of Basic Skills (ITBS) and Iowa Tests of Educational Development (ITED) were at record levels (Hoover, 1995). They continued to rise until 1966, when they began a decade-long decline, only to return in the 1990s to levels above those of the 1950s and thus to new record levels.

The Iowas (as ITBS and ITED are called) are a particularly useful gauge in evaluating test score trends. Unlike most commercial achievement tests, the ITBS and its high school companion, the ITED, are carefully equated from form to form, permitting trend analyses not available for other commercial tests. Other tests maintain a floating standard: when the test is re-normed, whatever raw score equates to the 50th percentile becomes the national norm.

In 1955, a major change in the content of the ITBS and ITED led the staff at the Iowa Testing Program to discontinue reporting earlier data. Still, H.D. Hoover, longtime director of the Iowa Testing Program and developer of the ITBS and ITED, reports that when the 1940 versions of the tests were administered to Iowa students in 1965, those students "nailed" the test in comparison to their earlier peers (Hoover, 1995). Note that this improvement in test scores took place during a period of rapidly increasing schooling. It also took place in a state with few demographic changes: Iowa has no large cities even today and remains 98 percent white. These results are consistent with the summary of "then-and-now" studies in reading by Karl Kaestle and colleagues in their book *Literacy in America: Reading and Readers from 1880 to 1980*. Although these studies are plagued with interpretive difficulties because so many variables change at the same time, then-and-now studies tend to favor now, at least in reading (one study by Dale Whittington of Cleveland State University strongly implies that this conclusion holds for American literature and history also).

One survey, commissioned by the *New York Times* and prepared by Allan Nevins, a professor of American History at Columbia University, had found that the knowledge of history and geography of American college freshmen was scandalously low:

A large majority of the students showed that they had

virtually no knowledge of elementary aspects of American history. They could not identify such names as Abraham Lincoln, Thomas Jefferson, Andrew Jackson, or Theodore Roosevelt....Many students attending Southern colleges thought that Jefferson Davis had been president of the United States during the Civil War....Some students believed that George Washington was President during the War of 1812. Others listed for this war include Alexander Hamilton, John Adams, Theodore Roosevelt, Andrew Jackson, Thomas Jefferson, Abraham Lincoln, and John Jay....Most of our students do not have the faintest notion of what this country looks like. St. Louis...was placed on the Pacific Ocean, Lake Huron, Lake Erie, the Atlantic Ocean, Ohio River, St. Lawrence River, and almost every place else.

Given the task of identifying famous Americans' professions, students claimed that Walt Whitman was a missionary to the Far East, a pioneer, a colonizer, an explorer, a speculator, an unpatriotic writer, a humorist, a musician, a composer, a famous cartoonist, the father of blank verse, an English poet, and a columnist. "Hundreds of students listed Whitman as being an orchestra leader".[4]

The *Times* ran the results at the top of Page One, just to the left of its principal headline, "Patton Attacks East of El Guettar." One might want to rethink "a rising tide of mediocrity" with the results of this survey in mind. The survey was published in April 1943, two years before life adjustment education was conceived. Slightly less than 50 percent of students finished high school, and only about 20 percent of these went on to college. Many of the students who enrolled in college had attended private college preparatory schools.

Such ignorance on the part of college students is in no way an attempt to justify it. This is not a "Forrest Gump" defense of American public schools. But it is to note that many evince a tendency to look yearningly back to some hazily seen "Golden Era" of American education. No such era ever existed. Indeed, while many American schools need much improvement and most could be more intellectually exciting than they are, the history of education is a history of progress toward something not yet attained, perhaps never attainable: a nation of learners.

The Iowas were, from the 1930s, a nationally calibrated test battery. The SAT was at the time of Sloan Wilson's essay still very much used only in the Northeast and Atlantic Seaboard South. The *Times* survey was large but it is not clear that it was national. Beyond these three indicators, there is nothing save anecdote and impression to indicate the quality of U.S. schooling, one way or another. It is curious, then, that people were able to reach such forceful conclusions about the condition of schools on the basis of so little empirical information. Thirty-five years later, Clark Kerr, President Emeritus of the University of California, would look at the statements of the school critics and declare that "seldom in the course of policymaking in the United States have so many firm convictions held by so many been based on so little convincing proof" (Kerr, 1991).

Nevertheless, in the 1950s the notion that American schools had failed was firmly implanted. Lawrence Cremin's question about why the great expansion in schooling was accompanied by a sense of failure finds its answer in a variety of causes, both national and international. *How* schools had failed would change from time to time as would the arguments for how to fix the broken system. Failure would be the one constant.

Even as Bestor and Rickover were leveling their criticisms and as the "new" math, science, and social studies curricula were being developed, events were conspiring to make the new curricula obsolete. A new spirit was developing that held that even the best schools in America, the kinds that Bestor and the rest wanted to see everywhere, had failed. A report appeared from the Rockefeller Brothers' Fund in 1958 entitled *The Pursuit of Excellence*, which sought to make the case for high performance as a national goal. Two years later, A.S. Neill's *Summerhill* was published. It is not recorded how many copies of *The Pursuit of Excellence* were snapped up, but within a decade, *Summerhill* was selling at 200,000 copies a year (Ravitch, 1983, p. 236). *Summerhill* proposed a kind of child-centered, child-driven, come-to-class-if-you-want-to curriculum that would have made all but the most radical Progressives blush.

Summerhill was soon followed by Paul Goodman's *Compulsory Mis-Education*. Before the Sixties were over, the decade had witnessed the publication of Herbert Kohl's *Thirty-Six Children*, Jonathan Kozol's *Death at an Early Age*, Nat Hentoff's *Our Children Are Dying*, James Herndon's *The Way It Spozed to Be*, George Dennison's *The Lives of Children*, John Holt's *Why Children Fail*, Jerry Farber's *The Student as Nigger*, Neil Postman and Charles Weingartner's *Teaching as a Subversive Activity*, George Leonard's *Education and Ecstasy*, and Stephen Joseph's,

The Me Nobody Knows. These books painted a picture of schools that couldn't do anything right. Conditions might be worse for black children than white, but as with war, schools were not healthy for children and other living things.

It was not just schools, of course, that came under heated attack. The 1960s brought virtually every national institution into question. One cartoon of the period depicted two men on stools at a bar. One says to the other, "The Supreme Court! What do they know about law?" It captured the spirit of the time.

But given the perception of schools as places that hurt people, it should come as no surprise that as the 1970s dawned, educator-ideologues such as Ivan Illich began writing about "deschooling" society. Sociologist Philip Slater delivered a stunning critique of American society in *The Pursuit of Loneliness.* Theodor Roszak described *The Making of a Counterculture.* The joys of playing Frisbee in bell-bottoms while stoned on marijuana were limned, by, of all people, a Yale University law professor, Charles Reich, in *The Greening of America.*

The early 1960s had been, in spite of the Cuban missile crisis which threatened a nuclear Armageddon, a period of high optimism. Racially segregated schools, ruled unconstitutional in 1954, were finally being targeted for elimination. College students roved over the South to register blacks to vote. In the hereditarian-environmentalist debate on the nature of intelligence, environmentalists temporarily gained the upper hand and determined that what poor youngsters needed was a "head start" before school. John F. Kennedy, youthful, manful, and buoyant, along with his beautiful, arts-loving wife, brought a new spirit to the White House and the nation.

But behind this outer exuberance there lurked a potent force of disaffected youth. Already, people were looking back on the Eisenhower years as dull and sad. "Togetherness," the motto of the decade, was being parodied, as was the colorless symbol of the 10 years, Sloan Wilson's novel, *The Man in the Gray Flannel Suit.* In 1956, C. Wright Mills had published *The Power Elite* decrying the centralization of power, the small cliques that controlled the economy and most important decisions, and hoodwinking the ordinary person. Nineteen-sixty saw the founding of Students for a Democratic Society dedicated to building a "new left." In his 1960 "Letter to the New Left," Mills asked "[Who is it] that is getting fed up? Who is it that is getting disgusted with what Marx called 'all the old crap'? Who is it that is thinking and acting in radical ways? All over the world—in the bloc, outside the bloc and in between—the answer is the same: it is the young intelligentsia."

In 1960 also, some black college students tried to obtain food at a Woolworth's lunch counter in Greensboro, North Carolina. That action, coming on the heels of Rosa Parks's refusal to give up her seat to a white man on a Birmingham, Alabama, bus, launched the civil rights movement. In a few years, the tactics of the movement would be applied on campuses all over the country, often by the same activists, to different ends. The civil rights movement, though, served to change America's focus on what were its most pressing problems. By the end of 1962 the Russians had backed down over Cuba, and America had begun to launch satellites that circled the earth with men in them; in 1969 one of them would take men to the moon. Sputnik phobia was fading.

Within the schools, the voices of disaffection became very loud. The decade that started out so promising quickly clouded over. In 1963 President Kennedy was assassinated. The next year, a protest at the University of California, Berkeley over restrictions of on-campus political activity galvanized the disaffected across the land. Although not everyone agreed with all of the demands of the protesters, they came to symbolize the downtrodden (in fact, some of the leaders such as Mario Savio saw their cause as identical to that of civil rights, for which many of them had worked in the South over the previous summer). On the other hand, Berkeley president Clark Kerr, his administrative staff, and the University of California Regents came to symbolize an unfeeling, unresponsive "Establishment," people emblematic of the soon-to-be-common aphorism, "Don't trust anyone over 30." The Berkeley phenomenon spread across the country, although most colleges quickly acceded to student demands: no administration wanted to go through what Berkeley had been through.

Diane Ravitch has speculated that if the Free Speech Movement (FSM), as it was known, had been contained to the Free Speech Movement, it might have been contained to Berkeley, but the FSM soon had another issue to exploit: the Vietnam War (p. 226). Vietnam would chew up America as nothing had before or has since, and it still sticks in America's craw—witness the uproar over then-Secretary of Defense Robert McNamara's recent book in which he claims that while the goal was worthy, he knew as early as 1965 that the war was unwinnable. Kennedy's ideas for helping the poor and minorities became embodied in Lyndon Johnson's Great Society programs, then became entombed in Southeast Asia. Johnson, who had been elected in 1964 by a landslide, declined to run for re-election in 1968.

In 1965 the Watts riots in Los Angeles opened what would be years of urban disturbances. Black Panthers prowled. Nineteen sixty-eight saw both Robert F. Kennedy and Martin Luther King, Jr., assassinated and many injured in a "police riot" during the Democratic Nominating Convention in Chicago. *The Sixties: Years of Hope, Days of Rage*, was the accurate title University of California sociologist and Sixties demonstrator, Todd Gitlin, took for his chronicle of the decade.

Naturally, what was happening in the nation as a whole was reflected in the schools. In addition, the great curriculum reforms generated in the 1950s were sputtering to an end. But as the curriculum builders struggled with pedagogy, "they were unaware of the fact that almost everything they said had been said before, by Dewey, Whitehead, Bode, Rugg, etc.; and they were unaware that almost everything they tried to do had been tried before, by educators like Frederick Burk, Carleton Washburne, and Helen Parkhurst, not to mention Abraham Flexner and Dewey himself" (Silberman, 1970, p. 179).

Worse, most of these curricula had been created by people like MIT's Jerrold Zaccharias—well-known university professors—and this was seen initially as their great strength. Later, it came to be seen as their great weakness. The curriculum makers had little experience with schoolroom dynamics. They tried to create curricula that "would permit scholars to speak directly to the child" (Schaefer, 1967). They assumed that if the teachers used the materials properly, the child would learn what the curriculum had to teach. Teachers were seen, at best, as technicians. The phrase "teacher-proof" entered the vocabulary as something to strive for in curriculum making.

Thus, against the general backdrop of social unrest, was the picture of failing school reform. Schools might be most destructive to poor black youngsters, critics said, but they oppressed and killed the spirit of all who inhabited them. Charles Silberman, in his 1970 tome, *Crisis in the Classroom*, asks, "Why are schools so bad?" While some of the earlier listed titles were polemics of personal experience, Silberman's book was authoritative-sounding with footnotes on every page. It received a great deal of attention. Silberman answered that schools are so bad because they are obsessed with order and control. Teachers are demeaned and depressed by this obsession, and they often toil in dreary buildings under terrible work conditions. But it is the children who suffer most. Wrote Silberman:

> Because adults take schools so much for granted, they fail to appreciate what grim, joyless places most American schools are, how oppressive and petty are the rules by which they're governed, how intellectually sterile and aesthetically barren, what an appalling lack of civility obtains on the part of teachers and principals, what contempt they consciously display for children as children. (p. 10)

"The most important characteristic schools share in common is a preoccupation with order and control," Silberman wrote elsewhere in his book. He cited progressivist "giant" Carleton Washburne as saying, "Every child has the right to live fully and naturally as a child. Every child has the right also to be prepared adequately for later effective living as an adult." Said Silberman commenting on Washburne, "In the grim, repressive, joyless places most schools now are, children are denied both rights" (p. 116).

As it turned out, there was an educational philosophy, developed in England, that critics thought would restore both rights and improve learning, too. "Schools For Children" was the title of the first of a three-part series by Joseph Featherstone in the *New Republic* (1967). Featherstone reported on the growth of "open education" in English primary schools, fostered by a commission report that endorsed an activity-centered approach. Featherstone portrayed English youngsters as happy, busy, and learning in ways that American children were not.

Timing is everything, and Featherstone's message caught the moment: within a year, over 100,000 reprints of the series had been sold. While Featherstone was very careful to emphasize that the schools had been developed for children five to seven years old, as the movement became a crusade, American educators assumed the concept was appropriate first for all of the elementary grades and then for high school as well. Notions that had initially been presented as no more than notions were now taken as research-proven precepts, unchallengeable.

Much confusion soon surrounded the ideas of "open education." In many places, the concept degenerated to nothing more than open space. Learning became confused with play, assisted, no doubt, by misinterpretations of Jean Piaget's idea that play is the work of childhood. By 1974, at least one person was able to write an article called "When Open Education Died." In many places open education had been an instance of what had been labeled "The Rockefeller Technique of Reform," which went this way: about the same time that open education was becoming popular, then-New York Governor Nelson Rockefeller, declared that in six months the Long Island Rail Road, a source of much complaint, would be the best commuter rail line in the world. Six months later, Rockefeller declared the Long Island Rail Road the best commuter rail line in the world. He presented no evidence.

Some began to see open education as no more than an extension of the much discredited progressive education. The time was ripe for a return of education's get-tough, law-and-order mentality. It arrived in the form of the "Back to Basics" movement.

In some quarters, the back-to-basics thrust was assisted by public events. In 1974 in Virginia, in an attempt to return test scores to schools in time for use in remediation or planning, the state Department of Education shifted its testing period from mid-to-late-October to September. The norms for the test, though, assumed that it had been administered in October. The loss of over a month from the norms and the administering of a test before schools had really settled in for the year, combined to send test scores downward—"plummeting" was a word often used, although that profound a slide was really only apparent: as with most tests, two or three questions would convert into much larger changes in percentile ranks. The next year, the usual testing dates were restored, and the scores jumped back up to where they had been previously. But it was too late. An alarmed legislature enacted a Basic Learning Skills program that required first the development of basic learning skills objectives and then tests to assess whether or not kids and schools were meeting those objectives.

Similar lists of skills were being constructed all over the country. At the elementary school, "basic skills" became a mantra. In many instances, these skills reflected an implicit theory of knowledge that doesn't really accord with cognitive psychology or developmental psychology. The lists presumed that complex skills could be broken down into discrete, small basic skills; that these basic skills were necessary to the acquisition of complex skills; and that complex skills consisted of nothing more than accretions of basic skills. This epistemology was still common among those in the testing field as late as 1991 (Shepard).

At the high school level, another round of criticism was heard to the effect that students couldn't read the labels of what they sold, couldn't compute or make change, and so forth. Once again, critics alleged that students were being "socially promoted" and graduated on the basis of "seat time." These complaints often led to some form of "minimum competency test" (MCT) to be used, in many cases, as a requirement for receiving a high school diploma. Typically, the impetus for the test came from either the state house or the governor's mansion. By 1980 some 35 states had some version of MCT (the rise and fall of MCTs is treated in Chapter Two).

Paul Woodring, an education reformer of long standing at Western Washington University, noted that the criticism of the 1970s was remarkably similar to that of the 1950s, even though two of the favorite 1950s targets, Progressivism and teachers' colleges, had disappeared (Woodring also observed that most teachers had never come from such colleges [1978]). Ironically, in the same issue of *Phi Delta Kappan* in which Woodring wrote his "open letter to teachers," Michigan State University psychometrician Robert Ebel made his case for MCT by asserting that Progressivism *was* still around and was to blame:

> There is, I believe, a fundamental and powerful cause for the decline in achievement. It is the widespread acceptance in our schools of a specious, unsound, anti-intellectual philosophy of education. At various times in this century the philosophy has marched under the banner of progressive education, life-adjustment education, and, most recently, humanistic education. It has given us two generations of warm-hearted but soft-headed pedagogy. (Ebel, 1978)

It is hard to reconcile all this "warm-hearted," "soft-headed" education with Silberman's grim and joyless classrooms, and no doubt both writers overstated the case. This time, though, Ebel at least had some data on his side:

> College admission test scores, National Assessment of Educational Progress [NAEP] test results, norms on standardized tests of school achievement—all tend to confirm the impressions of professors, parents, and teach-

ers that many pupils are learning less from their schooling today than they did in the past. Equivalent scores on
the 1964 and 1973 editions of the Stanford Achievement
Test indicate that a typical student beginning the eighth
grade today can read about as well as a typical student
in the middle of the sixth grade ten years ago. (p. 547)

Not all of the data actually supported Ebel's contentions.
NAEP reading scores, for instance, were slightly up at all three
ages, which makes one wonder about the results on the Stanford
test. But math and science scores and scores for one of the three
ages for writing were at this point down, though only the science scores of 17-year-olds were down significantly. There is,
incidentally, an unexplained contradiction in trend lines of various tests: Most NAEP tests did not show the kinds of declines
seen on the SAT and achievement tests. The scores on the ITBS
and ITED, for instance, peaked around 1967 and were bottom-
ing out when Ebel wrote his article in 1978 (they have since
attained record levels).

But Ebel's concerns captured the day. Just prior to his article, the report of the College Board-sponsored panel to examine SAT declines, *On Further Examination*, had appeared and
received much publicity. *Educational Technology* magazine had
devoted its June and July 1976 issues to 15 articles discussing
the varieties of tests that were falling and what it meant. The list
of tests showing declines was impressive: many achievement
tests, the SAT, the ACT (American College Test), and some NAEP
scores. To some, the declines seemed even more awful because
IQ scores were up.

Not everyone in the profession blamed the schools. A background paper for the College Board simply listed the hypoth-
eses put forth to explain the SAT decline: 79 had been brought
forward, not including the one that it was produced by the ra-
dioactive fallout from the nuclear testing program of the 1950s.
Robert Zajonc hypothesized that it was due to family size that
had some years previous undergone increases. Thus, there was
a consequent decrease in the amount of time any given child
spent interacting with adults. Zajonc pointed to rising elementary scores and falling family size as changing the trend. Building on this, Herbert Walberg at the Chicago campus of the University of Illinois hypothesized, "It is likely that by 1982 college
applicant scores will be rising sharply because of the earlier
large reductions in family size." The SAT decline did stop then,

and only large shifts in the demographics of SAT test takers—more minorities, more low-income students, more females—kept Walberg's prediction from coming true.

Education had reached a point where schools were supposed to demonstrate that all children could learn a little—at least enough to get through the minimum competency test.

The worries over the flood of apparent bad news about test scores did not occur in a vacuum, of course. And much of the other news was debilitating as well. The United States had just exited from Vietnam in 1975, and in defeat. Starting in the fall of 1973, the country—the world!—was preoccupied and overwhelmed by the Watergate scandal that climaxed with Richard Nixon resigning the presidency in August 1974.[5]

The bombing of the Marine barracks in Lebanon and the OPEC oil embargo had left people feeling that America was vulnerable to much more than just the Soviet nuclear threat. We had previously scoffed at Chinese charges that we were only a "paper tiger." Now it seemed possible. Shortly after becoming president in 1976, Jimmy Carter found himself combatting double-digit inflation and announced that the country was suffering from "malaise," a statement that hastened his departure from office, even though it was accurate. In such a state of affairs, in a country with a recent history of steady school criticism, the schools could hardly escape more withering attention for the perceived decline in achievement.

As the presidential election of 1980 approached, those who were advising then-candidate Ronald Reagan had their own interpretation of the decline of education. Looking at the test data mentioned above, they contended:

> The level of learning, the knowledge and skills which our students acquire and possess on graduation from high schools and colleges has been declining for some years. This has become, as it should be, a subject of grave public concern.
>
> A prime reason for this ominous downward trend in the outcome of education has been an increasing interference by the federal government in the policy direction and management of educational institutions, the growing control which federal bureaucrats wield over the goals and practices, over staff and students, of our

schools and colleges. The goal of federal activities is not academic excellence, but egalitarian mediocrity...

One effective step the federal government could take in helping to arrest and reverse the declining trend in educational quality would be not only to abolish the Department of Education but to relinquish interference by federal agencies and courts in the policies and operations of educational institutions altogether. The direction of education should be left to the thousands of boards elected or appointed for that purpose, to administrators and teachers and to the communities themselves through out the country. Dozens of grant programs, each now run separately to different rules, could be combined into block grants, to be used at the discretion of state legislatures, governing boards or schools systems or institutions. There is no reason to assume that Washington possesses a monopoly on knowledge, wisdom and judgment required to direct our educational enterprise. (Unsigned, "Draft Education Memo," October 22, 1980, p. 1)[6]

The last sentence must be taken as tongue-in-cheek. Elsewhere, the document charged:

The Department of Education—and its predecessor the Office of Education—are a major cause of the appalling conditions in many of the public schools. They are responsible for much of the forced busing which is lowering educational quality; they bear a good part of responsibility for the wide discrepancies within many schools and classrooms. (p. 12)

Reagan did state that he would abolish the Department of Education, although his immediate action was to appoint Terrel Bell as Secretary. Bell apparently was to oversee his own demise. Jokesters commented that when Bell received the phone call in Utah, he was told not to bother packing a suitcase for the trip to Washington.

Bell later reported that he had heard "constant complaints about education and its effectiveness" (Bell, 1985, p. 114). Although the ferment in education was great, Bell claimed that we needed something to shake us "out of our complacency." He looked nostalgically upon the launching of Sputnik as such a tremor. Lacking a Sputnik-like event, he decided to establish a commission to examine the condition of education. In his recounting of the events, the resulting commission was not really to openly, objectively examine the condition of American schools. Rather, it was to formally document the deplorable condition which had caused all the complaints Bell was hearing.

Naturally, an administration aiming to diminish the federal role in education was not excited at the prospect of such a commission. Even if the outcomes were foretold, Reagan feared that such a report would imply a larger, not smaller, federal role. "Diffidence and scorn" were the words Bell himself used to describe the White House reaction. Still, in late 1981, using the personal power of newly appointed University of California president David Gardner, Bell managed to form his National Commission on Excellence in Education.

A lot of rumors circulate about how the commission's report was produced. One contends that the commissioners were handed the report at their first meeting and told that it was to be their treatise. Another holds that the commissioners ended up with a 400-page report and hired writers to slice it to manageable size. Neither of these stories appears to have any substance. Chairman Gardner steered with a strong hand, bringing the group to consensus at the expense of some cherished comments of individual commissioners.[7] James Harvey, then of the Department of Education and writer Bruce Boston, then of Editorial Experts, provided most of the continuity—the institutional memory, Boston calls it—to the many drafts. At one point, the document had suffered through what Boston called "the death of a thousand qualifications." It had lost its intensity. At this point, Harvard University physicist Gerald Holton produced what came to be known as "The Holton Draft," from which was crafted the final report. The Holton Draft restored the tone of a "clarion call," which the commission felt was needed.

The Holton Draft led to a document often referred to as "the paper Sputnik," *A Nation At Risk*. The introduction of the document commented that "the commission was impressed during the course of its activities by the diversity of opinion it received regarding the condition of American education...." No such diversity cluttered the text itself:

> Our nation is at risk. Our once unchallenged preeminence in commerce, industry, science and technological innovation is being overtaken by competitors through-

out the world...the educational foundations of our society are presently being eroded by a rising tide of mediocrity that threatens our very future as a nation and a people. What was unimaginable a generation ago has begun to occur—others are matching and surpassing our educational attainments.

If an unfriendly foreign power had attempted to impose on America the mediocre educational performance that exists today, we might well have viewed it as an act of war. (1983, p.5)

In a 1991 Kappan article titled "Why Can't They Be Like We Were?" I called *A Nation At Risk* a "xenophobic screed." I see no reason to alter that judgment now. The commissioners found the state of affairs unthinkable—*unimaginable!*—a generation ago. But a generation prior to 1983, much of the world was still recovering from World War II. Did the authors of *Risk* simply expect other nations to sit still and allow the United States to be Number One in everything?

In any case, after the opening cold-warrior rhetoric, *Risk* went on to present a set of factors that showed how and why we were at risk. These factors constituted a highly selective presentation of data and sometimes a presentation of contentions for which no data existed. For instance, although the College Board panel went to some pains to describe the causes for the decline of SAT scores, many of which had nothing to do with schools, the commission simply noted that the scores had fallen for 20 years.

The commission wrote that "there was a steady decline in science achievement scores of U.S. 17-year-olds as measured by national assessments of science in 1969, 1973, and 1977" (p. 9). This was true. But one could then ask why the commission had targeted science and 17-year-olds. The answer would be that it was the only trend that supported the crisis rhetoric. Of the nine NAEP trend lines (reading, mathematics, science for 9-, 13-, and 17-year-olds), *only* the science scores of 17-year-olds showed a "steady decline." Most scores were stable or increasing.

The commission also observed that the "average achievement of high school students on most standardized tests is now lower than 26 years ago when Sputnik was launched" (p. 8). This, too, was true, but it was the "glass-is-half-empty" view of looking at the data. Again, it was not true for many grades. The lower grades had never seen a decline; the upper grades had seen a decline in scores followed by a turnaround. The Commission could have said, "test scores for high school students declined in the 1960s and 1970s, but have risen for five consecutive years since then." It chose not to.

For at least two of the indicators no data existed: "Average tested achievement of students graduating from college is also lower" and "Over half the population of gifted students do not match their tested ability with comparable achievement in school" (p. 8). We do not measure the achievement of college seniors. The commission did not have in mind the Graduate Record Examination, administered to only a small minority of students, but it is not clear what they did have in mind. I have asked several researchers in the field of gifted-and-talented education, and none have been able to point to any research. Given that achievement tests are the most common means of identifying gifted students, the commission's statement about gifted students is curious indeed.

Some of the recommendations were naïve. For example, *Risk* called for colleges to raise admissions standards during the sixth of what would be 17 consecutive years when the number of 17-year-olds was declining (p. 27). Colleges were switching from selecting students to recruiting them as the baby boom passed, and a new emphasis was put on enticing "nontraditional" students to go to colleges (whose professors then complained that they were not as well prepared as previous generations). Further, *Risk* called on local officials to take responsibility for funding the reforms, but failed to note that, since schools were financed largely by property taxes, such funding could not be accomplished where it was most needed.

There have been reports, not corroborated by primary sources, that Reagan was furious at the report because it did not address his primary interests in education reform, tax credits and vouchers. Certainly it split the White House. White House adviser Edwin Meese and the right wing argued that Reagan should reject it precisely because it did not deal with the three issues he had campaigned on: abolition of the Department of Education, vouchers, and school prayer. Chief of Staff James Baker and adviser Michael Deaver, on the other hand, urged Reagan to accept it because it contained enough negative ammunition for his speeches about education.

Bell later wrote that the report, due in February, was delayed until April because commission members could not reach consensus. Bell also wrote that Reagan was pleased with the report, but he received word that Reagan's speech when releasing it would address mostly tuition tax credits and school prayer. This, apparently through the machinations of Bell's perennial enemy, Meese, was what Reagan did talk about. "As the President launched into that part of his speech that treated the prayer issue," Bell recalled, "I looked over into the foyer just off the State Dining Room to see [White House staffer] Ken Cribb give a congratulatory gesture and victory sign to his fellow defenders of the right. Ed Meese was standing there with a big smile on his face" (Bell, 1988, p. 131).

A Nation At Risk was an immediate hit. Lawrence Feinberg, then the education writer for the *Washington Post* (currently with the National Assessment Governing Board), offered a typical lead paragraph: "American education has deteriorated so drastically in the past two decades that 'our very future as a nation and a people' is threatened, an education commission warned yesterday in a study released by the White House." The news stories hit the papers on April 27, 1983. In the next month, the *Washington Post* carried no fewer than 28 stories on the report. All of the newspapers accepted it, although it did serve as something of a Rorschach test for various pundits. Joseph Kraft excoriated conservatives for using it to beat up liberals in their lamentable tradition of blasting liberal follies without offering anything constructive. This is a national problem, he said. William F. Buckley, Jr., welcomed the report, chided the commission for recommendations that "you and I would come up with over the phone," and wondered why it didn't offer the obvious solution, tuition tax credits. And so forth.

The articles about the report were uniformly accepting. If they criticized it at all, it was for recommending the obvious and the historical. Or, in the case of George Will in the *Washington Post*, why it didn't recommend more history. Another *Post* columnist, Richard Cohen, worried that since test scores were on the rise and schools had always worked pretty well for white people, we were headed for another period of neglect for groups the system had failed. Judy Mann, also a columnist of the *Washington Post*, wondered why there wasn't more of an uproar. If the report had said about our health care system the same things it said about our schools, Mann declared, the nation would be incensed. Of course, it could well be argued that a similar report on health care would have been greeted by at least some journalists with a *soupçon* of skepticism. Like science, journalism, after all, is supposed to insist that people warrant their claims.

From the journalists perusing *Risk*, however, no such incertitude arose. An editorial in the *Post* probably provides the reason why:

> National commissions more often ratify changes in the country's thinking than lead it. The value of the report a few days ago by the Commission on Excellence in Education is precisely that it marks a point already reached by a great many people—a large majority, we should guess, of those who take a serious interest in the schools. There's a wide consensus that this country has become depressingly tolerant of mediocrity in its school systems...

Interestingly, the *New York Times* took a much more reserved perspective on the report. Then-education writer Edward Fiske did present the results on Page One, but no pundit spoke, and the single editorial on May 2 was mild. The *Times'* Russell Baker looked at the sentence on "a rising tide of mediocrity" and declared that "a sentence like that wouldn't be worth more than a C in tenth-grade English." He was bothered by the tired cliché and a grammatical error. "I'm giving them an A+ in mediocrity," he said about the writing overall.

Within the education community, the report was accepted for mostly the wrong reasons. The reaction of the American Association of School Administrators (AASA) was typical. It reprinted the document, sandwiching it between AASA commentary. In front of it was a statement by AASA executive director Paul B. Salmon. At the back, were "key concepts" that needed to be understood, questions that needed to be asked, and suggestions for using the report. Salmon wrote:

> AASA welcomes the Commission's report. We are pleased that education is back on the American agenda. We know that recently school administrators have been frustrated by state lids on taxes, cutbacks in federal funds, and White House support for tuition tax credits, but we believe that this report can be an important first step in redefining and reexamining our national commitment to education.

Educators welcomed the bright light of attention. They believed that if people really understood what was going on, funds would be more readily available. It was not to be.

Terrel Bell was looking for a report that would do for education what the Flexner Report had done for medicine: revolutionize it. This *Risk* did not do. The recommendations from the commission did not call for anything *different*, only for *more*: more science, more mathematics, more foreign language, more computer science, more homework, more time in class, more time on task, a longer day, a longer year, higher salaries. The implication of the recommendations is clearly that the fundamental structures and processes of schooling are healthy; we just need higher standards, better prepared teachers, etc. Five years later, Bell would close a book with recommendations that also assumed the basic institution of school was fine and that the only thing needed was a return to quality. Still, in terms of turning the spotlight of scrutiny on schools, *Risk* succeeded like nothing before or since, save Sputnik itself.

There was another aspect of the reaction to *Risk* that bears comment. Each new wave of reform acts as a jolt of electro-convulsive shock that induces immediate amnesia for the preceding wave. Each time, there is a wistful nostalgia for the way things used to be. Said Bell in his book, *The Thirteenth Man*:

> If we are frank with ourselves, we must acknowledge that for most Americans...neither diligence in learning nor rigorous standards of performance prevail....How do we once again become a nation of learners, in which attitudes toward intellectual pursuit and quality of work have excellence as their core? (1988, p. 167)

How do we get back to the garden?

Only the curmudgeonly James J. Kilpatrick had enough sense of history to notice that *Risk* contained nothing new. In an essay titled "At Bottom, Americans Just Don't Give a Damn," Kilpatrick provided an abbreviated version of the history of education criticism presented here in the previous 70 pages. Citing, among others, Bestor, Rickover, and Silberman, Kilpatrick observed that

> they all said the same things, and they all made basically the same recommendations. They said the quality of education in our public schools is shamefully low.... These recommendations are sound. They have been sound for the last 30 years....Why hasn't anything been done about all these years of similar findings and recommendations? The cause, at bottom, is that the American people simply don't give a damn about their public schools.

As should be clear by now, the United States had never been "a nation of learners." When Charles Prosser proposed life adjustment education, it was assumed that only 20 percent of the high school graduates could qualify for, handle, and benefit from learning at the college level. And this was twice as high as had been thought a generation earlier. The graduation rate from high school was under 50 percent. And, as noted in the earlier mentioned 1943 survey, college freshman, an elite, didn't show too well in American history and geography.

It is common to hear people speak of the performance and high job-success rates of the immigrants of this earlier age who were tossed into a sink-or-swim situation. Those who so speak forget that most of them sank. Like stones. They weren't noticed because they simply joined the large majority of people who were high school "dropouts." Memory is fallible, and nostalgia is dangerous. As Karl Kaestle and his colleagues observed after a review of then-and-now studies in reading, there is no evidence that a given social class had ever learned more at any time in the past (Kaestle et al., 1991). Dale Whittington found similar results in history and literature and conjectured that, because of the low dropout rates of today, students might very well know more than their parents and grandparents (Whittington, 1991). The *New York Times'* 1943 survey cited earlier contains some weak evidence that she is right.

Nostalgia or not, interest in reform grew. Bell produced the infamous "wall charts" that grouped states into two categories, "ACT states" and "SAT states," depending on the dominant college entrance examination. Reagan announced a national goal of a 50-point gain in the SAT, a goal equivalent to a goal of increasing arm length by making shirt sleeves longer. Phrases like "effective schools" and "indicators of quality" became the currency of reform.

To some, however, the school in its current state seemed to have reached its maximum efficiency. To reform education did not mean just ratcheting up standards or increasing the number and difficulty of courses taken in high school. Reform began to take on a qualitative dimension. A word apparently first used by Ted Sizer in a 1983 *Phi Delta Kappan* article began to be heard more often and in many quarters. It would be necessary, said some, to "restructure" schools.

"Restructure" soon became a favorite word among educators and, as a consequence, acquired a great deal of surplus meaning and muddiness. Some spoke to the need for "systemic" reform.

Some borrowed the concepts of Total Quality Management (TQM) from W. Edwards Deming—or the words anyway. In 1991, the Bush administration launched the New American Schools Development Corporation (NASDC), with the goal of developing "break-the-mold" schools. In 1989, President Bush, meeting in an "education summit" with the National Governors' Association (NGA) established a set of six National Education Goals and, of course, a National Education Goals Panel to oversee progress towards them. These goals, which were amended in 1992 by the Clinton administration to include two more goals and additional wording (designated below in brackets), are:

1. All children in America will start school ready to learn.
2. The high school graduation rate will increase to at least 90 percent.
3. All students will leave grades 4, 8, and 12 having demonstrated competency over challenging subject matter, including English, mathematics, science, [foreign languages, civics and government, economics, arts,] history, and geography; and every school in America will ensure that all students learn to use their minds well, so they may be prepared for responsible citizenship, further learning, and productive employment in our Nation's modern economy.
[4. The Nation's teaching force will have access to programs for the continued improvement of their professional skills and the opportunity to acquire the knowledge and skills needed to instruct and prepare all American students for the next century.]
5. U.S. students will be first in the world in mathematics and science achievement.
6. Every adult American will be literate and will possess the knowledge and skills necessary to compete in a global economy and exercise the rights and responsibilities of citizenship.
7. Every school in the United States will be free of drugs, violence, [and the unauthorized presence of firearms and alcohol] and will offer a disciplined environment conducive to learning.
[8. Every school will promote partnerships that will increase parental involvement and participation in promoting the social, emotional, and academic growth of children.][8]

Reaching these goals was no mere challenge. It was absolutely crucial to the future of the nation. "For the country to change, the schools must change," said President Bush's Secretary of Education, Lamar Alexander. As noted earlier, the schools have always been expected to solve large social problems, but this was likely the first time that the nation had been made the dependent variable, the hostage, to what transpired in the schools.

In spite of all the ferment, schools continued to receive a great deal of criticism, much of it actually false. "In mathematics and science, American high schoolers finish last or next [to] last in virtually every international measure," said Louis V. Gerstner, chief executive officer of IBM, in his 1994 book, *Reinventing Education*. "We've gotten used to...coming in dead last in international math comparisons," said pundit Charles Krauthammer in the summer of 1994. Albert Shanker, president of the American Federation of Teachers, hammered as hard as any of the outside critics. In three consecutive opening sentences in three consecutive columns in the *New York Times*, Shanker tossed these bombs: "The achievement of U.S. students in grades K–12 is very poor" (1993a); "American students are performing at much lower levels than students in other industrialized nations" (1993b); and "International examinations designed to compare students from all over the world usually show American students at or near the bottom" (1993c).

None of these statements is true.[9]

Jefferson desired to "rake the best geniuses from the rubbish." The Committee of Ten thought only an "insignificant" proportion could sustain college level material and only a small proportion would graduate from high school. Charles Prosser held that only 20 percent of American students were up to college-level work. But in the 1980s, the new restructuring reforms opened up a new era of optimism and a new refrain was heard over and over: "all children can learn." Actually, the statement was not so new. Benjamin Bloom had suggested in the 1970s that 90 percent of our students could learn what we had to teach them through high school. Ralph Tyler had made a similar suggestion in 1974. Now, though, what we had to teach them had changed. The 1970s had witnessed a call for all children to learn at least "minimum competencies" before leaving high school. These minima were, in most instances, minimal indeed. In the 1980s reformers had pleaded for higher standards. Now, increasingly, people were incensed that *anyone* could get a high school diploma and not be capable of college-level work. The Commonwealth of Virginia's Secretary of Education, Beverly Sgro, was quoted in the *Richmond Times-Dispatch* in September 1994 saying, "It's unacceptable for us to have students graduating from high school unable to do college work. We've got to set standards that they will have to meet." (She confirmed by phone that she was not misquoted.) Take *that* Thomas Jefferson, Committee of Ten, Charles Prosser, and the rest: all of Virginia's students should be able to handle college. That they are not is the fault of the schools, not the kids.

In many quarters the notion surged that the means to get all children to learn was through the establishment of standards. Standards would give us something to shoot for, would let our students compete with those in other nations, and would let our workforce be as competitive as those of other nations (in fact, ours already is the most productive in the world).

The nation was scandalized recently when reports surfaced in Kentucky that not all people there thought all people can learn. It seemed that some folks in that state were carrying an implicit bell curve in their heads. Worse, that kind of thinking was found more in teachers than in laypeople. Still, a revolution of sorts occurred against the notion of outcomes-based education in which all children would learn. To the man on the street, the only way to teach all children the same things was to not teach any of them very much. (The issues surrounding standards and outcomes are covered in Chapters Three and Four.)

The fate of recent reforms is much in doubt. One recent report analyzing data from the 1988 National Educational Longitudinal Study found that schools that had restructured (practices considered to be restructuring are defined in the report) showed more gains from eighth grade to 10th grade in reading, mathematics, and science, than schools that had done nothing or schools that had adopted more of the traditional "more-type" reforms. It is unlikely, however, that these changes, even if they become widespread, will be sufficient to quiet critics. Looking back over the last century of criticism of American education up to the quote in the Prologue from *Business Week*, it is clear that however well the schools are performing, it is never good enough.

Chapter Two

The Evolution of Assessment

*That the schools will ever be free from the
tyranny of diploma and examination may
be an Utopian expectation.*
—Walter Ballou Jacobs, "The Dangers of
Examinations," *The School Review* (1896)

*With all, it was now clear that among say
eight kids reading at 4.5–4.8 grade level,
making errors A, B, and D (but not C), there
were in fact eight kids, some of whom were
reading all kinds of stuff, some who would only
read the newspaper, some who would only read
Mad magazine— or look at it anyway— and
some who wouldn't read anything at all. Thus
the test could only mean something if you
never looked at the kids themselves.*
—James Herndon,
How to Survive in Your Native Land (1971)

As the aphorism of Santayana from the Prologue could only be from an American philosopher, so could this chapter only be written for an American book. In no other nation did tests and assessments become as ubiquitous and important as they did in the United States, the current "exam hell" of Japan notwithstanding. This is interesting, for in the view of many, the tests are unnecessary to the educational enterprise and even interfere with it. (No one doubts the importance of assessments, which are not the same as tests.)

This chapter provides a short history of testing and assessment, particularly as it pertains to the testing and assessment of school achievement. We are not concerned here with specific tests. This chapter does not detail the history of IQ (intelligence quotient) measurements, controversial as those have once again become with the publication of Richard Herrnstein's and Charles Murray's *The Bell Curve* in 1994.[1] Neither does this chapter detail the history of the Scholastic Aptitude Test (SAT), controversial as that history has been.[2] However, the National Assessment of Educational Progress (NAEP) is accounted a separate section here, as it has emerged from near-total obscurity to assume the role its early detractors feared it would: as an instrument of the federal government to influence the curriculum.

For the most part, though, we are concerned in this chapter with three aspects of assessment: (1) how achievement has been measured, (2) to what uses the assessment has been put, and (3) what those who developed measurements assumed about schools and the nature of learning.

One might think that the discipline of assessment would have grown out of a concern for educational outcomes. One can easily imagine a group of people sitting around in the nineteenth century saying, "OK, now we know what we want to have happen as a result of education, but how do we—how can we know—if it happened?" However rational, the development of assessment involved no such meetings. As noted in Chapter One, education in the nineteenth century was still viewed in terms of civic responsibility and socialization, and when people did speak of outcomes, they assumed that these were safely reposing in the institutions of higher education.

Indeed, until about the second decade of this century, many would have sided with Walter Ballou Jacobs of Brown University, whose quote opened this chapter. Jacobs raised all of the objections that are raised today: Some people don't test well; tests are backward-looking, and education should be forward-looking; students studying for examinations forget tomorrow what they regurgitated today; tests encourage students and teachers to view each other as enemies; tests "overpressure students and cause nervous strain, especially to girls"; tests produce "mechanical uniformity in our scholars, they crush out spontaneity"; tests cause both teachers and students to "overvalue that which can be readily examined" (p. 680).

What to do?

> Simply this: Not that the examination be abolished, but that it be put in its proper place, in the eyes of the scholar and the eyes of the public; that we have faith in the judgment of the teacher, and the teacher have faith

in his own; that the classes be small enough for the teacher to know his pupils, and teachers good enough to make it worthwhile for their scholars to know them; that there be an abundance of written work, for much writing makes the accurate man; and that the end of education before our eyes be not knowledge merely, but greater and higher than that, strong, vigorous, moral manhood. (p. 680–681)

When people in Europe and, especially, in America, began to be interested in testing, they wanted to measure not the outcomes of school, but the capacity, the ability, the intelligence of other people. The French ministry of education had set for clinical psychologist Alfred Binet the task of determining which children had so few intellectual assets that they could not benefit from instruction in regular schools. Another psychologist, Sir Francis Galton in England, was interested in capacity and the transmission of such capacities from one generation to another.

Although this chapter does not delve into the history of IQ testing, there are aspects to the measurement of "intelligence" that greatly affected both the American perspective on testing and how the tests in schools were to be used. Binet, for his part, was concerned with what he called "intelligence in general," and he was quite aware of the tentative nature of his investigations. He declared that the tests were

> not an automatic method comparable to a weighing machine in a railroad station....The results of our examinations have no value if deprived of all comment; they need to be interpreted....A particular test isolated from the rest is of little value;...that which gives a demonstrative force is a group of tests. This may seem to be a truth so trivial as to be scarcely worth the trouble of expressing it. On the contrary, it is a profound truth....One test signifies nothing, let us emphatically repeat, but five or six tests signify something. And it is so true that one might almost say "It matters very little what the tests are so long as they are numerous." (quoted in Wiggins, 1993, p. 13)

It matters little as long as they are numerous. This is appropriate for "intelligence in general," a concept implying observation of many behaviors. An individual might be deficient on one but make up for it on another and, in general, exhibit a certain amount of intelligence. But when Binet's tests crossed the Atlantic, intelligence in general quickly became "general intelligence," something viewed as a unitary trait affecting virtually every behavior in every setting. There were, to be sure, debates among those who believed in Spearman's "g" or general factor, and those who felt that Thurstone's multifactor intellect was the better conceptualization, but most of the early proponents of the tests were also proponents of "g."

Today, still, some not only cling to this notion but also proselytize animatedly for it, as seen recently from Herrnstein and Murray in *The Bell Curve*: [It is] "by now beyond technical dispute [that] there is such a thing as a general factor of cognitive ability on which human beings differ" (p. 22). This general factor is measured by all standardized tests of aptitude or achievement, claim Herrnstein and Murray, but it is most accurately measured by IQ tests which are stable, and which "are not demonstrably biased against social, economic or ethnic groups when properly administered." Heredity accounts for no less than 40 percent of IQ and no more than 80 percent.

While most contemporary theorists allow some role for the environment's influence in the determination of intelligence, sometimes a substantial one, in the early days of IQ tests many thought in more deterministic veins. If there were but a single, unidimensional factor in intelligence, it's an easy conceptual leap to the conclusion that intelligence is genetic in origin and determinate in quantity (the rediscovery of Mendelian genetics also corresponded in time with the development of testing). This conceptualization had profound implications for tests and their use. For instance, confronted with the notion that schooling improves intelligence, testing pioneer Robert Yerkes had this to say:

> It is quite commonly believed that intelligence increases with schooling. This however, is flatly contradicted by results of research, for it turns out that the main reason that intelligence status improves with years of schooling is the elimination of the less capable pupil. (1923, p. 362)

The implications of such a view were profound. For instance, from the results of tests, it seemed wildly ineffectual and inhumane not to group students by ability. Why frustrate the less able with material they could not handle? As Stanford University psychometrician Lee J. Cronbach put it in 1975, to these testing promoters "it was so obviously cruel and inefficient to instruct everyone in the same things at the same pace, and so obvious that systematic measurement was providing better information for teachers, that the testers of the 1920s could conceive of no risk or error save that of failure to take the tests seriously."

Terman cast it this way in 1922:

> Preliminary investigations indicate that an IQ below 70 rarely permits anything better than unskilled labor; that the range of 70–80 is pre-eminently that of semi-skilled labor; from 80–100 that of skilled or ordinary clerical labor; from 100–110 or 115, that of the semi-professional pursuits; and that above these are the grades of intelligence which permit one to enter the professions or the large fields of business. Intelligence tests can tell us whether a child's native brightness corresponds more nearly to the median (or one or another of these classes). This information will be of great value in planning the education of a particular child and also in planning the differentiated curriculum. (p. 58)

From this perspective, it is only a short hop to the conclusion that, since different ethnic groups differ on intelligence tests, intelligence is distributed differently among the different ethnicities.

There is another quality to the words people such as Lewis Terman, developer of the Stanford-Binet IQ test, and Yerkes expressed in talking about IQ tests: certitude. They knew without question that they were right. They often turned sanctimonious in rebutting critics. Even today some psychometricians act more like members of a religious brotherhood than a collection of disinterested scientists when it comes to discussing and defending their profession.

In this country as in England, the initial interest in educational testing focused on measuring sensory attributes with an implicit, sometimes explicit, assumption that those who had fast reaction times or highly attuned perception were also brighter. American psychologists were under the sway of the British empiricist school of philosophers who held, among other things, that information could only get into the brain via the senses. Highly refined senses, therefore, could well point to an acute intelligence.

During World War I, though, as scientists tried to predict who among the recruits would make good officers or specialists, the interest in measurement broadened to other areas that seemed more directly akin to intellectual functions. In any event, the fundamental goal of measurement in most instances was to separate sheep from goats. That function would increase in power until the 1960s. If education were a sorting machine, tests would be the principal engine to drive it.

The exact moment when educational measurement first began is somewhat clouded and depends, in part, on what aspects of measurement one considers. In 1918, Leonard Ayres claimed that the history of educational measurement was 50 years old if one looked at the "oldest beginnings of which we have record," 25 years old if one began with the comparative studies of J.M. Rice, but only 10 years old if one started with the work of E.L. Thorndike (p. 9). Ayres was apparently distinguishing between "measurement" and simple examinations which, said early psychometrician, Giles M. Ruch in 1929, "appear to be as old as formal education itself."

Not that examinations and measurement hadn't undergone changes. In 1845, Horace Mann argued at length for the superiority of the written examination over the then-traditional oral examination, using a line of argument later applied for objective examinations. The written examination, said Mann,

> submits the same question not only to all the scholars who are to be examined, in the same school, but to all schools of the same class or grade. Scholars in the same school, therefore, can be equitably compared with each other; and all the different schools are subjected to a measurement by the same standard. Take the best school committee-man who ever exposed the nakedness of ignorance, or detected fraud, or exploded the bubbles of pretension, and let him examine a class orally, and he cannot approach the exactness in judging of the relative merits of the pupils by any very close approximation. And the reason is apparent. He must propound different questions to different scholars; and it is impossible that these questions should be equal, in point of ease or difficulty. (Caldwell and Courtis, 1924, p. 37)

In fact, the oral examination, said Mann, often puts the good scholar at a disadvantage. Given 30 students and an hour for testing, the examiner can allot each student only two minutes. This alone is sufficient argument for a written test that provides each student the entire hour, but this lengthening of time is more important for the better performers. "Now it often happens that a sterling scholar is modest, diffident, and easily disconcerted under new circumstances. Such a pupil requires time to collect his faculties. Give him this, and he will not disappoint his best friends" (Caldwell and Courtis, p. 40).

Mann also observed that teachers often undermined examinations by providing leading information or by asking questions in ways that suggested a particular line of answer. Although Mann's arguments were 80 years old, Ruch was impressed by their power and modernity. He distilled them into 12 points in the language of then-contemporary testing (Ruch, like many psychometricians, was fond of making his points in numbered lists).

Whatever the starting point, "mental testing," a phrase first used by James McKeen Cattell in 1890, made a huge leap of "progress" sometime during World War I. The military needed quickly to classify some two million recruits and to assess their various abilities. We are so accustomed today to mass testing that we can scarcely imagine what a daunting task this must have seemed in the absence of contemporary scoring procedures. As it turned out, one Arthur Otis, then a graduate student working with Lewis M. Terman at Stanford, had developed a test that did not require individual assessment. It could be administered in groups. It also contained a feature that elicited little comment at the time: the use of question formats that would become known as "new-type" or "objective," including the multiple-choice item. Until recently, this type of question has been so taken for granted that most people fail to understand how important its development was and what a drastic turn in measurement it occasioned.

Though slow to gain a substantial foothold, the multiple-choice format increased in popularity over the years after its invention, especially after University of Iowa psychometrician E.F. Lindquist invented ways in which the answer sheets could be rapidly scored by machines. Up to the mid-1980s, it enjoyed a virtual stranglehold on item formats on all assessments, save those in the vocational and the fine- and performing-arts arenas. Little noticed and, indeed, actively resisted was a spin-off from the Heisenberg uncertainty principle in physics: how you measure something may well influence what you see. Until recently, those of us who have challenged the utility of multiple-choice questions have been dismissed, accused of "tossing out a host of shopworn attacks on multiple-choice tests" (Popham, 1987, p. 688).

As noted, the advent of the multiple-choice question caused little excitement at the time. In 1918, E.L. Thorndike, writing generally on assessment, made no mention of multiple-choice items, but only the "products" of education. In his brief 1918 essay, Thorndike laid down a "Credo" that is still a canon in many quarters:

> Whatever exists at all exists in some amount. To know it thoroughly involves knowing its quantity as well as its quality. Education is concerned with changes in human beings; a change is a difference between two conditions; each of these conditions is known to us only by the products produced by it—*things made, words spoken, acts performed,* and the like. To measure any of these products means to define its amount in some way so that competent persons will know how large it is, better than they would without measurement. To measure a product well means so to define its amount that competent persons will know how large it is, with some precision, and that this knowledge may be conveniently recorded and used [italics added]. (Thorndike, 1918, p. 16)

One wonders how Thorndike might have gone about measuring a Monet.

Thorndike's statement reflects the tenor of the times for those in educational psychology. Many experimental psychologists viewed their principal goal as developing psychology into an experimental science on a par with physics. Science is sometimes defined as a discipline adequate to its subject. For many early psychologists, unfortunately, the nature of the subject to be studied was often sacrificed to the quest for scientific legitimacy. Educational researchers and test developers such as Thorndike took experimental psychology as their model (outside the fields of educational research and psychometrics, thinking was influenced by a wider band of philosophers including Hegel and Herbart, particularly Herbart).

Thorndike also noted problematic areas in educational measurement that bedevil many investigators today—generalizability and validity:

> Great care should be taken in deciding anything about the fate of pupils, the value of methods, the achievement of school systems and the like from the scores

made in a test, unless the significance of the test has been determined from its correlations. For example, it cannot be taken for granted that a high score in checking letters or numbers is significant of a high degree of accuracy and thoroughness in general....A pupil's score in a test signifies first, such and such a particular achievement, and second, *only whatever has been demonstrated by actual correlations to be implied by it.* (1918, p. 22)

Thorndike hinted in this paper that there was an additional problem: a vague criterion about what it was the tests should indicate. He fumed that all we really had in our possession was normative data. In a *Psychological Review* article a few years later, he made these concerns more precise:

When we assert that a man is found by measurement with the Army Alpha to have the intellect of an average recruit in the draft, all that is really asserted is that he does as well in that particular battery of tests scored and summated in a particular way, as the average recruit did. Just what the intellects of recruits were and how closely their Alpha scores paralleled their intellects, we do not know. The measurement is one thing, the inference to intellect is a different thing....We do not know how closely the rating or score in the Stanford Binet or the Army Alpha or any other instrument correlates with a perfect criterion of intellect, because we do not know what such a criterion is, much less its correlations with these tests. (Thorndike, 1973, p. 8)

In addition, said Thorndike, the tests themselves are imperfect in several ways. He was not happy with the necessity of measuring the products of the intellect, and he speculated on the direct observation of intellect through the activity of the thyroid gland or perhaps the intensity of certain chemical processes, or "the intensity of the fibrillary action of certain neurones." He was not sanguine, however, about accomplishing this any time soon:

At present, we know so little of the neural correlates of intellect that if twenty freshmen were immolated to this inquiry, ten being the most intellectual of a hundred, and ten being the least intellectual of a hundred, and their brains were studied in every way by our best neurologists, these could probably not locate sixteen out of the twenty correctly as at top or bottom. Moreover, what we do know of neural correlates is of little avail during life, the living neurones being extremely inaccessible to present methods of observation. (Thorndike, p. 12)

What is "intellect?" Thorndike first considered that it was the ability to obtain truth in the service of improving prediction, quite the same as a scientist might seek. He rejected that notion, though, contending that psychologists, people in general, and makers of intelligence tests meant by intelligence "what Pericles and Washington and Gladstone had as well as what Aristotle and Pasteur and Darwin had" (p. 15). After some further considerations, Thorndike concluded that the intellect, whatever it might be, was not a singular entity:

Any system of units of measurement [of the intellect] that is to be adequate must then apparently be flexible enough to a wide variety of operations such as we may call attention, retention, recall, recognition, selective and relational thinking, abstraction, generalization, organization, inductive and deductive reasoning, together with learning and knowledge in general. (p. 22)

For a first approximation, let intellect be defined as that quality of mind in respect to which Aristotle, Plato, Thucydides, and the like differed most from Athenian idiots of their day, or in respect to which lawyers, physicians, scientists, scholars, and editors of reputed greatest ability at constant age, say a dozen of each, most differ from idiots of that age in our asylums. (p. 25)

It is not clear if the inclusion of editors was a sop to his own, but, clearly, under this definition one cannot be intelligent and crazy at the same time. It concerned Thorndike that we had no external criterion for deciding what made different tasks differentially difficult. He wanted to know why, say, the study of physics was more difficult than the memorization of words, but he simply had to accept that it was. It was performance on tasks of increasing difficulty, normatively and empirically defined, though, that permitted the measurement of intelligence.

Following what he said was psychological theory, psychometric theory, and common sense, Thorndike decided that he could measure intelligence—exclusive of social intelligence and mechanical intelligence—with sentence completion, problem solving, comprehension, and discourse questions (both oral and written). Some of the questions resemble those common to most forms of IQ tests others require specific knowledge. For instance, among the sentence-completion items were many similar to the following:

The Declaration ____ _____ affirms that the Creator _____ all men with certain inalienable _____.
(p. 77)

Vocabulary items were assessed with multiple-choice format questions, as were, in a way, some of the comprehension questions. These often took the form of a quotation with four possible interpretations, sometimes themselves quotations. For instance:

"It is one thing to see that a line is crooked and another thing to be able to draw a straight one."

____It is one thing to see the mote in our neighbor's eye and another to see the beam in our own.

____Those who see mistakes cannot always correct them.

____As the eye is trained to accuracy the hand develops skill.

____We may recognize faults that we are unable to overcome. (p. 79)

Outside of these areas, Thorndike did not invoke multiple-choice questions.

Thorndike did not appear to have the common view of intelligence as unitary. He also seems not to have been the nativist that most other testing people were. Thorndike was well aware that his tasks measured both nature and nurture, that they depended in many instances on education and training. "We are measuring available power of intellectual achievement without any specification as to its genesis." It might be interesting to try to measure pure "original capacity," but Thorndike did not think that was possible until adequate measurement of intellectual achievement, as found in the real world, had been attained. And besides, he said, "there is also danger that, if we include in a series of intellectual tasks only those in whose accomplishment differences of education can make little or no difference, we shall have a collection of freakish puzzles, irrelevant to the actual operations of the intellect…" (pp. 95–96).

Thorndike was a giant of educational psychology and psychological testing, but his approach had the ironic effect of helping make the field virtually irrelevant to people in schools. In 1899, at the age of 25, Thorndike had written an essay, characteristically titled, "Sentimentality in Science Teaching," in which he declared that "one can readily show that the emotionally indifferent attitude of the scientific observer is an ethically far higher attitude than the loving interest of the poet." At no time in the ensuing 50 years of his career did he moderate this overarching trust in the capacity of science to solve all problems—even after, as David Berliner noted in 1993, the events of the Holocaust and Hiroshima caused many to question their faith in science.

Thorndike's "emotionally indifferent attitude of the scientific observer" led him away from schools. One can imagine him virtually holding his nose over the messy problems that real educational settings present. His stance was most in opposition to that of John Dewey. Whereas Dewey saw the school as a laboratory for his work, Thorndike wanted to establish a research laboratory where he could control events. Thorndike's attitudes contributed mightily to a psychometry and educational psychology that ignored the realities of schools.

This remoteness of educational psychology and testing from the ecology of the classroom continued until recently. As late as 1984, Elliot Eisner at Stanford University and Eva Baker at the University of California, Los Angeles could engage in a debate in the pages of *Phi Delta Kappan* as to whether educational research could ever inform educational practice (Eisner, 1984, and Baker, 1984). Eisner took essentially a negative position and won in a walk, noting, among other things, that the average duration of "treatments" in experiments published in articles of the *American Educational Research Association*, the flagship journal of the American Educational Research Association (AERA), lasted only about three-fourths of an hour (a situation happily changed in the last decade).

Teachers, by and large, never saw educational research as attending to their problems, nor did they see the tests developed from the Thorndikian approach as validly representing what they were about in the classroom—even though many of them emulated the tests' formats and took on the assumptions about what tests did or did not reveal. The disjuncture between teaching and testing was of no consequence as long as testing itself was of no consequence to teachers, a condition that prevailed until the 1960s.

The phrase "high-stakes testing program" would have been

meaningless until after the Great Society programs of Lyndon Johnson's administration began in 1965. That landmark legislation also produced a marked change in the evaluation of educational innovations. To that point, most social programs were evaluated in terms of how they spent their money. Now the grantors of federal funds held the grantees accountable for showing that their interventions actually produced some improvement. When the program evaluators looked around for tools, what they found, by and large, were tests. The Thorndikian attitude had inhibited the development of school-relevant program-evaluation instruments.

Not all testers were so dismissive of school problems. Ruch, as noted, took as the starting point for his ruminations on testing the arguments for classroom written tests put forward 75 years earlier by Mann. Ruch first observed that "there is no convincing evidence that examinations are essential to the complete procedure of instruction. There is similarly no indisputable evidence that they are not....The worth of examinations is open to crucial experimental determination, and nothing short of this will be convincing in the long run" (pp. 8–10).

Ruch posited four justifications often given for examinations: they motivate students to learn; they maintain standards of achievement; they train people in the use of the English language; and they measure achievement. Ruch thought that most tests had failed as motivators but that this was a fault of how they had been used. If the exam were impartial, he argued, students would esteem it and be motivated to perform well on it. He thought tests should come frequently—an end-of-semester test was too remote a goal to stimulate students. In addition, students should keep cumulative records of their performance as a means of plotting their progress, something that Thorndike had earlier posited as a means of motivating students. Thorndike's formulation came close to making the distinction between norm-referenced and criterion-referenced measurement, a distinction formalized in the 1960s that assumed considerable importance in the 1970s and thereafter. Finally, Ruch said, tests that are of "detailed, specific, and diagnostic character" would not be seen as drudgery. If these four conditions could be met, Ruch contended, tests would function as motivators to learning.

As for the use of tests in maintaining standards of accomplishment, he was more skeptical. He observed that many city-, county-, and statewide testing programs were developed in the hopes of evaluating teachers' efficiency. He noted that pioneer

J.M. Rice had been severely criticized by the National Education Association (NEA) around the turn of the century for using tests for this purpose. Ruch's analysis is quite contemporary:

> It was first thought that the standard tests would serve to evaluate teaching upon the principles that if pupils showed high accomplishment, the teaching was good, but if pupil achievement was low, teaching was, perforce, unsatisfactory.
>
> The dangers inherent in this point of view were soon exposed. The standard test method made no allowances for differences in pupils' mental equipment, the most important single factor controlling the rate of learning yet found. It was soon realized that standard tests were unadaptable to local conditions, that they were open to abuses through coaching, that they were not as unerring guides as first supposed, and that they often misfired in reaching the essential activities of the classroom. (pp. 12–13)

If Ruch was skeptical of tests as keepers of standards, he absolutely dismissed the idea that tests helped students organize their thoughts and put them down in good English. Most student tests, he declared, are far worse written than other products—they may actually be destructive of good English. Students have to write too fast to pay attention to composition or style. Students also know that teachers will grade on facts, not style. Finally, he said, "Language habits are complex....It is unlikely that they will arise as by-products of frenzied efforts at setting down facts in limited time" (p. 14).

So far as Ruch saw the situation, there were four types of examinations available: oral, written, standard, and the objective or new-type. As noted earlier, he dismissed the oral examination, but he now also pronounced the written test unfit because "*experience and experiment have shown that the results of an essay examination cannot be evaluated fairly by the human mind*" (p. 20, emphasis in the original). What are we to make of it, he asked, when the same paper receives scores from 40 to 90 out of a possible 100 when graded by different people?

For Ruch, the standard test, which we would today call a norm-referenced standardized test, had numerous advantages over the written essay. It strove to "standardize the conditions of the examination period with respect to directions, time allowances, method of responding, etc....They are objective or impartial....They provide norms or standards" (p. 22). Despite this, Ruch alleged that most of the then-current standard tests were of little value and suggested that if "100 of the best were selected and the rest destroyed, the loss would be negligible" (p. 23).

The only other serious limitation of the standard test was that it "cannot be adapted to the idiosyncrasies of local school conditions." For this reason, the objective test was also needed, it being a teacher-constructed test similar to standard tests but lacking norms, item tryouts, and the other refinements put to a well-constructed published test. Formats of the standard or objective tests could take the form of recall, completion, true-false, or multiple-choice items.

The advantages of the objective test led Ruch to conclude that the traditional written examination was destined for oblivion:

> Looking back over the five-year period in which the author has been engaged in studying experimentally one phase or another of examination construction, the story of the progress of objective examination methods is ample ground for predicting that something like the objective examination, when perfected, will be the principal reliance of the classroom teacher for the next few decades to come. There will doubtless be a place for the traditional examination in the future, but it seems likely that it will tend to become a last resort, to be employed when other methods are not at hand. It may be possible to perfect the ordinary examination so as to control some of its vagaries, but progress to date leaves small reason to hope for marked success. (p. 25)

Ruch's notions of reliability and, especially, validity approximate some current conceptions. While validity "is the degree to which a test or examination measures what it is intended to measure," a valid test is also a worthwhile test, a test that incorporates the essential elements of the topic, a test that parallels the curriculum and good teaching practice, and a test that is used to measure the abilities it was intended to measure.

Ruch realized that the new tests permitted guessing, but he argued that the traditional examination permitted "bluffing," writing about material only tangentially related to the question, which the new tests did not. Said Ruch, "on the whole, exchanging the disturbing factor of bluffing for the admitted danger of guessing is a gain, since there is no mathematical formula for minimizing bluffing, but there is a more or less adequate statistical means of allowing for guessing" (p. 110).

In other areas of measurement, Ruch and his compatriots were remarkably naïve. For instance, one of his students devised an experiment to test the argument advanced by critics of the objective test that it did not measure all that a student knew and that discussion questions elicited more knowledge (p. 53). For this he presented students with essay examinations such as "Discuss fully Ireland, Scotland, and England." He also presented them with objective tests "covering the same ground." Essays were scored for number of facts presented and points made, objective tests for number correct. Over a variety of subjects, the experimenter found that the students got more than twice as many multiple-choice questions correct as they made points in the essay setting and that they took, on average, only half as long to make the twice-as-many points. The ratio of essay points to correct answers on the objective test was, on average, .44. "It seems likely," Ruch concluded, "that the essay test calls forth less than half (.44) of the pupil's real knowledge of the subject" (p. 54). And it takes twice as long to boot. Fifty-five years later, Norman Frederiksen and colleagues at Educational Testing Service (ETS) would demonstrate that constructs measured by essay and other performance tests could not be captured in multiple choice formats. That is, the different tests measured different "things." This revelation contributed quickly to a rising interest in "authentic" assessment (Frederiksen, 1984).

There are several qualities about the writing of Ruch and others of the time worth noting. First, the student is nowhere seen as a person. He is a student, a pupil, or a scholar, but in reality he is a manipulable subject of the tester. To determine scientifically how much a student knows requires only the proper instrumentation and method. While Thorndike believed that students' interest in the test would vary in ways that could not be controlled, Ruch proposed methods to get everyone motivated.

Second, the teacher is seldom seen, as well, although she is more visible in Ruch's writings than in Thorndike's. Again, there is a concentration on perfecting the method, a perfection certain to be attained.

Third, Ruch's reflections very much represent Thorndike's credo that if a thing exists, it exists in some quantity. And while Thorndike spoke of measuring only the products of intellect,

Ruch appears to believe that direct measurement of "real knowledge" and the like are possible. Although Werner Heisenberg would receive the Nobel prize for his Uncertainty Principle in 1932, only three years after Ruch's book appeared, it is unlikely that his reasoning was known to those in the fledgling field of psychological testing. While Ruch speaks of variables that can distort or prevent accurate measurement, there is no hint of any awareness that the very *what* of what is being measured can be affected by the very *how* by which it is measured. Ruch, Thorndike, and the rest inhabited a Newtonian rather than an Einsteinian universe.

Fourth, there is in Ruch, as in Thorndike, a concern for efficiency and a faith that science will allow efficiency to prevail. Ruch's acceptance of his student's comparison of essay and multiple-choice questions "covering the same ground" is so naïve from an otherwise astute observer that it suggests Ruch wanted to believe the results.

Against the charge that objective questions measured only memory, whereas thought questions caused students to think, Ruch mounted both anecdote and reasoning. He recalled a letter from an acquaintance who had written that his recent professor had for six weeks "waxed warm and loud in his praises of the thought question—and never once provided an example" (p. 121). Whether a question is a thought question or not depends on the background of the examinee, said Ruch. He gave an example: "Why do many taxation authorities believe that the income tax is the fairest form of taxation yet developed?" (p. 121). An intelligent person unfamiliar with the topic *could* reason out some whys, Ruch contended. But a student in a course of economics might well have seen the reasons listed by number in a page on his textbook, rendering the so-called thought question one of mere memory.

When he came to the objection that objective formats were unnatural and unpedagogical, Ruch invoked a line of argument and observation that would be recapitulated 60 years later by Lauren Resnick at the University of Pittsburgh:

> It would be most instructive and valuable to study the exact forms in which school-acquired knowledge is used in actual life. These modes would then be our answer as to what are the natural or pedagogical forms of questions. As a rough substitute for such experimental investigations, the author has made a conscious effort to ob-

serve the ways in which adults use their concepts and information. One fruitful source of hints has been the conversations in the smoking compartments of Pullman cars. Thus far, nothing has been found which resembles closely any variety of school question-and-answer with the possible exception of a sort of true-false statement. Certainly no person after leaving the public schools has ever been called upon to write or to recite answers to such a question as "Give the causes of the Revolutionary war" or "Explain in full the digestion of carbohydrates." We do hear adults make statements to the effect that "the League of Nations is a flat failure" or that "the Monroe Doctrine is nothing more or less than a chip on America's shoulder." To such an assertion there is speedy and dogmatic challenging, attempted support and refutation, and a final settling down to argument. Whether it be the riding qualities of the new Ford, the payment of European debts, or the batting of Babe Ruth, nothing closely akin to the question of the traditional examination emerges.

We are densely ignorant of what is "natural" as a type of examination question....As has been stressed before, *the examination should be nothing more or less than a sampling of the kinds of activities which go on daily in the classroom.* (Ruch, 1929, p. 127)

For Ruch and almost all others, the value of tests lay in their ability to discriminate among students and to classify them. Tests were the instrument of the sorting machine. Classification, as noted earlier, was important because it allowed students of different ability to receive instruction tailored to that ability. As a secondary function, tests could be used to assign grades. Norms, useful for interpretation, were not essential:

The value of norms has been badly over-estimated, even in the case of standard tests. Carefully derived norms have unquestionable value, but local conditions relative to the course of study, ages of children in different grades, differences in racial and economic background, variations in mental ability, etc., make general or "blanket" norms uncertain business.

The constructor of objective tests must seek other means of interpretation than through the use of norms. Local norms may be derived with the accumulation of records, and in the long run, interpretations may be made quite as accurate as practical demand suggests. (Ruch, 1929, p. 66)

The above seems an appropriate stance when thinking of a nation whose 60,000-plus school districts were still very much buffeted by local conditions, where technology did not really link the various districts in any meaningful way.

If norms did not provide a useful handle by which to interpret tests, neither did the normal curve:

> *The number of A's which should be given is wholly a matter of definition.* Each school must settle for itself such questions as a matter of administrative policy. There is an idea current that such letter-grade distributions are somehow derived from and fixed by the normal curve. The normal curve is totally impotent in the matter, unless we except the fact that the normal curve does suggest the relative proportions of letter grades in contrast to absolute numbers. (p. 67)

Ruch's admonitions about norms and the normal curve were overwhelmed by the normative concerns of most test developers. And, as tests became more homogeneous in form, more and more attention was paid to their statistical properties. When mechanical and then electronic scoring procedures became feasible, the economy and efficiency of multiple-choice questions and scorable answer sheets gradually squeezed out competing forms. With the advent of high-speed computers, people were able to do tasks in nanoseconds without wondering if they should be doing them at all. Such an emphasis on the technical considerations of tests drew the wrath of *Mental Measurements Yearbook* editor Oscar Buros, who in 1978 wrote that

> Statistical methods such as these [item validation procedures] greatly simplify the task of the testmaker. The selection of the most discriminating items on the basis of a tryout requires no knowledge of the content matter of the test. It is a task which any testing specialist can perform. There is still another advantage in using discriminating items only—they will result in higher reliabilities....Although these [item validation] techniques are widely used by our very best test makers, it is my thesis that these techniques have been harmful to the development of the best possible measuring instruments. These statistical methods of item validation con-

fuse differentiation with measurement and exaggerate differences among individuals and between grades. I would like to see their use discontinued. (p. 1975)

Buros went on to note that the technical procedures resulted in some instances in the inclusion of items that subject matter experts and teachers thought poor and the exclusion of some that subject matter experts and teachers thought both good and important. Elsewhere, Buros observed that test makers made it nearly impossible for test users to use raw scores. By converting to some norm-referenced score, Buros hinted, the test makers could obscure where there hadn't been any learning.[3]

No doubt, this obsession with the statistical properties of the test was responsible for less technical but no less astute comments, such as those of teacher James Herndon in one of the epigraphs to this chapter.

At times, the obsession with the statistical properties of tests was so overwhelming that the nature of education got lost. Nowhere was this more evident than in the multifarious (and sometimes nefarious) procedures for keeping tests "secure"—that is, for keeping people ignorant of their contents. When I was in graduate school, a fellow student once said that the University of Minnesota could give its introductory psychology test over and over again because there was such tight security surrounding it. I recall thinking at the time that this totally perverted what I thought to be the goal of the university; the institution had to hide from its students those parts of psychology it deemed most important. But I tossed the matter aside as another peculiarity of the Dust Bowl Empiricism which had been rampant for years in the Midwest.

The secrecy aspect of testing is something that has not been much noted in its evolution, but it is a critical aspect of most testing programs and of social control in education in general. As Allan Hanson has observed in *Testing, Testing: Social Consequences of the Examined Life*, concerning not only academic achievement tests but also drug tests, lie detection tests, and, indeed, all tests: "the testing situation entails the application of power over the subjects of tests. Such power is to a degree in the hands of the persons who order and administer the tests, but it inheres more importantly in the organizations they represent and especially in the total social system" (1994).

Grant Wiggins of the Center on Learning, Assessment, and School Structure (CLASS) discerned in *Assessing Student Perfor-*

mance (1993) that the secrecy surrounding tests is so common that we—"we" doing the testing and, often, "we" taking the tests—never think about it:

> It is so common that we barely give it a second thought: the tests that we and others design to evaluate the success of student learning invariably depend upon secrecy. Secrecy as to the questions that will be asked. Secrecy as to how the questions will be chosen. Secrecy as to how the results will be scored. Sometimes secrecy as to when we will be tested. Secrecy as to what the scores mean (if we are not given back our tests and an answer key). Secrecy as to how the results will be used. What a paradoxical affair! Our aim is to educate, to prepare, to enlighten, yet our habits of testing are built upon procedures that continually keep students in the dark—procedures with roots in premodern traditions of legal proceedings and religious inquisitions. (p. 72)

Wiggins later brings these "premodern traditions" into part of the modern world:

> High stakes and large-scale secret tests (such as the SATs), in which the only apparent judges are electronic, threaten intellectual integrity even further, because they heap harmful suspicion on human judgment. Intellectual freedom is thus threatened by secure testing in the same way that it is threatened by political rule that emphasizes ritual and secrecy above the consent of the governed. Is it cavalier to suggest that the centrally mandated and secret testing of students in this country parallels the centrally planned and secret-dominated political systems now collapsing throughout Eastern Europe? I think not, for in Poland and Czechoslovakia, workers and citizens learned to do what many students and school districts regularly end up doing here: obey the letter of the law only; do no more and no less than the state directives require; see no incentives—indeed, see many disincentives—to set and honor more authentic standards. (p. 102)

In the command-economy days of the Soviet Union, Poles told this joke: "They pretend to pay us; we pretend to work." The typical testing system produces an educational analog: "They pretend to teach us; we pretend to learn."

Wiggins presents means by which this defect of the system might be addressed, but he also offers reasons why it will not be: the victims of the system by and large can't vote and, therefore, have no clout. In addition, when Wiggins discusses what he calls "An Assessment Bill of Rights," he finds it often makes teachers openly hostile. One can hope, however, that the "Standards for Educational and Psychological Testing," promulgated jointly by the American Psychological Association, the American Educational Research Association, and the National Council for Measurement in Education and currently under revision, will take test consumers' needs and rights more into account than did the previous editions.

By 1927, according to Oscar Buros, testing was well-established in its largely contemporary form. Most changes had more to do with scoring than with the testing process. By the 1960s, however, there was considerable ferment both in education generally and in the field of assessment. Chapter One documented the pre-Sputnik criticisms of schools. Within testing, the typical norm-referenced test (NRT) had come to be used almost exclusively—and almost exclusively for ranking students. In 1963, Commissioner of Education Francis Keppel wondered if it might be possible to conduct a "census" on the knowledge and skills of American students. The gathering of medical statistics about health and the incidence of disease had led to improvements in health programs. Could the same thing happen in education? In addition, Keppel as commissioner, was required to submit periodic reports to Congress about progress in education. Most of these had to do with time and money. Keppel was interested in reporting on performance, no doubt because he thought the performance of the American educational system was so low. In any case, Keppel undertook to construct what we now call the National Assessment of Educational Progress (NAEP).

Also in 1963, a short article by Robert Glaser was languishing in the *American Psychologist.* This article made reference to "norm-referenced measurement" on the one hand and "criterion-referenced measurement" on the other, a distinction first made by Thorndike, though not in those words. The first, as implied in the title, refers to a relative standard, while the second "depends upon an absolute standard of quality." One might, without doing terrible damage to the notion, call the original NAEP the first criterion-referenced testing program. In the 1990s,

NAEP and criterion-referenced measurement would become inappropriately fused in a different way, but that is getting ahead of our history.

THE NATIONAL ASSESSMENT OF EDUCATIONAL PROGRESS

Keppel turned to Ralph Tyler, then director of the Center for Advanced Study of the Behavioral Sciences at Stanford, to explore the possibilities of such a census. Tyler, in turn, with money from the Carnegie and Ford Foundations, put together the Exploratory Committee on the Assessment of Progress in Education (ECAPE).

One possible way of getting the information that Keppel sought would have been to give some extant norm-referenced test (NRT) to a random sample of students. This the committee rejected for a variety of reasons. One was simply that NRTs were too closely associated with ranking. Another was that Keppel and the ECAPE had in mind assessing 10 areas: art, citizenship, career development, occupational development, literature, music, reading, science, social studies, and writing. In many of these areas, NRTs were silent.

In addition, the committee was interested in what is now known as performance assessment. Students were to be assessed in science by doing experiments, in writing by essays, in art by creating things. ECAPE referred to its assessments from the beginning as "exercises," not items, that were "objective-referenced," not norm-referenced. Tyler, especially, was at pains to correct anyone who referred to the material as a "test."

Moreover, NRTs were structured according to grades, but there was much variance, nationally, in who learned what and when. Tyler echoed Ruch in worrying about the inapplicability of uniform measures and uniform ages across such widely varying systems.

Finally, the committee did not want NAEP to be constrained by the statistical considerations imposed on NRTs. About half of all students respond correctly to the typical item on an NRT, and few items are very hard or very easy. (This kind of item selection maximizes the dispersion of students' scores, the NRT goal that Buros was earlier cited as disparaging.) In contrast, the exercises for NAEP were to be written so that one-third could be correctly answered by 90 percent of the test takers, one-third by about 50 percent, and one-third by only 10 percent. This distribution of scores reflected Tyler's opinion that it was important to assess what has been learned, as well as what has not:

The assessment exercises will differ from current achievement tests in two other important aspects. An achievement test seeks to measure individual differences among pupils taking them. Hence the items are concentrated with those which differentiate among the pupils. Exercises which all or nearly all can do as well as those which only a very few can do are omitted, because these do not give much differentiation. But for the purpose of assessing the progress of education we need to know what all or almost all of the children are learning and what the most advanced are learning, as well as what is being learned by the middle or "average" children. To get exercises of this sort will be a new venture for test-constructors. (1965, pp. 14–15)

Tyler saw NAEP as producing something akin to indices found in other fields:

The need for data on progress has been recognized in other spheres of American life. During the depression, the lack of dependable information about the progress of the economy was a serious handicap in focusing efforts and in assessing them. Out of this need grew an index of production, Gross National Product, which has been of great value in guiding economic development. Correspondingly, the Consumer Price Index was developed as a useful measure of the changes in cost of living and inflation.

We need to apply this logic to education, said Tyler, because education has become so important:

Education, today, is of great concern to all Americans. Without education our young people cannot get jobs, are unable to participate intelligently and responsibly in civic and social life, and fail to achieve individual self-realization. Education is increasingly recognized as the servant of all our purposes. (1965, p. 13)

Tyler could not see any reason for objections to the assessment, because "it is clear that assessing the progress of education is not the same as mounting a nationwide testing program" (p. 14). He said this in spite of the fact that all of ECAPE's contracts at the time were with organizations that had experience only in producing the kinds of tests that Tyler eschewed: Educational Testing Service, Science Research Associates, the Psychological Corporation, and the American Institutes for Research.

In fact, the difference between tests and Tyler's proposed NAEP was not clear to most people. The zeitgeist at the time was adamantly against any collection of data that would permit state-by-state or district-by-district comparisons. Some educational organizations such as the American Association of School Administrators (AASA), the National Education Association (NEA), and the Association for Supervision and Curriculum Development (ASCD) were against the enterprise in general, no doubt because of Keppel himself and the alliance he put together to launch NAEP, a group described by one chief state school officer as having an "Eastern, ivy-league, foundation syndrome."

When Keppel later wrote of his experiences, he sounded much like Arthur Bestor, disdaining the schools and the professional educators in the universities' schools of education. Indeed, Keppel was Eastern and Ivy League—his father was the dean of admissions at Columbia University; he, himself, had attended Harvard and later became its dean of education through the considerable machinations of Harvard president J.B. Conant. Conant believed that "there might be some little trouble in selling Keppel to the school people" since Keppel had no advanced degree and no public-school experience and was only 32 years old. But Conant appointed him and apparently was quite happy with his performance (Hazlett, p. 58).

Keppel, for his part, while disdaining professional educators, also thought that the U.S. system of local control had become obsolete. While he had Bestor's faith in liberal arts, unlike Bestor, he also had Sputnik and the years afterward as additional guides: education was too important to leave to just the locals any longer; the national interest was at stake and that meant there was a federal role in the enterprise. Although it is never stated, it is not too remote to speculate that Keppel might have seen NAEP as one means of systematizing the curriculum and perhaps even of stimulating the growth of a truly national curriculum. This, at least, was what he was accused of by Harold Hand, professor of education at the University of South Florida, at an ASCD convention. Hand called the proposals for NAEP "a fiendish innovation which the [Carnegie] Corporation and the United States seemed bent on perpetrating..." (Hazlett p. 95).

Hand elaborated his position in *Phi Delta Kappan* in September 1965:

I am opposed to a national testing program set up for purposes of comparing schools chiefly because (a) it would set up new obstacles to realization of our goal of equality of educational opportunity, (b) it would be the nose under the tent which would be followed by a monstrous camel in the form of a centrally controlled curriculum, (c) it would stultify the curriculum, (d) it would stifle local innovation and experimentation in respect to the curriculum, (e) it would result in unbearable pressures on classroom teachers and school administrators, and (f) it would encourage cheating on the part of students and teachers alike. (Hand, 1965, p. 9)

Also in the September 1965 *Kappan* was a report of one panel's discussion of NAEP at a White House Conference on education. Most of the panelists seemed against one or more of the possible NAEP outcomes. Jack Arbolino, director of advanced placement at the College Board, asked, "Can we assess student achievement without encouraging conformity?" Hedley Donovan, editor-in-chief at Time, Inc., said, "I question our ability to construct any valid system of central assessment." Sister Jacqueline, president of Webster College, commented, "Any unit—town, state, or nation—that employs a monolithic set of standards is stifling growth. It doesn't have to be a national test." Jerrold Zaccharias, developer of the New Physics, stated that "we do not need to hang a sword of Damocles over the head of the child by instituting ruinous pressure of competition" (*Phi Delta Kappan*, September 1965, pp. 17–18).

These statements reflect the fears and misunderstandings—and the psychology—prevalent at the time. Among the panel's advocates for a national assessment was John Goodlad, at the time director of the University Elementary School at UCLA. Goodlad addressed the need to break the iron group of norm-referenced tests:

Today we are happy if a fifth grader with an I.Q. score of 100 reads at the sixth-grade level, unconcerned with where he should be reading based on *his* ability, not the group average of attainment. All fifth graders can be reading at fifth-grade level and *all* be deficient in some aspect of reading going undiagnosed. We have done almost no assessment based on criterion measures rather than norm-based standards. (p. 17)

Resistance was widespread. In early 1967, AASA's executive committee sent a letter to affiliates advising them not to cooperate with the tryouts of the materials and giving them four reasons why. First, it will be a uniform test that does not take diversity into account. Second, NAEP "*is a national testing program*, and as such it will be coercive, it will inevitably lead to the pressures of regional, state, and local comparisons, and it will have national overtones in the dispensing of federal aid." Third, only comparisons would be relevant to those who would sit in judgment of the schools. And finally, "The national assessment project would yield very little, if any, information on the performance of students in public and private schools which is not already known" (Hazlett p. 188).

Although the NEA had passed a resolution withholding support the previous summer, that resolution had been lost in a host of resolutions, and it was, therefore, the AASA letter that caused articles in the media and reactions from educators all over the country. The AASA letter had also been more sophisticated in articulating the fears people had about NAEP.

Later, after much correspondence with Tyler, AASA shifted its position. In addition, as the project moved toward actuality, governance disputes were resolved by placing the enterprise with the state-operated Education Commission of the States, effectively removing the threat of federal control. Still, in the years leading up to the first assessments in 1969, there was tension between NAEP on the one hand and educational organizations and the Department of Education on the other; there was also tension between the Department of Education and Congress. Each entity was suspicious of the other's motives.

While most NAEP exercises were multiple-choice and machine-scorable, such formats were not seen as part of the long-range plan:

> The early planners of NAEP felt that more accurate and responsive results could be obtained from assessees if bound booklets were used on which the assessee could write directly rather than on answer sheets separated from the exercise itself. Moreover, it was the plan that, increasingly, forms other than multiple-choice would be used which would not lend themselves to the ease of machine scoring." (Hazlett, p. 17)

It is worth noting that the originators of NAEP felt that "all exercises should have *face* or content *validity*. This means that the content material to which an exercise addresses itself is worthwhile in itself as a bit of knowledge, as a skill, or as a situation around which attitudes and feelings can be developed in a school setting. There should be no content triviality, nor should an item be selected as a contributor in the setting of test norms. Indeed, conceivably, the character of the response on a single exercise might be the basis for a significant judgment" (Tyler, 1965, p. 10). Tyler emphasized this face validity and contrasted it with the usual kind of testing:

> The other important difference [between NAEP and an NRT] is the requirement that each assessment exercise be intelligible to the thoughtful lay citizen and something which he recognizes as desirable for children to learn. Current achievement tests report in numerical scores, and items are often included which are correlated with grades or other criteria but which are not apparently sensible or significant for children to learn. (Tyler, p. 15)

It should be noted that "face validity," one of several types of validity describable for tests, had become an ignored aspect of tests. It is only recently (1993) that Grant Wiggins points once again to its importance in *Assessing Student Performance.* If students don't see a test as having face validity, they will not take it seriously, Wiggins contends.

There were to be three levels of reporting. The first was to determine the accuracy of the results, the second to organize the objectives (some exercises could be included, for instance, in both biology and physics), and the third would border on

> interpretation and speculation....Such an approach would seek to answer such questions as: Why is the median "p" value in the Southeast in the first four subjects reported uniformly lower than in the rest of the country? How does one account for the low proficiency in simple writing mechanics at ages 9 and 13? Why do young people possess as little knowledge of the structure and function of local and state government as National Assessment results seem to indicate? (Hazlett, 1974, p. 20)

Apparently, at least some were disappointed in NAEP's findings from the beginning.

A report from a 1964 conference of the planning committee

with Carnegie officials indicates its founders had multiple hopes for NAEP:

- It would increase the knowledge about education in the United States.
- It could show relationships between expenditures and results.
- Competitive aspects of the assessment would spark community effort.
- There would be more reliable data for decision making.
- Progress in education could be measured over time.
- There would be the possibility of international comparisons. (Hazlett, 1974, p. 48)

Conferees expressed fears about what might happen if the results were made public, if the public felt that NAEP only added one more test in schools where there were already too many tests, and whether NAEP would deflect and narrow curricula.

There were numerous exchanges between the NAEP developers, members of educational organizations, and members of Congress, the latter two groups fearing a federal takeover of education. Recall that the development of NAEP was occurring during the launch of the Johnson administration's Great Society programs, a massive federal initiative. Many citizens, not the least among them Southerners, were coping with desegregation; their school systems were at risk of being exposed as deficient if a federal program were able to report state-by-state data.

The worries about a federal strike into the heart of local control, the schools, were abetted by events in other spheres. Even the development of new types of exercises was cause for concern and suspicion. Many felt at the time that norm-referenced assessment was sufficient. Hazlett reports being told by members of Educational Testing Service that there was nothing a criterion-referenced test could do that a norm-referenced test couldn't. If there were no technical need for new forms of measurement, what were the motives of those who would develop them? (1974, p. 391).

It is interesting that since 1980, a period in which the federal government has pushed more initiatives for the states, NAEP has expanded in scope and visibility. It will be interesting to see if the radical power-to-the-states-block-grants-solve-all-problems philosophy displayed after the election of 1994 alters NAEP's role.

Certainly in its formative years, NAEP received little attention from anyone outside its immediate circle. To some extent, this was by design. As noted, school officials of the day were adamantly against any national system of testing that permitted reporting by student, district or state. As a consequence, NAEP reported only national and regional statistics. It reported by age, not grade. In addition, Hazlett argues that the complexity and novelty of design impeded the use of the results because they didn't fit the normative model people were used to. While Keppel and later Harold Howe II, as commisioners of education, both supported NAEP, Keppel's motivations were "suspect" and Howe was a less enthusiastic supporter. In addition, Office of Education staff members gave contradictory statements, increasing an already considerable amount of confusion. Finally, Hazlett reports that while the committee that developed NAEP diligently sought professional technical expertise, it was negligent in tending to its public relations problems, particularly in view of the fears that NAEP aroused in some people and groups.

NAEP's developers wanted state-level results. They felt that the state was the basic unit of education. Although there were some 30,000 local school districts, the Constitution, being silent on education, placed it in the hands of the states. Keppel, for his part, felt that the competition that state-level results would produce would actually help education in general:

> My enthusiasm for having a national mean [what we would today call a national norm] can be restrained. I am more interested in using the national competitive quality of it, you see, if this can be used to push the whole damned thing [quality of education] up. (Greenbaum, 1977, p. 24)

Despite these enthusiasms, the politics of the time prevented state-level reporting. During the 1970s and early 1980s, though, the sentiment for having some measure that reported nationally at the state level was seen as important. The "Wall Chart" for the states, started in 1982 by Secretary of Education Terrel Bell, was greeted in almost all quarters with groans. These charts categorized states into two groups, depending on whether the SAT or ACT was the dominant college admissions test. Within each category, the charts presented figures for numerous other variables for the states, such as per-pupil costs, percent enrolled in special education, etc. There was, however, no meaningful way of combining any of the figures to obtain a meaningful picture of the quality of education in any given state (if, indeed, these statistics could even be called indicators of quality). William Bennett, who succeeded Bell as education secretary, acknowledged that the wall charts were not useful, but he declared that he would continue to produce them until someone offered him something better. (Bennett has recently begun again to publish them through two groups with which he is affiliated, Empower America and the American Legislative Exchange Council.)

In 1981, the U.S. Department of Education hired Willard Wirtz and Archie Lapointe of the consulting firm Wirtz and Lapointe to conduct an evaluation of NAEP. Wirtz was a former Secretary of Labor and chairman of the panel that had analyzed the SAT decline in 1977, while Lapointe was a former vice president of what was then the educational testing division of IBM, Science Research Associates. After making its study, the firm was dissolved. Lapointe was hired by Educational Testing Service to direct NAEP even though ETS did not have the contract for the program—yet. Some organizations had been pressuring the Department of Education to put NAEP up for bid rather than awarding it perennially to the Education Commission of the States (ECS) on a sole-source basis.

When the program was put up for competitive bid, ETS used its rather formidable array of psychometric expertise to win the contract (only ETS and ECS bid). Some thought it also rather convenient for ETS to have hired one of two critics of the current program, but the competition apparently was an honest one. Since winning the contract, ETS has improved the technical quality of the assessments, but the most interesting developments in NAEP have occurred outside of ETS and largely outside of the technical realm.

When NAEP moved to ETS, Lapointe and then-ETS president Gregory Anrig took to referring to NAEP as "the nation's report card," a name with vastly different implications from what NAEP's developers intended. Shortly after the transfer of NAEP to ETS, people began to mention the possibility of a state-by-state assessment. In 1984, through the auspices of the Southern Regional Education Board, Florida, Virginia, and Tennessee agreed to an exploratory assessment to determine the feasibility and economy of gathering state-level data. The Hawkins-Stafford Amendments of 1988 authorized state trial assessments, and in 1990, a broader array of states participated in such a feasibility study. In 1992, 41 states took part in a trial that reported state-level data in mathematics at grades four and eight and in reading at grade four.

Some want to use this state-level data to assess the quality of the various states' educational systems. This, of course, is precisely what Keppel had in mind and precisely what everyone else opposed when NAEP was born. The pros and cons of state-by-state comparisons have divided people over NAEP, with the psychometric community largely against it. The psychology for some indicators was put forward well in a report by former Secretary of Education Lamar Alexander and Thomas James, Stanford professor and former director of the Spencer Foundation:

> Today state and local administrators are encountering rising public demand for thorough information on the quality of their schools, allowing comparison with data from other states and districts and with their own historical records. Responding to calls for greater accountability, state officials have increasingly turned to the national assessment for assistance.

But therein, responded Daniel Koretz of the RAND Corporation (now with the Urban Institute), lies the rub:

> State NAEP cannot tell us what policies and programs are effective....NAEP is purely cross-sectional, which eliminates a large number of the designs that could be used to draw causal inferences. Moreover, the cross-sectional nature of NAEP means that even when differences in scores do reflect differences in programs, we won't be able to ascertain *which* differences in policy or practice are responsible. A state that has a lousy middle-school mathematics curriculum, for example, may have a strong enough elementary curriculum to score better than its neighbor on the Grade-8 state NAEP nonetheless.
>
> The NAEP also does not provide the type of data that would be required for reasonable cross-sectional causal modeling. It does not allow one to rule out other entirely plausible explanations of state differences. One reason is its limited individual-level background data. Some important variables—such as family income, which is a very powerful predictor of student performance are lacking entirely....School- and community-level background factors are also problematic. (Koretz, 1991, p. 20)

A 1994 study by Glen Robinson and David Brandon of Educational Research Service found that Koretz's concerns, stated prior to the release of the first state-level NAEP tryout, were well-taken. Robinson and Brandon determined that 83 percent of the variance in state-level NAEP scores can be accounted for by only four variables: number of parents at home, parental education, type of community, and state poverty rates. The "83 percent of variance accounted for" is a technical term, but in lay language such a large figure means that one can make almost perfect predictions about state scores using only the four variables named. Because these four variables are not under the control of the schools, Robinson and Brandon conclude that their near-perfect predictions for state-level NAEP scores mean that NAEP is not valid as an indicator of state-level school quality. They argue that NAEP state-level data are more appropriately seen as indicating the difficulty facing the various states in educating their citizens.

The Hawkins-Stafford Amendments wrought another major change to NAEP. It established a National Assessment Governing Board (NAGB, pronounced "nagbee") to consist of two governors or former governors, two legislators, two chief state school officers, one member of a local board of education, three classroom teachers from the grades assessed by NAEP, two curriculum specialists, two measurement experts, one nonpublic-school administrator, two principals, and three additional members from the general public. Where the appointees are political agents, they must be from opposite parties. NAGB is responsible not only for setting NAEP policy but also for establishing performance standards.

To date, the attempts to establish performance standards have not been successful, although this has not stopped people from talking as if they have been set in place. The directors of NAEP at ETS abandoned Tyler and ECAPE's concerns for face validity, converting the plain-language interpretations of results into scaled scores that vary from 0 to 500. Reports by Richard Jaeger of the University of North Carolina at Greensboro and RAND's Daniel Koretz indicate that, at least in reporting the first state trials, these scaled scores were widely misinterpreted by the media (Jaeger, 1991; Koretz, 1991). There had been a concern all along that NAEP was not well-disseminated into the public domain. It now appears that misinformation is making its way into the public's reading material.

In addition, people began to make criterion-referenced interpretations of NAEP scores. This is not surprising, since the performance levels of NAEP sound like criterion-referenced indicators:

Basic. This level, below proficient, denotes partial mastery of knowledge and skills that are fundamental for proficient work at each grade—4, 8, and 12.

Proficient. This central level represents solid academic performance for each grade tested—4, 8, and 12. It reflects a consensus that students reaching this level have demonstrated competency over challenging subject matter and are well-prepared for the next level of schooling.

Advanced. This higher level signifies superior performance beyond proficient grade level master at grades 4, 8, and 12. For twelfth grade, the advanced level shows readiness for rigorous college courses, advanced technical training, or employment requiring advanced academic achievement.

Given this format for the levels of NAEP performance, it is not surprising to see statements such as these:

Each June, only $7^1/_2$ percent of our three million high school seniors leave their secondary school experience with an ability to integrate scientific information with other knowledge and skills they have learned in school or through life experience. (Lapointe, 1991, p. 61)

More than half of the nation's 17-year-olds appear to be inadequately prepared either to perform competently jobs that require technical skills or to benefit substantially from specialized on-the-job training. The thinking skills and science knowledge possessed by these high school students also seem to be inadequate for informed participation in the nation's civic affairs. (Mullis and Jenkins, 1988

The assessment results for 17-year-olds who are still in school are particularly dismaying. Most of the 25 percent of high school students who drop out are gone. The 17-year-olds who are there to be tested are our successful students, the ones who are about to march down the aisle and get diplomas. Yet the findings of the NAEP indicate that few of these students are ready to do real college-level work or to handle a good job. (Shanker, 1990, p. 346)

Are such criterion-referenced, generalized interpretations of NAEP results proper? Are they even permissible? "I would answer, without reservations, 'no.'" Thus spake University of Iowa psychometrician Robert Forsyth in 1991 (p. 9).

As mentioned earlier, the scales constructed by ETS run from 0 to 500, with most performances between 150 and 350. ETS selected some items to represent "anchor points" for performance at 150, 200, 250, 300, and 350. But the selection technique had no criterion-referenced process. It was purely technical, based on the proportion of students who got the items right and wrong.[4]

Says Forsyth, "the subject matter and the cognitive skill addressed by the item are not directly considered in this classification." That is, the scales ask nothing about what the item actually assesses, only what proportion of students get it right or wrong.

Forsyth then wonders how well-defined the NAEP domains are. It is impossible to construct a criterion-referenced test from an ill-defined domain. Following a widely used classification scheme, Forsyth asks whether the NAEP science domain is (a) well-defined and ordered, (b) well-defined but unordered, (c) ill-defined, or (d) undefined. Forsyth concludes that "the NAEP science domain is an ill-defined domain at best." Moreover, "it is highly doubtful that learning within this domain will proceed through neat sequential stages along some ordinal dimension" (1991, p. 5). Forsyth's analysis of the science domains assessed by NAEP turns up a hodgepodge of dimensions. He makes a similar analysis of the mathematics domain.

From such considerations, it would not seem likely that the NAEP scales could yield the proficiency levels mentioned earlier in any clear, well-defined way, but NAGB attempted, according to its charge, to establish such levels. These levels represent a form of standards—NAGB wanted and wants to use such levels to specify not only what students do know but also what they should know. As part of the effort, NAGB hired a team headed by Daniel Stufflebeam of Western Michigan University and including Jaeger and Michael Scriven of Western Australia University and the U.S.-based Nova University to evaluate the outcome of the standard-setting process. These three evaluators are among the best known and most highly regarded in their field. The team determined that the process had failed. They began by questioning the expertise of NAGB to conduct the process:

> The problems attending NAGB's lack of technical exper-
> tise seem to present a serious policy issue rather than an

> operational issue…it probably cannot fulfill its responsi-
> bility if the technical community is not represented on
> the Board at a level equivalent to that of the NAEP user
> groups. (Stufflebeam et al., 1991, p. 9)

This last statement refers to the widespread perception that having only two psychometricians on NAGB leaves it vulnerable to being co-opted by political concerns. The team noted that a number of people assigned to set levels had found many items themselves lacking in quality. They also found the definitions of "basic," "proficient," and "advanced" too vague. Finally, the team also found that the level-setting process was neither technically sound nor professionally credible.

In response, NAGB fired the team—or at least tried to: the wording of the contract did not permit it. The report of the team was suppressed, however, with each of its 53 pages carrying the stamps "CONFIDENTIAL" and "DO NOT REPRODUCE OR CIRCULATE." In reaction to this, Congressman Ford of North Carolina asked the General Accounting Office (GAO) to investigate. The GAO reached conclusions similar to those of the original evaluation team, deciding that while the levels represent different levels of performance on the test, "they do not necessarily imply that students have achieved the item mastery or readiness for future life, work, and study, specified in NAGB's definitions and descriptions" (1993, p. 3).

The GAO report made no mention of the previous evaluation. This led Jaeger to write a letter to Congressman Ford inquiring why these events had been ignored. The result was a letter from the GAO to Ford stating that the original evaluation team had been correct in its conclusions.

The NAGB standard-setting attempt continues, with several contracts now in place with the American College Testing organization. (At the time of this writing, ACT's reports have not been cleared for release.)

As educational winds shifted, the perspectives with which people viewed NAEP also changed. Initially NAEP was *deliberately* constructed so that no more than 10 percent of students would get the most difficult items correct. If we consider that this approach established one form of an "advanced" level, then NAEP was deliberately constructed so that not many people would be considered "advanced." Now people looked at the results organized by proficiency level and complained that too few students attained high performance.

THE ADVENT OF CRITERION-REFERENCED MEASUREMENT

While Robert Glaser was not the first to contrast norm-referenced against criterion-referenced measurement (as noted earlier in this chapter, E.L. Thorndike formulated the distinction in 1913), he apparently coined the phrase "criterion-referenced measurement" in 1962 and used it again in a more widely known *American Psychologist* article in 1963. Said Glaser:

> Underlying the concept of achievement measurement is the notion of a continuum of knowledge acquisition ranging from no proficiency at all to perfect performance. An individual's achievement level falls at some point on this continuum as indicated by the behaviors he displays during testing. The degree to which his achievement resembles desired performance at any one specified level is assessed by the criterion-referenced measures of achievement or proficiency. The standard against which a student's performance is compared when measured in this manner is the behavior which defines each point along the achievement criterion. The term "criterion" when used in this way, does not necessarily refer to final end-of-course behavior. Criterion levels can be established at any point in instruction where it is necessary to obtain information as to the adequacy of an individual's performance. The point is that the specific behaviors implied at each level of proficiency can be identified and used to describe the specific tasks a student must be capable of performing before he achieves one of these knowledge levels.
>
> Along such a continuum of attainment, a student's score on a criterion-referenced measure provides explicit information as to what the individual can or cannot do. (1963, p. 519)

If the behavior being measured were, for example, ice-skating skill, the criterion might be "pupil completes double axel with proper landing." A criterion-referenced measure might initially show "pupil cannot stand on ice without assistance" and end with a description of the criterion behavior. As the pupil became more proficient, other performances could be assessed with respect to the ultimate criterion or intermediate criteria established along the way. A norm-referenced measurement would show only a relative status: "pupil performs as well as 70 percent (or 10 percent or 90 percent, etc.) of other pupils his age."

There are some highly questionable assumptions in Glaser's exposition. First, the notion that there is a continuum of achievement. This implies a unidimensionality of achievement that is seldom seen except where artificially *imposed*.[5]

Similarly, there may well be no agreement on the ultimate criterion, at least for complex behavior. Glaser has recently commented that "in the original paper, when I used the phrase 'continuum of knowledge acquisition,' I was thinking in the context of then-prevalent stimulus response theory of learning and of cumulative behavioral components of acquired performance" (1994a, p. 9). Glaser had learned his stimulus-response psychology from William Estes and B.F. Skinner. Later Glaser comments reveal a much more current view of learning derived from developments in cognitive psychology, but they do not fully clear up the matter.

Glaser acknowledged that the notions were not new, and he later produced a 1913 quotation from Thorndike saying, among other things, that "To be seventeenth instead of eighteenth or twenty-third instead of twenty-fifth does not approach in moving force and zeal to beat one's own record, to see one's practice curve rise week by week, and to get up to the standard which permits one to advance to a new feat" (1971, p. 51). Although Thorndike lived in an era in which the power of "We're Number One!" was diminished compared with today, his observation is acute (and accounts for some of the hypnotic attraction of computer games).

Glaser's article did not generate much interest for quite a while. In 1969 James Popham and T.R. Husek observed that "other than adding new terms to the technical lexicon, the two constructs have made little difference in measurement practices" (p. 1). William Clark Trow in 1971 observed one reason for the inertia of norm-referenced thinking: "Perhaps the main reason for the lag (in using criterion-referenced measurement) is that World War I psychology was concerned with norm reference and so promoted this one style, while nothing equivalent to it or Sputnik has acted to generalize and motivate the use of the criterion score" (p. xi). Trow went on to say that this "style" was not sufficient by itself and speculated that too many people had been trained in norm-referenced psychology and had invested too much of their careers in it to admit that maybe they had been wrong and needed to learn something new.

Popham, in any case, undertook to popularize criterion-referenced tests (CRTs). Popham, along with fellow UCLA professor Robert Mager (1975), was among the most ardent advocates of behavioral objectives at the time, an advocacy later recanted (throughout his career Popham has shown an extraordinary ability to devote intense energy to a cause, then to abandon it entirely, even ridicule it). Popham declared that a behavioral objective specifies in behavioral terms what students should know or be able to do after instruction. That is, he said, it sets a criterion or a standard. A criterion-referenced measure, then, is just what an evaluator would use to determine if the objective had been met. This is one means of solving the criterion problem that so vexed Thorndike.

Later, the concept of CRT was broadened to "a well defined behavioral domain" (Popham, 1977, p. 93). The identification of CRTs as involving standards occurred not only because behavioral objectives were enjoying some vogue at the nation's universities at the time, but also because Popham campaigned for criterion-referenced measurement at the same time that many states were establishing criteria for high school graduation in the form of something called minimum competency tests.

As noted in Chapter One, the rise of minimum competency tests came from claims that students were being sent through the grades via "social promotion" and on the basis of "seat time," with the result that the diploma had become meaningless. Some concluded that "standards" had to be set and then assessed with a test to make sure that students had learned the "minimum" necessary for a high school diploma. A test was needed that would establish a minimal level of knowledge. We saw in Chapter One that Sloan Wilson had called in 1958 for something to establish the "absolute achievement" of a high school diploma. Denver, Colorado, moved in that same year to establish such a test, although there was no link to Wilson's *Life* essay. The Denver test sprang from complaints of a group of businessmen. The MCT movement, though, did not really gather momentum until the mid-1970s, Oregon being among the earliest entrants with requirements established in 1972.

Within a few years after the first states put such requirements into place, 35 states had enacted some form of minimum competency testing. It was a favorite tack of governors and legislatures, the educational analog of getting tough on crime.

From one perspective, CRTs appeared custom-made for minimum competency testing. An NRT's goal was the maximum dispersion of scores in order to discriminate among individuals. The goal of a CRT, on the other hand, was to see if a group or an individual had benefited from instruction and could now do things that couldn't be done before the instruction. However, Popham and Husek's assertion that you can't tell an NRT from a CRT by looking at a test *became* true. Although Glaser had specified that CRTs should reference specific behavior, the items on NRTs did not produce observable criterion behavior. Save for a few writing samples, they were multiple-choice questions. Nor were the "well-defined behavioral domains" well-defined or even specifiable. We saw earlier that NAEP, among the most ambitious of assessments, is built around ill-defined domains. For most tests called CRTs, all the more so. They were norm-referenced tests without norms. The "criterion" in criterion-referenced test was reduced in many instances to being one and the same as a cut score. There was no behavioral referent, nothing that looked like a usual "criterion," only a pass-fail decision based on whether or not the person answered the required percentage of questions correctly. You *couldn't* tell a CRT from an NRT by looking at the test.

From another perspective, the use of CRTs to establish minimum competency looked like a scam, a supposed technical solution to a problem that did not admit of a technical solution. "I have read the writing of those who claim the ability to make the determination of mastery or competence in statistical or psychological ways," wrote Gene V. Glass, then of the University of Colorado. "They can't. At least, they cannot determine 'criterion levels' or standards other than arbitrarily. The consequences of the arbitrary decisions are so varied that it is necessary to reduce the arbitrariness, and hence the unpredictability, or to abandon the search for criterion levels altogether in favor of using test data that are less arbitrary and, hence, safer."

Glass alleged that "the vagaries of teaching and measurement are so poorly understood that the a priori statement of performance standards is foolhardy." As an example, Glass gave two second-grade items from the Stanford Reading Test, items that were identical in the skills required but which had vastly different passing rates.

Glass's mistake, however, was to assume that the problem had to do with teaching and testing. The MCT programs were political in nature, hence not malleable through the kinds of technical arguments Glass advanced. As Harvard's Jerome Murphy put it:

The reason for the problems surrounding assessment

are political. People simply realize that collecting test score data for policy making purposes is a patently political activity, particularly when there isn't any scientific base for choosing the objectives for testing. Information can be and will be used as a political tool....Because of the stakes involved, people are going to fight over who is tested, what is tested, when it is tested, and by whom and how the data ought to be used.

Murphy's comment is applicable to any assessment program, but it is especially germane to minimum competency testing (MCT) programs.

In addition, however arbitrary, MCTs caused little disruption in most places. Most MCT programs might, in fact, be considered a kind of consumer fraud. Cut scores were typically set at a point where enough students initially failed to satisfy those who had called for the test in the first place, but the scores were also set at a point where virtually no one ultimately failed. One informal study in Virginia determined that if eighth graders scored at the chance level on the state-mandated norm-referenced achievement, only then were they at risk of failing the minimum competency test the next year as ninth graders. That is, a student had to be nearly three years below grade level at the eighth grade to be in danger of failing the MCT. Those who failed the test typically came from groups that had minimal clout in affecting school policies.

The winter 1994 issue of *Educational Measurement: Issues and Practices* offered a retrospective on Glaser's original article. Most authors concluded that the distinction he made fundamentally altered the course of assessment. Robert Linn of the University of Colorado observed that the original concept has been "clouded by surplus meaning." That is, elements not essential to the concept have been grafted on, elements such as the assumption that all criterion-referenced measures have cut scores. In addition, says Linn, "Criterion referenced measurement is often associated with an outdated behaviorist conception of the accumulation of discrete skills in a hierarchical fashion." Lorrie Shepard, also of the University of Colorado, had earlier observed that most psychometricians believed that complex skills were simple accretion of simple skills, a view very much at odds with current conceptions in cognitive psychology. It is somewhat ironic to find that people who build tests to measure learning have peculiar notions about how people learn.

In Popham's own contribution to the retrospective, he completely abandons the notion of behaviorism for an approach that is naïve to say the least:

> I suggest that we focus our future criterion-referenced descriptive effort exclusively on the score-based inference that we wish to make....In educational terms, we need to try to get inside the student's head so that we understand the *essence of the intellectual operations that the student must perform in order to satisfactorily complete the tasks represented in the test's items.* (1994, p. 17)

For his part, Glaser reflects on the origins of his original article. "We noted that the weak link in the construction of proficiency tests was the analysis and definition of the behavior to be measured....In retrospect, we seemed to be looking for principles of what is now called *authentic assessment*" (1994a, p. 10).

THE RISE (AND FALL?) OF "AUTHENTIC" ASSESSMENT

While large segments of the country were mesmerized by minimum competency testing, some other parts were growing increasingly dissatisfied with multiple-choice tests used for any purpose. One essence of our discontent had been long ago captured by one T.C. Batty in a March 15, 1959, letter to the *Times* of London:

> Sir:
>
> Among the "odd one out" type of questions which my son had to answer for a school entrance examination was, "Which is the odd one out among cricket, football, billiards, and hockey?"
>
> I say billiards because it is the only one played indoors. A colleague says football because it is the only one in which the ball is not struck with an implement. A neighbor says cricket because in all the other games the object is to put the ball into a net; and my son, with the confidence of nine summers, plumps for hockey "because it is the only one that is a girl's game." Could any of your readers put me out of my misery by stating what is the correct answer, and further enlighten me by explaining how questions of this sort prove anything, es-

pecially when the scholar has merely to underline the odd one out without giving a reason?

Perhaps there is a remarkable subtlety behind all this. Is the question designed to test what a child of nine may or may not know about billiards—proficiency at which may still be regarded as the sign of a misspent youth?

Yours faithfully, T.C. Batty

Many respondents produced additional reasons for choosing one or another of the options, but none produced a letter to satisfy Batty's initial query. It being England and the 1950s, no one bothered to question the wisdom of giving school entrance examinations to nine-year-olds. Batty's letter makes it clear that neither NRTs nor corrupted CRTs can tell you much about what a person can do if the tests consist of multiple-choice questions. One has no idea how students reach the answers that they do.

The dissatisfaction with multiple-choice tests took a while to result in actual attempts to construct something else aside from the nearly invisible exercises of NAEP. Events started to take shape toward the end of the 1970s. In 1979, S. John Davis, the newly appointed superintendent of schools for the state of Virginia, gave his maiden speech in his new role at the annual state testing conference. He announced a new K–12 testing program. Since most of us in the testing division (I was director of research, evaluation, and testing for the state at the time) had had bad experiences with the minimum competency test and an earlier K–6 basic learning skills test, the announcement was, for us, less than thrilling. Nevertheless, the various subject areas were parceled out to members of the testing service, who then worked with the curriculum staffs in those areas.

In the same way that Neil Postman and Charles Weingartner referred to teaching in their book, *Teaching as a Subversive Activity*, the Virginia Standards of Learning Program, as it was known, might have been called "Authentic Test Development as a Subversive Activity." The program was also what would now be called an "unfunded mandate," a shortcoming that would be important from the beginning. We could not follow the usual procedure of promulgating a Request for Proposal to various commercial contractors. Instead, we collected hundreds of teachers, supervisors, and professors for weeks at a university dormitory vacant for summer vacation. They were instructed to write objectives that would be appropriate to all students. Over objections, they divided themselves into elementary and secondary, but they otherwise approached the task with some relish.

The following school year, the compiled objectives were distributed to other teachers for review. Does this objective make sense? Is it teachable? Assessable? And so forth. A second summer was devoted to revising the objectives based on the feedback. This second summer of development brought some of the previous year's teachers back to provide continuity, but it also involved many new teachers. Only after this second round of objective refinement did the construction of assessments begin.

Different areas approached their subjects differently. The mathematics group produced a highly traditional set of outcomes and multiple-choice tests to go with them. Science emphasized process skills. Foreign language and language arts produced what we would now call performance assessments (as did some areas of science).

The language arts developers had been particularly creative and articulate. For each assessment, a prologue described the purpose of the objective, why it was important for anyone to learn the objective in the first place, how the objective built on earlier objectives and led to later ones, how to teach the objective, how to get ready for the assessment, how to conduct it, how to score it. Many of the scoring schemes were rating scales like those adopted by California a decade later. Some required the observation and rating of complex performances.

Considering what had preceded it and the lack of funding, the Standards of Learning Program was remarkably forward-looking. There were some problems: a complete set of the Language Arts Assessments K–12 occupied two notebooks, each about six inches thick. It was daunting to behold. More important, the novelty of many of the assessment procedures called for a large inservice program, but no funds were available for it. With adequate funding, the program could have been, for some curriculum areas, a national model. With no appropriation, it hung on but was never properly implemented.

Also in the late 1970s, Richard Stiggins of the Northwest Regional Laboratory had called for performance assessment in the area of writing, a call he later broadened in the 1980s to other areas. ETS's Norman Frederiksen wrote an essay in 1984 that is now cited by everyone but which seems to have been discovered only after the rise of authentic assessment. Still, it is an important piece that, like Batty's letter, illustrates many of the issues.

Frederiksen reviewed the rise of group testing involving multiple choice, charting immense growth but observing, as we have earlier, that testing was largely unrelated to instruction until Congress passed the Elementary and Secondary Education Act of 1965. For the first time, federally funded programs had to be evaluated. Tests were the most common instrument of evaluation. The link between instruction and testing became strong when a Florida judge ruled that before a student's diploma could be withheld because that student had failed Florida's minimum competency test, the state had to show that the student had an opportunity to learn the material covered by the test.

These events caused curricula and instruction to be aligned with tests in ways not previously seen. Because of our testing history, "teaching to the test" is typically viewed as something bad. But, said Frederiksen, teaching to the test is OK under certain circumstances, and in the grand tradition of *plus ça change*, he produced a citation from an *Atlantic Monthly* of 1926:

> The question of studying for marks rather than for knowledge, and the kindred matter of cramming for examinations are not uninteresting and are often misunderstood. The peculiar impression is that a student whose primary object is a higher grade devotes himself to memorizing small, and comparatively unimportant, points in a course and thereby makes a better showing than a classmate with a larger real command of the subject. As examination questions are often made out and marked this way this result may, and does occur. But if all examinations were so conducted as to be an accurate and complete measure of the education the course is intended to give, then there would be no reasons why the student should not work for marks, and good reason why he should. To chide a tennis player for training himself with a view to winning a match, instead of acquiring skill in the game, would be absurd because the two things are the same.

The problem in education, said Frederiksen, is that the two things are *not* the same. Multiple-choice tests are highly efficient and, for that reason, tend to replace other forms of testing. Frederiksen then produced evidence to show that when he measured complex skills with open-ended questions, an attempt to measure the same skills with multiple-choice tests did not produce the same result (recall Ruch's student who measured the "same" material with both formats in 1929).

The problems that can be presented by a multiple-choice format are highly structured. And because what gets tested is what gets taught, teaching is aimed toward highly structured problems. But, writes Fredericksen, "Most of the important problems one faces in real life are ill structured, as are all the really important social, political, and scientific problems in the world today. But ill-structured problems are not found in standardized achievement tests....The real test bias has to do with the influence of tests on teaching and learning. Efficient tests tend to drive out inefficient tests, leaving many important abilities untested—and untaught. An important task for educators and psychologists is to develop instruments that will better reflect the whole domain of educational goals and to find ways to use them in improving the educational process."

How much Frederiksen's article influenced the rise of tests to reflect the "whole domain of educational goals" is not clear. However, two events not long after his essay was published seemed to set it all off: a speech by Brown University's Ted Sizer at ETS in 1986 on the nature of exhibitions, and a symposium on authentic assessment at the annual Education Commission of the States Assessment Conference in Boulder, Colorado, in 1987. I chaired the symposium, which featured Mary Diez of Alverno College and Grant Wiggins, then with the National Center on Education and the Economy. I was surprised to see the conference well-attended, because we were up against another symposium that featured John Cannell taking on all of the major testing companies. Cannell, a pediatrician from West Virginia, had uncovered what has since become known as testing's "Lake Woebegon Effect"—all the children are above average. For a variety of reasons, far more people than should be were turning out to be above the national norm. That finding, amplified through Secretary of Education William Bennett and Assistant Secretary of Education Chester E. Finn, Jr., had become, for the staid field of psychometrics, quite a scandal. Against what promised to be fireworks, though, the Diez-Wiggins talk drew about one-fourth of the conferees, some 100 people in all.

After the Diez-Wiggins symposium, authentic assessment was all the rage. People who had never questioned the efficacy of the multiple-choice format were now heard saying that writing skills must be assessed by writing. If you're in an airplane, you don't care if the pilot can get a passing score on a multiple-choice navigation test; you want to know if he can get the plane into the air and down again safely at the right airport. People noticed that architects and artists had always used portfolios in evaluations and that foreign-language and instrument-playing skills could be assessed only by actual performance. And on and on. As Allan Hanson had observed, testing tends to produce that which it attempts to assess. Some psychometricians had a homelier example, the Law of WYTIWYG: What You Test Is What You Get.

Ruch and many psychometricians, long after Heisenberg's uncertainty principle had become well-known, continued to think that tests were a neutral form of obtaining information about what a student knew (some still hold such a position). Many now recognized, however, that the procedures for measuring something could, indeed, alter that something—that what you saw depended in part in how you looked for it. This, in part, was what Frederiksen's research had affirmed.

Perhaps the most well-known (notorious?) instance of the Law of WYTIWYG at work occurred in Prince George's County, Maryland, where one John Murphy became superintendent of schools. He promised, among other things, to get scores up and to close the gap between black students (about 70 percent of the district's population) and whites. Murphy established a room in which he displayed all of the test-score trends of the various buildings, a room he named the "Applied Anxiety Room." Scores did rise. Black students scored above the national norm. The gap between blacks and whites narrowed. Some people, however, became concerned that instruction in Prince George's schools had come to resemble preparation for the California Achievement Test, the state mandated NRT. Classroom activities, came reports, often involved going to the blackboard to choose one alternative out of four or five.

There were additional concerns that Maryland's edition of the test had been in use for a long time, something associated with rising test scores. Many psychometricians also felt that the norms for this particular edition of the California Achievement Test were too easy, another factor that could produce elevated scores. Murphy rebuffed several attempts by institutions to conduct objective evaluations of the test scores, which, of course, increased the suspicion that something foul was afoot. When the state of Maryland finally changed tests, scores all over the state declined, but those in Prince George's plummeted and the racial gap yawned as wide as ever. Some scores sank as low as the 18th percentile. Murphy, in the meantime, had taken a job elsewhere.

In his book, Grant Wiggins observes that we have excellent assessment programs at the extremes of our educational system: kindergartners and graduate students get thoughtful assessments. But, he says, "from first grade through at least the beginning (and often the end) of the undergraduate years in college, standardized and short-answer tests—and the mentality that they promote—are dominant. Students are tested not on the way they use, extend, or criticize 'knowledge' but on their ability to generate a superficially correct response on cue" (Wiggins, 1993, p. 2).

The word "assessment" is related to the French *s'assoir*—to sit down—and apparently to an Old French word meaning "to sit down beside the student." And not just once—a good assessment is a long-term process involving multiple observations that include, at least for those such as Wiggins, Dennie Wolf, Ruth Mitchell and a variety of others, patterns of behavior that we refer to as "habits of mind" and "style." This is rather more ambitious a program than Mann, Thorndike, or Popham had in mind, and it apparently goes against the cult of efficiency. (Wiggins would argue that ultimately it does not, since inappropriate measures cannot be considered efficient, no matter how cheaply and quickly they can be obtained.)

When some teachers consider how many students they have to deal with, they pronounce authentic assessments of complicated behaviors impossible. Yet such assessment occurs in schools. "Why have the band director, debate coach, science fair judge, play director, and volleyball coach not succumbed to the same thoughtless or fatalistic expediency [of multiple-choice tests]?" asks Wiggins (p. 3). "Because," he continues, "they understand that the 'test' of performance *is* the course, not something you do after it. Because they understand that both validity and reliability of judgment about complex performance depend upon many pieces of information gained over many performances."

This understanding, it should be noted, goes against the grain of at least 150 years of academic testing. There is nothing like it in Mann, Ruch, Thorndike, Glaser, or Popham. Although Ruch called for tests that were samples of classroom behaviors, his testing was still something you do *after* you're done teaching. For Wiggins and many others, assessment is ongoing, often invisible. Although the various protagonists for "authentic" assessment differ on some issues, I think that most would agree with the postulates that Wiggins put forth for a thoughtful assessment system:

1. Assessment of thoughtful mastery should ask students to justify their understanding and craft, not merely to recite orthodox views or mindlessly employ techniques in a vacuum.

2. The student is an apprentice liberal artist and should be treated accordingly, through access to models and feedback in learning and assessment.

3. An authentic assessment system has to be based on known, clear, public, nonarbitrary standards and criteria.

4. An authentic education makes self-assessment central.

5. We should treat each student as a would-be intellectual performer, not as a would-be learned spectator.

6. An education should develop a student's intellectual style and voice.

7. Understanding is best assessed by pursuing students' questions, not merely by noting their answers.

8. A vital aim of education is to have students understand the limits and boundaries of ideas, theories, and systems.

9. We should assess students' intellectual honesty and other habits of mind.

In the interest of having 10 of everything, a 10th postulate: a thoughtful assessment should *improve* performance, not just monitor it, something implicit here, but which Wiggins discusses elsewhere in his book.

Seen naked here without the explanatory text that accompanies them in the book, Wiggins's postulates appear as a radical departure from current practice. And they are. We might, in fact, call them a Declaration of Independence from testing. They are perhaps too strong for those with loyalties to the current approach. They will certainly be rejected by certain groups of fundamentalists who see education as the direct transfer of knowledge—orthodox knowledge—from teacher to pupil. As with the original Declaration, though, "a decent respect to the opinions of mankind requires that they should declare the causes which impel them to the separation." Wiggins declares the causes (and I enthusiastically commend the reader to his book to read them).

The Wiggins postulates are unlikely to be received enthusiastically by a wide audience. They represent a return to a John Dewey model of education when the nation is virulently anti-

Dewey, though it never expresses itself in those terms. Dewey saw education as growth. Growth for what? More growth. For its own sake. Because children became the adult society of the future, how they were treated in school could predict a lot about how society would change.

Currently there is a call for developing skills that will be useful in a society already changed and changing—apparently without anyone's being capable of directing the change. The change in psychology is analogous to the similar changes during the administration of President Ronald Reagan. Reagan entered snarling, "The buck stops here." After the Iran-Contra scandal, he left sniveling, "Mistakes were made." The active voice had been lost to the passive.

The current calls to prepare children for a changing society where no one controls the change is a call for education that molds children to society, rather than for an education that molds society as a result. It is widely asserted that businessmen find high school graduates deficient in skills. But, as noted, national surveys reveal this is not so. What surveys find is that businessmen want workers who will reliably show up on time, will be polite to customers, and will get along with fellow workers. We have already quoted in Chapter One Alan Wurtzel, chairman of the board at Circuit City, on what business wants.

It should be emphasized that authentic assessments or alternative assessments are not simply different formats for measuring the same "thing" as multiple-choice tests, nor do they simply reflect a different purpose of education. Beyond that, the approaches to authentic assessment represent a different *epistemology* from that found in traditional testing. Whether such an epistemology can become a daily part of school routines remains to be seen.

At the moment, the alternative assessments are at best in a holding pattern. They have been linked to outcomes-based education, which has, in many places, taken a beating (the story of outcomes-based education is discussed in Chapter Four). At the annual assessment conferences sponsored by the Council of Chief State School Officers (CCSSO) in June 1995, it was clear that multiple-choice tests were back in favor in many quarters.

In some instances, this had occurred because alternative assessments had not yielded (yet) the kinds of data policymakers wanted for accountability purposes. Issues of reliability and validity swirl about these assessments. In other instances, it seemed as if newly arrived politicians or politically appointed officers (such as chief state school officers) did not have the patience to await the development of technically sound measures. The multiple-choice question has been in its current form for about 75 years, while work on the more complex alternatives is not yet a decade old. Still, at this point in time, there might well be a return to multiple-choice questions for accountability purposes while alternatives are championed for instructional purposes. This would, in my opinion, be a terrible regression and would stifle the needed progress in developing authentic measures. But expediency may yet rule the day.

Chapter Three

The Evolution of Standards

The lack of standards is education's dirty little secret... many countries are educating everybody to higher levels than we are. One of the main differences between us and them is standards: they have them and we don't.
—Robert R. Spillane, *Education Week* (1993)

Many maintain that the three Rs and formal drill are neglected, that the work of pupils and teachers, owing to the fads and frills which are included, is superficial and that promotions from grade to grade are made without much regard to real attainments.
—Andrew W. Edson,
American School Board Journal (1914)

Different educators in this country seem to have two different time frames in mind when asked when educators began speaking about standards. One line of reference holds that the national concern with standards in U.S. education is a rather recent event that appeared about the same time as the post–World War II criticisms described in Chapter One. The other perspective takes a longer view, generally starting with the work of the Committee of Ten in the 1890s.

With regard to the short-term view, the post–World War II perspective on standards can be summarized with extracts from the testimony of Commissioner of Education Francis Keppel in 1963:

It has often been pointed out that America lacks standards by which it can measure educational results, and stimulate its students to greater accomplishment. One means to solve this national problem is to work out ways of taking samples of the achievement of students at critical points in their school. With this information, it becomes possible to plan the needed reform in a precise and pinpointed way....A partial step, therefore, in an overall plan, would be some kind of voluntary examination by which parents and students alike, as well as the schools themselves, could assess their position.

We are all aware of the lack of adequate qualitative measures of the outputs of our schools. While we applaud individual instances of obvious academic excellence and decry equally obvious failures of educational achievement, we have no reliable means by which to judge the vast output of some 33,000 heterogeneous school districts. With a fifth of our population moving each year, often into quite different school situations, and with the mounting need of industry, business and government not only for better educated men and women, but also for more predictably well trained employees, we need, as never before, national guidelines to evaluate our manpower in all its strengths and weaknesses. (Hazlett, pp. 352–353)

Allowing that a precipitous move into this area might have many unintended consequences, Keppel declared, "I intend to seek scholarly and expert advice in the desirability of developing voluntary national academic standards" (Hazlett, p. 353).

Many in Congress opposed Keppel's notions, seeing in them a desire for a federal takeover and standardization of education. "One More Step Down the Road Toward National Testing," was the title of an anti-NAEP speech given by Congressman Robert Michel of Illinois to the House of Representatives in 1965. Michel cast a jaundiced eye on the statements of Keppel, Secretary of Health, Education, and Welfare John Gardner, and various communications between them and officials at ETS. Michel saw in them the workings of the "Eastern, Ivy League, foundation syndrome" and a plot to subvert Congress. Gardner, after all, was on leave as president of the Carnegie Corporation and had been a member of the ETS board when ETS received a contract for the Equal Educational Opportunities Survey, which Michel confused with a national testing program. Michel saw a plot:

Mr. Speaker, the Office of Education has used the Civil Rights Act of 1964 to establish a benchmark for National

Testing. I can visualize next year, or the year after that, Secretary Gardner and Commissioner Keppel, coming to the Congress with the established precedents of these school surveys, requesting a more formal type of survey. Probably something with the euthenistic [*sic*] title "National Assessment," but well known to those knowledgeable in this field as "National Testing." Let me repeat—without prior approval of Congress—the Office of Education has proceeded with a national testing program....Unless at this juncture—when there is still time—we have some open and free discussion on this issue, there will be no turning back and we will be headed hell-bent down the road toward a giant, monolithic, federalized educational system. (Hazlett, p. 358)

In their 1982 report on NAEP, Willard Wirtz and Archie Lapointe captured the short-term view of the situation well when they said that "although 'high educational standards' have always been an article of national faith, the term stood historically simply for a broad belief in quality and excellence. It meant doing the teaching job well." We assumed the system was succeeding in this quest for quality, and any notion that we needed actual measurements of student performance to prove it would have been seen, at best, as irrelevant, but, more likely, as a threat to individualized instruction, educational diversity, and academic freedom. "That quiet confidence lasted until the middle of the century," they said (p. 2). And then it collapsed under the criticisms documented in Chapter One, particularly those of Arthur Bestor in *Educational Wastelands* and Rudolph Flesch in *Why Johnny Can't Read*.

They note that, in reaction to Sputnik, the National Defense Education Act activated a review of curricula and teaching methods. Nothing was said about examinations. That happened later:

By the early 1970s, however, the national sense developed that educational quality was deteriorating rapidly and dangerously. It is not entirely clear how far this went, how general it was, or what measure of fault was the schools'. But the judgment was made clearly and firmly. The reaction to this alarm took a dramatically new form. For reasons rooted in other developments, many people had lost confidence in the government and in the professions. The strongly sensed deterioration in education seemed confirmation of the failures of both of these services. So it was decided not to rely this time on either of these agencies. The decision, instead, in one State and community after another, was to move in directly on the schools, not with funds but with "*standards*." (Wirtz and Lapointe, pp. 2–3)

When most people think of higher education standards, said Wirtz and Lapointe, they think simply of "moving the passing grade up whatever number of notches is determined to be available. But this narrow definition does serious disservice to the 'standards' concept." Standards, they argued, have an "infinitely larger potential for improving education" if we first establish what students ought to be learning, then develop "measuring systems" that are "carefully tuned" to whatever we think students should be studying. Otherwise, they said, we risk simply raising the passing grade on tests that measure the wrong things.

Their definition of an "educational standard" combines what today would be separated as content standards and performance standards (definitions of which are given later in this chapter in a general discussion of the meaning of the word "standard").

An "educational standard" is taken, for purposes of this report, as being the measuring instrument or process used to determine the level of students' educational achievement. Setting a standard includes determining how the responses to all the items or exercises that make up the instrument are to be scored and what significance is to be given various scores. A "better" educational standard is one that measures and reports more accurately on what are rationally determined, in constructing the standard, to be the critical elements of desired student achievement. A standard can be made "higher" either by improving the educational objectives on which it is based or by raising scores or grades that are required for "passing" and for being considered superior or excellent. (Wirtz and Lapointe, pp. 4–5)

The longer view of standards starts with Horace Mann in the 1840s then quickly jumps to the work of the Committee of Ten and other turn-of-the-century reform efforts. The Committee of Ten, formally the Committee on Secondary School Studies, was established by the National Education Association in 1892. Charles Eliot, president of Harvard University, directed the committee and college presidents dominated it.

The committee had organized a series of conferences to study the state of the various courses taught in secondary schools. Interestingly, unlike today's study conferences, which are almost exclusively formed from institutions of higher education, those who worked with the Committee of Ten were almost equally divided among colleges and K–12 schools (although the academics apparently monopolized the agenda and the discussion). The conferences were to study Latin, Greek, mathematics, English, other modern languages, natural history, physical science, geography, history, civil government, and political economy and to consider their possible places in secondary education. Of these topics, only the first three were regarded as college preparatory subjects at the time. The conferences addressed 11 questions:

1. In the school course of study extending approximately from the age of six to eighteen years—a course including the periods of both elementary and secondary instruction—at what age should the study which is the subject of the conference be first introduced?

2. After it is introduced, how many hours a week for how many years should be devoted to it?

3. How many hours a week for how many years should be devoted to it during the last four years of the complete course, that is, during the ordinary high school period?

4. What topics, or parts, of the subject may best be reserved for the last four years?

5. In what form and to what extent should the subject enter into college requirements for admission?

6. In what form and to what extent should the subject enter into college requirements for admission? Such questions as the sufficiency of translation at sight as a test of knowledge of a language or the superiority of a laboratory examination in a scientific subject to a written examination on a text-book, are intended to be suggested under this head by the phrase, "in what form."

7. Should the subject be treated differently for pupils who are going to college, for those who are going to a scientific school, and for those who, presumably, are going to neither?

8. At what age should this differentiation begin, if any be recommended?

9. Can any description be given of the best method of teaching this subject throughout the school course?
10. Can any description be given of the best mode of testing attainment in this subject at college admission examinations?
11. For those cases in which colleges and universities permit a division of the admission examination into a preliminary and a final examination, separated by at least a year, can the best limit between the preliminary and final examination be approximately defined?

Although two of the questions addressed to some degree the issues of outcomes and standards, these concerns were secondary to issues of what was to be studied in high school and which of those studies would be valuable in applying to college. Educators of the time saw education as playing very much the same role that Arthur Bestor would describe for it 60 years later: developing a disciplined mind through the exercise of "faculties."

The interest of secondary school people in the Committee of Ten's work lay in trying to get colleges to standardize their entrance tests. The interest of the college people lay in trying to get the high schools to better prepare students for college. Many colleges at the time had preparatory departments through which remedial-program students had to pass before embarking on a regular university course of study. (It is not recorded if professors then complained as loudly about such remedial efforts as they do today.) The interest of the entire committee lay in establishing the proper relationship between the traditional "classic" high school program of study and the newer subjects in the natural and social sciences.

Elsewhere, a concern for standards—and outcomes—was emerging in a number of quarters. In 1897, researcher James Mayer Rice had scandalized a meeting of school superintendents in Indianapolis by revealing that students who studied spelling 40 minutes a day for eight years spelled no better than those who spent only 10 minutes a day learning how to spell. The scandal erupted not over the lack of effectiveness of the longer term but over Rice's temerity in judging teachers on the basis of student performance. The teachers might be held to standards, the superintendents contended, but certainly not on the basis of student outcomes. In 15 years these attitudes toward student outcomes had changed substantially. This will be discussed in Chapter Four, "The Evolution of Outcomes."

THE NATURE OF A STANDARD AND STANDARDS

This is a good point at which to stop the chronology of the evolution of standards and to examine the various definitions of the term and the ways that educators have meant to use standards. Actually, it is not always clear which meaning various writers and commentators have in mind when they use the word.

Too often the word "standard" appears with no definition at all. At the state and district level, various documents can be found using the term interchangeably with goals, outcomes, and objectives. Many school documents confuse these words with process goals such as this: "It is the goal of this curriculum to provide each student with weekly periods of computer use." This "goal" refers merely to some process that will take place. A true goal or standard would likely impute what will happen as a result of the experience.

The first definition of standard given in the 1992 edition of the *American Heritage Dictionary* is: "a flag, banner, or ensign, particularly one with heraldic figures, signifying a head of state, or an emblem of an army, hence a rallying point." This definition is not of great import in education save for the most general of conversations. In many discussions and debates about standards, a vague notion of standards does serve as some kind of rallying point for doing better—we need to raise our standards, or the standards of American education are too low, etc.

A second dictionary definition presents standard as "an object that under specified conditions defines, represents, or records the magnitude of a unit." This definition begins to approach what most educators have in mind when they think of standards, but it lacks any value judgment. A platinum rod defines the various units of length, but it is silent as to whether these units are any good or not.

Next, we see "a degree or level of requirement, excellence, or attainment." Now we are on more familiar territory. This definition comes close to establishing a scale against which performance can be judged, as some have argued for using criterion-referenced measurement and outcomes-based education.

Unfortunately, these nominative uses of standard are confounded because the word is often used also as an adjective: for a model, as in "a standard reference work"; for something less than perfect, as in "a standard grade of beef"; for something common or familiar, as in "the standard excuse"; or something commonly supplied as in "standard car equipment." None of these uses is connoted in this chapter. Indeed, some of these uses are antithetical to the notion of a standard because they imply standardization rather than standards.

As synonyms for standard, the *American Heritage Dictionary* provides: "benchmark, criterion, gauge, measure, touchstone, or yardstick." It notes that "the central meaning shared by these nouns is 'a point of reference against which individuals are compared and evaluated.'"

In Chapter Two we saw that in the world of testing the initial concern was the comparison of individuals with other individuals in terms of relative standing. Since the onset of criterion-referenced measurement, however, that concern has yielded significantly to a concern for evaluations in reference to some kind of absolute standard. Where normative comparisons are still in vogue, they typically concern comparing American performance on assessments to the performance of students in other nations. These comparisons often take the form of benchmarking. In benchmarking, a competitor's performance on something is measured and used to improve one's own or one's company's performance. The performance of Asian nations on mathematics tests is often (wrongly) taken as a benchmark against which to measure American performance.

In education, the closest thing to a standard that defines or records magnitude would seem to be the "content standards" for the various curriculum areas much discussed of late. And even here, as we leave the world of physical standards, we also leave the world of objectivity, because in the various content standards, judgments have been made that these are what students *should* learn. In recent years, the establishment of these standards has been accomplished largely by the various organizations of teachers with particular specialties, for instance, the National Council of Teachers of Mathematics.

In contrast to content standards are performance standards. Such standards attempt to specify not only what should be taught but also what degree of learning and subsequent performance using what was taught should be considered good enough. In NAEP or in the California Learning and Assessment System (an ambitious program of complex performance assessment, now defunct), those who grade the various exercises and examinations are provided with scales and, for each point in the scale, a set of criteria to use in deciding how many points to award. If the system works in writing, for example, the scale will capture the criteria of good writing, and these criteria can then be shared by all.

While most people can define and accept content and performance standards, another set of standards has emerged as crucial to some, anathema to others. These have been referred to under several names, the most common being "school delivery standards" or "opportunity to learn" (OTL) standards. The latter phrase concerns the ability of schools to provide adequate learning opportunities. Often the phrase also connotes concerns that range beyond the school and into the family and community. Indeed, it was in the face of such concerns that the initial name of school delivery standards was changed to OTL.

The various professional organizations devising content and/or performance standards have not yet agreed on what would constitute an appropriate set of OTL standards. They are still more removed from any agreement as to what would constitute meeting the OTL standards. That is, no one has proposed to determine how many working science laboratory stations a school should have, or how old the textbooks can be before they fail to meet the OTL standards, or the minimal level of support families must provide to meet OTL standards.

The lack of agreement on what constitutes OTL standards has not prevented them from becoming the most controversial aspect of the recent debates about national standards and assessments. Defenders of OTL standards argue that it would be unjust, given the "savage inequalities" that exist among schools, to hold all children to the same level of performance when their schools, families and neighborhoods differ immensely in the resources they can bring to bear on education.

Critics of OTL standards attack from two separate lines of argument. One has nothing to do with the value of such standards themselves: it is concerned with how such standards might be used by the federal government to interfere with what should be a state and local function and how they might be used either to obtain more federal funds for education or, more likely, to operate as unfunded mandates from the federal government, putting yet another burden on the states.

The other line of argument is similar to that raised against the use of local norms to evaluate schools. The problem with local norms is summarized nicely in the tale of the man who walks into a doctor's office and says, "Doc, I'm only getting two hours of sleep a night. Am I normal?" Before answering, the doctor elicits information from the man, and discovers in the process that his wife has left him, that he has recently lost his job, and that he sips vodka all day and chugs a half pint of Scotch before retiring. Entering these figures into his computer's database, the doctor concludes, "Yes, for a divorced, unemployed alcoholic, you're normal."

Thus, the problem with local norms, or OTL standards, is that they can be used to conceal very real and important problems. Some school districts and states have conducted statistical analyses to show that, if they didn't try to teach hungry, poor kids from single-parent families, they'd do as well as the schools in the suburbs or more affluent states. "We're doing as well as you can expect," they offer as a counter to criticism. This is a nice fantasy. The problem, though, is that they do have to teach such children and that these children are performing at low levels. Certainly, local norms or OTL standards can be used to prevent high-poverty schools from being unjustly criticized. If local norms or OTL standards are used to determine what resources are needed to improve performance, and if they are used to obtain those needed resources to improve performance, they serve a real purpose. If they are used only to obscure problems, they perform a real disservice.

STANDARDS VERSUS STANDARDIZATION

It is said, sometimes in envy and sometimes in derision, that the French minister of education knows at any moment what page students are reading in all of France. Such standardization of student coverage is not what most people have in mind when they propose standards, although it must be said that those who have advocated standards have not clearly delineated how different students might meet the standards differently, except in the most general, and therefore, vague terms. This lack of clarity, coupled with the mantra "all students can learn," causes some to be anxious that a set of standards will lead not to improved performance but only to standardization.

There can be cause for concern over this. For instance, Kazuo Ishizaka, a former teacher and principal and a current member of the Japanese Institute for Educational Research, reports that first-grade teachers in Japan are directed to teach 80 characters or *kanjis*, Chinese characters that remain part of the Japanese language corpus. Some students will arrive knowing these 80; some arrive capable of learning in a few weeks; and some leave at the end of the year not knowing them. But the teachers dare not tailor performance to these differences among students and to teach beyond the 80 *kanjis*, says Ishizaka. They concentrate on the slow learners, with the result that students bring small toys, which they hide in their desks and spend most of their time playing with. In this instance, standardization—teaching 80 *kanjis*—has little to do with standards (Ishizaka, 1993).

Some of those who call for standards do, in fact, also make an (unnecessary) call for standardization. For instance, in her 1995 book on national standards, Diane Ravitch writes that "the mathematics in one modern country are not—and should not be—different from the mathematics and science taught in other modern countries. Number systems operate in exactly the same way regardless of race, gender, ethnicity, or religion of the person performing the mathematical operation. Nor are the principles of science culturally determined" (Ravitch, 1995, p. 10). Although there is some hint that Ravitch has combined standards with benchmarks, this statement overall belies a remarkable ignorance of the fact that both science and mathematics are human constructions subject to revision as new data arrive. More important for the discussion here, because not all of science or mathematics can be taught, one could create a number of equally useful curricula that produce different outcomes. One teacher might, for instance, prefer to structure her presentation of geometry on Euclid's postulates and systematically explore them. Another might choose to present Euclid as largely a historical figure. Another might familiarize students with Euclid's postulates and general approach in order to contrast them with the equally logical non-Euclidean geometries that have appeared in this century.

Elliot Eisner, an art educator at Stanford University, also expresses fears about standardization. Eisner notes that there are any number of ways of teaching any particular curriculum area and that some ways will work for some children, some for others. Beyond that, says Eisner:

> Education is about learning how to deal with uncertainty and ambiguity. It is about learning how to savor the quality of the journey. It is about becoming critically minded and intellectually curious, and it is about learning how to frame and pursue your own educational aims. (Eisner, 1992a, p. 722)

In fact, standards do not inherently give rise to standardization, although they will tend to do so. Author Grant Wiggins writes:

We surely do not need a single set of mandated academic standards (and pressure to meet them). I watched sixteen students build a beautiful $250,000 house to contract and code at a Finger Lakes-area vocational high school. But all the students were academic "failures" in New York's Regents syllabus-and-exam system and in terms of the national standards debate laid out by the governors and the president a few years ago. (Wiggins, 1993, p. 283)

Wiggins and Eisner disagree on whether human performance can be held up to standards, but their disagreement may be more verbal than anything else. Eisner asks people to imagine a Monet and a Picasso. What standards can anyone apply to such different artists? Yet both are recognized as superb in their respective styles. You can apply criteria for good art, says Eisner, but not standards that imply some communality (Eisner, 1992b).

Wiggins would agree in the instance of Monet and Picasso, as he gives very similar examples from the world of music (Yo-Yo Ma versus Wynton Marsalis) and literature (Mark Twain versus Tom Wolfe). The exemplars all represent high, but different, standards. I doubt that the debate over standards in this country will generally reach the high level at which Wiggins and Eisner conduct their discussions.

Standards versus Norms

Standards are often confused with norms, and, indeed, in the dictionary, one definition of standard is that of a norm. However, in assessment circles, "norm" has quite a different meaning, one devoid of any connotation of quality. It is the norm of norm-referenced tests discussed in Chapter Two. This norm is nothing more or less than the average (median in this instance, not mean) score obtained by the test publisher from a norming sample. To obtain a norming sample, the publisher seeks a group of students who represent the nation in terms of ethnicity, family income, and other demographic variables. The average score obtained by these students, the 50th percentile rank, is then called the norm. For almost all commercial achievement tests, this average is calculated independently of earlier calculations each time the test is re-normed. It is, thus, a floating "standard" that does not indicate anything about the quality of performance at the time of testing or over any period of time (norms on the Iowa Tests of Basic Skills and Iowa Tests of Educational

Development, which are equated from form to form, are an exception to this statement).

STANDARDS AND QUALITY

At one point in his 1993 book, Grant Wiggins warns against the use of external standards that deal only with authority:

> "'My English teacher doesn't like my writing'...conveys the view that the subjective and hazy desires of Authority are being taught, not clear standards. But if the correctness of answers and arguments is justified only because Authority says so, careless and thoughtless work is the inevitable result. So is passivity: students learn by such mysterious and one-way assessment that they cannot reframe questions, reject questions as inappropriate, challenge their premises, or propose a better way to prove their mastery. The moral and political harm is significant. Too many students learn to just "give them what they want" and to accept or acquiesce in bogus but "authoritative" judgments. (Wiggins, 1993, pp. 100–101)

I resonate to this passage because it evokes a memory of an argument, all too typical, with my daughter when she was attending one of the more highly reputed school systems in Colorado. At the time, I was writing two columns a week on food and restaurants for a newspaper and one a month on education for *Electronic Learning* and *Phi Delta Kappan* magazines, as well as various occasional pieces. She was struggling with the concept of the "topic sentence" for the opening paragraph of an essay. I tried, in vain, to show and convince her that there were various ways of opening a topic and that such an opening might, in fact, require more than one sentence. She would not buy it. She quite literally said precisely what Wiggins quoted generically above: "You've got to figure out what they want and give it to them." Anything else risked a low, or at least lowered, grade.

Appeals to authority are particularly common in math and science instruction in the elementary grades. In these two fields, elementary teachers are often ill-prepared. For instance, many teachers, asked to explain why one cannot divide by zero, could offer no more than "it's a rule."

"Careless and thoughtless work" raises the issue, not yet dealt with here, of that ineffable yet important concept, quality. Perhaps the best, certainly the most popular, treatise on quality in recent years is Robert Pirsig's *Zen and the Art of Motorcycle Maintenance*. At one point in the book, Pirsig, or rather, his alter ego, Phaedrus (a character from Plato's *Republic*), is teaching philosophy and rhetoric at a university. He is becoming obsessed with the nature of quality.

"Tell us what quality is," his students say. "You already know," he tells them. They dispute this. He gives them two essays of notably different quality. They have no trouble distinguishing the better one from the poorer one. The exercise continues throughout the semester with little disagreement among the students or between the students and Phaedrus. Although the nature of quality remains difficult to define, it is clearly seen by all. Pirsig then demonstrates that the rules of rhetoric are useful in attaining high-quality writing. He has thus moved to a position that Wiggins advocates, where rules—standards—have a meaning in terms of known and justifiable demands, not just authority (unfortunately for Phaedrus's sanity, he later went well beyond this position). It is possible, though, that Pirsig obtained his result because the samples of writing were so dramatically different. Early educational research, discussed below, did not find such uniformity of judgment.

THE EVOLUTION OF STANDARDS, CONTINUED

As used by American educators, the words "standard" and "standards" have taken on a variety of meanings over the years. The changes that occurred after the work of the Committee of Ten can be seen in the studies of grading reported in 1912 by Daniel Starch and Edward C. Elliott of the University of Wisconsin. "The reliability of the school's estimate of the accomplishment and progress of pupils is of large practical importance," they write. Marks are of "practical importance" in determining

> transfer, promotion, retardation [retention in grade], elimination, admission to higher institutions; to say nothing of the problem of the influence of these marks or grades upon the moral attitude of the pupil toward the school, education, and even life. The recent studies of grades have emphatically directed our attention to the wide variation and the utter absence of standards in the assignment of values. (Starch and Elliott, 1912, p. 442)

According to Starch and Elliott, though, these studies did not fully control or eliminate other variables in order to study only the "personal factor" in the assignment of grades. To do that, they contended, different teachers must grade the same papers. They acquired two actual papers written by high school students, made plates of them, and printed hundreds of copies on the same kind of paper that students had used, thus preserving not only the handwriting but also the appearance of the originals. The papers were written by students at the end of the first year of high school English in response to this examination:

1. Give five rules for the use of the comma, two for the period, and illustrate each use by a sentence.
2. Give five requirements to be observed in the structure of a paragraph.
3. Write a brief business letter.
4. Define narration, coherence, unity; classify sentences rhetorically and grammatically. Illustrate or define.
5. Name all the masterpieces studied this year, and name the author of each. [Starch and Elliott provided their readers with answers to this item]
6. Write a three-paragraph essay, narrative, descriptive, or both combined.

But for the last item, there is little room for individual variation in "complex performance." If open-ended, the business letter could be a source of variability, but the examples Starch and Elliott provided to their readers consisted of either one or two sentences only. The test is largely the kind of examination that the Progressives later dismissed as "mere verbalism" in contrast to the learning for understanding they were promoting.

Like Pirsig later, Starch and Elliott chose two student papers they thought were of different quality and sent them to 200 high schools of the North Central Association, requesting that the principal teacher of first-year English grade these two papers "according to the practices and standards of the school."

They received back almost 150 usable papers, which they divided on the basis of what was considered a passing score at the various schools, 70 in some instances, 75 in the others. No matter which "cut score" the schools used, the median scores of both papers were quite similar: 88.3 and 87.2 for the better paper and 80.4 and 78.8. for the lesser attempt. However, the range across all papers and graders was enormous, running from 60 to 98 for the better exam and 50 to 98 for the other.

Although in actuality, the student who had submitted the poorer paper received a passing mark from his teacher, 22 teachers in the experiment flunked him. One conclusion, then, was that a student's fate on an examination depended to a certain extent on the luck of the draw. When Starch and Elliott repeated the experiment using University of Wisconsin students in a course on the teaching of English and in a course on educational measurement, the large variability appeared again.

Starch and Elliott then considered the argument that differences in absolute standards among teachers were of little import, because their relative judgments would be the same. That is, students who rank high with one teacher will rank high with another. While Starch and Elliott did find some substance in this claim, they also found that 19 teachers had scored the poorer examination higher than the better one. Clearly, neither absolute nor relative standards were in operation in American classrooms.

The work of Starch and Elliott dovetailed nicely with yet a third source of standards, the concern of many administrators in the 1910–30 period with application of "scientific management" to schools. Franklin Bobbitt of the University of Chicago argued long for the establishment of standards in school similar to standards in industry. Who was responsible for such standards? Certainly not educators. "A school system can no more find standards of performance within itself than a steel plant can find the proper height or weight per yard for steel rails from the activities within the plant" (Bobbitt, 1913, p. 34). Business and industry should set the standards; it had just not occurred to them to do so. The role of educators was to seek out what business and industry needed, then bring their systems into compliance. Writing of this trend, Raymond Callahan expresses indignation: "Doubtless many educators who had devoted years of study and thought to the aims and purposes of education were surprised to learn that they had misunderstood their function. They were to be mechanics, not philosophers" (Callahan, 1962, p. 84).

Ellwood Cubberley, whose *Public School Administration* was one of the most influential textbooks of the time, endorsed Bobbitt's ideas enthusiastically, as well as those of Frederick Taylor, the best-known and most ardent advocate of applying scientific management to business and industry. Cubberley, in fact, endorsed the notion of the school as a factory:

> The work described in this chapter is new work, and work of a type which schoolmasters are as yet little familiar, but it is work of great future importance, work which will professionalize teaching and supervision, and work destined to do much to increase the value of the

public service rendered by our schools. By means of standards and units of the type now being evolved and tested out it is even now possible for a superintendent of schools to make a survey of his school system which will be indicative of its points of strength and weakness. And to learn from the results better methods and procedures...Our schools are, in a sense, factories in which the raw products (children) are to be shaped and fashioned into products to meet the various demands of life. (Callahan, 1962, p. 152)

The standards and units that Cubberley and others had in mind were not in any sense those that are discussed today. They never mentioned performance standards, norms, or benchmarks. The concern was largely with doing better, and most times "doing better" meant spending less money or saving time. Theodore C. Mitchell, superintendent of New York City schools, asked if the "recitation" in schools had made the same kind of progress as industry had made through scientific management. He advised teachers not to waste time scolding pupils. Time was also wasted when children borrowed paper or pencils from each other; the teacher should keep a satchel with the needed supplies available at all times. Other means of improving efficiency concerned an elaborate system of bookkeeping and changes in classroom management:

Only a teacher would think of trying to keep adequate records in one little book that can be slipped into the pocket....In recitation use should be made of all available time....Too often valuable time is lost when tasks assigned to each one by one, while all the rest wait their turn. As much as four minutes is spent by some....The cultured ease in the classroom, of drawing-room quiet and refinement...must give way to an ideal of timesaving through preparation for dealing expeditiously and variously with a variety of needs, to the end that maximum results may be attained under pressure of time and with economy of material. By better use of ground space, by better setting of machinery, by better placing of raw material, by cutting down of labor motions, by producing harder and more lasting tools—by these and other means the factories have increased their output, have lowered the cost of production, have met the demands of their very existence. (Callahan, p. 102)

The most common form of determining efficiency and setting standards was the rating form. A typical form rated teachers on a five-point scale from "very poor" to "excellent" on 42 qualities, such as general appearance, health, optimism, cooperation, moral influence, and care of light, heat, and ventilation. While a number of the items addressed the teacher's preparation and skills, only two referred to the achievement of students (Callahan, 1962, p. 106). Teachers, in turn, rated principals on a variety of personal qualities, as well as on management and supervisory skills.

As for students, they were largely ignored by the raters. One rating scale did ask students to rate themselves in response to 30 questions pertaining to their efficiency as students. However, many of these questions did not pertain to classroom activities—"Do you read magazines?"—and many did not refer to school—"Do you attend and enjoy church?"

The superintendent was largely immune from the rating scales, although a variety of articles encouraged self-rating. William Vance, superintendent of Delaware, Ohio, schools, provided a list of qualities of the successful superintendent. In the prefatory remarks to his list, Vance provided an interesting comment on the tenor of the time:

> In these days of scales and standards or norms, when there is a burning desire to reduce everything in the pedagogical universe to the fraction of something else, and then to hold it up to public view as a percentage, or a graph, or a segmented line, or a sectored circle, or groups thereof, one device seems to have escaped the diabolism of the experts, namely, a contrivance whereby the superintendent of schools may take his own measure, quickly, accurately, privately. But how is he to do this himself? How can he anticipate the inquisitorial methods of some Holy Office of a Survey? (Vance, NEA Proceedings, 1914, pp. 280–281)

Vance said the superintendent must be a "man of affairs":

> By this I mean not only that he should know the details of the school plant and equipment, from pens and ink to plumbing fixtures and vacuum cleaners, but that he should be an expert in warming, ventilating, school seating, decorating, and landscape gardening....In cities of less than 25,000 he is frequently the purchasing agent of

the board of education, and hence he must be a compendium of school and office supplies. Catalogues, samples, and price lists comprehensively filed are at his finger tips. He familiarizes himself with the quality of the manufactured output of the various houses. He inspects the school grounds, basement, furnace and engine rooms, toilets—the entire realm of which the janitor is king—and even ventures a suggestion or a correction, if need be, to that potentate.

The other major activity aimed at improving school efficiency was the school survey. Typically developed and administered by a group of college professors, some of whom identified themselves as "efficiency experts," the survey provided comparative information about the school or system in relation to others. They were often initiated by groups outside the school, but they sometimes served to defend the school and its staff against critics, either because the comparative data looked good or because the volumes of findings were constructed in a way that laymen "cannot interpret and which no one with the least grain of sense would attempt to read" ("An Unintentional Survey," *Journal of Education*, July 3, 1919, p. 8).

Again, the survey, like the rating scale, was an attempt to apply either what we would today call content standards or performance standards. The psychology of the survey was reflected well in the statement by the Taxpayers Association of California when it established a special Bureau of Educational Investigation:

> The Taxpayers Association of California, exists for the purpose of eliminating waste and promoting greater efficiency in the administration of public affairs. As a part of its operating program it will attempt to show the business men and taxpayers of California how they can get better educational results for the money spent. Educational leaders for many years have been demanding changes for the better, but either have achieved no results or else have had to be satisfied with so many compromises that it is generally admitted that the highest efficiency is not being obtained even with the large amount of money now being spent. (Callahan, p. 116)

The emphasis of the surveys was on the economic, not the educational, and this was fine with at least some of the educators who conducted them. In *The School Survey*, with an introduction by his mentor Cubberley, Jesse Sears wrote:

> With a critical public opinion demanding economy and efficiency, and with a new conception of education growing rapidly into a science of education, we had both the motive and the means by which the survey movement could take form. Under these circumstances it was not strange that the public should take readily to the survey idea. People were already familiar with the work of the efficiency engineer and the accounting expert in business and industry. Naturally, then, when boards of education called up educational experts to help point the way out of difficulties, the idea was promptly understood and sanctioned by the public, and the school survey movement had begun. (Sears, pp. 3–4)

Administrators, apparently willingly, accepted the survey, the teachers grudgingly. It was resisted only in large cities with strong unions—most teachers at the time did not have tenure. Administrators were similarly weak. There were dissenters. Typical of the dissent was that voiced in *The American Teacher* in 1912 by Benjamin C. Gruenberg:

> The organization and the methods of the schools have taken on the form of those commercial enterprises that distinguish our economic life. We have yielded to the arrogance of "big business men" and have accepted their criteria of efficiency at their own valuation, without question. We have consented to measure the results of educational efforts in terms of price and product—the terms that prevail in the factory and the department store. But education, since it deals in the first place with organisms, and in the second place with individualities, is not analogous to a standardizable manufacturing process. Education must measure its efficiency not in terms of so many promotions per dollars of expenditure, nor even in terms of so many student-hours per dollar of salary; it must measure its efficiency in terms of increased humanism, increased power to do, increased capacity to appreciate. (Gruenberg, 1912, p. 90)

Others questioned whether the essential qualities of teaching could be quantified by a survey or a test. Fred Newton Scott of the University of Michigan, speaking before the North Central

Association of Colleges and Schools in 1914 and documenting the rising tide of articles on efficiency as indexed by the *Readers' Guide to Periodical Literature*, expressed doubt that the tide would recede, then questioned the new science's applicability in terms that would echo till today:

> The results of the applications of these standards [of scientific measurement] are quantitative and can be expressed in mathematical or other abstract symbols. But the most efficient things in teaching are not, in my opinion, susceptible of adequate quantitative measurement. They are such things as personality, sympathy, sincerity, enthusiasm, intuiting of character, taste, judgment, love of truth, tact. These things are qualities, not quantities, and any judgment of them, to be adequate, must be made in terms of quality. To be sure, in the case of any quality, we can indicate the more or less of it in mathematical symbols, but how thin and ghostlike are such records compared with the living reality. (Scott, p. 35)

Scott then tried to turn the movement against itself by taking its logic to the extreme:

> Whatever may be said for and against it, the testing industry in education is likely to go on with unabated vigor. Like it or not, we must put up with it and turn it to the best uses we can. Since that is so, I would make a suggestion. It is that if such tests of efficiency are good for pupils and teachers, they are equally good for their superior officers. Why withhold this precious boon from principals, from superintendents?...But we must not stop here. We must go on to test school boards and boards of trustees, bodies which present curious variations of efficiency. We must test the people who elect these boards, and, ultimately, we must test the testers themselves, who are not free, I suspect, from the defects of our common mortality. We must even test college presidents....We can all imagine, I think, the expression which would flit over the president's face as he examined his curve [of successes and failures]. That expression would be worth preserving photographically. I suspect that it would not be the expression of a broken and a contrite spirit, but rather, in the words of the Psalter, the expression of a stony heart that is insensible of the burden of sin, stub-

born, rebellious, impenitent, and incorrigible. (Scott, p. 41)

Such dissenting voices were few. A goal of "increased humanism" sounded hopelessly fuzzy in the era of scientific management and the efficiency expert. No doubt Scott received a good laugh at his proposal to test the testers and college presidents, but the efficiency movement, immune to satire and irony, swept treatments aside.

Even granting that concern for efficiency was pervasive, one can still raise a question about the adequacy of Callahan's thesis. As cited earlier, Callahan was concerned that "educators who had devoted years of study and thought to the aims and purposes of education" were being asked by the efficiency experts to become "mechanics." He presented his concerns in an influential 1962 book, *Education and the Cult of Efficiency* (a number of other books and essays would adapt this title in the form of "[The Author's Concern] and the Cult of Efficiency").

Callahan offered the hypothesis that the obsession with efficiency turned administrators generally and superintendents most particularly away from scholarly activity and toward what we would refer to today as "administrivia." Administrators made such a deviation in part because business and industry were the twin heroes of American culture and these endeavors had discovered the wonders of "scientific management." In addition, Callahan contended superintendents had only a tenuous grip on their jobs. To make matters worse, there was an unprecedented barrage of criticism of public schools. These conditions conspired to make efficiency the focus of the schools and, especially, the superintendency. In the evolution of standards, the diversion to the cult of efficiency was a long trip to a dead end and, in Callahan's view, greatly impeded a genuine concern with standards appropriate for schools and educators.

Much of Callahan's treatise is correct. Certainly scientific management swept the nation. Certainly schools were under attack. Certainly superintendents were vulnerable. Certainly they got caught up in the efficiency craze. But there are aspects of Callahan's treatment that do not seem supported by the evidence.

In the first place, Callahan presents his assertion about the scholarly bent of superintendents in a curious fashion. The shift from scholar to mechanic would seem to represent a major proposition. And it is true that mobility from a K–12 setting to a university position was more evident then than now. Yet, in a book with several references on most pages, this contention appears only as a footnote containing a reference to an unpublished dissertation by one of his doctoral students: "A recent study of the older generation of superintendents indicates that they considered themselves scholars and gentlemen, never businessmen" (Callahan, p. 180).

Callahan's principal source of information about the obsession with efficiency are pages of the *American School Boards Journal (ASBJ)*, and over the years in question, 1910–20, these are indeed replete with articles on efficiency, standardization, and scientific management. Yet the years leading up to the era of efficiency do not provide evidence of the superintendent as scholar.

To be sure, *ASBJ* has always viewed itself as a practical periodical rather than as a journal of ideas. First drawings, then pictures of new schools dominate its pages. Articles about heating and ventilation abound, as do tracts on the often tendentious relationships between boards and superintendents. And occasionally a piece appears, as in March 1906, "The Value of Charcoal" (it absorbs gases and impurities in the stomach, sweetens the breath, cleans and improves the complexion), or in February 1906, "The Girl—How Educate Her?" (give her training in homemaking so she won't steal jobs from boys by doing the same work for lesser wages) (Fishel, 1906, p. 21).

In spite of this emphasis on the practical, one might expect some sign of scholarliness in the essays since most of them were penned by superintendents. Yet rarely do *ASBJ*'s articles from 1890 to 1910 contain any indication of scholarship or any references to the theoreticians who were influencing practice. The articles do contain information about improving efficiency well before what Callahan offers as the birthdate of scientific management, Frederick Taylor's 1910 testimony before the Interstate Commerce Commission.

Indeed, one senses from articles in *ASBJ* prior to 1910 that the profession of the superintendency is still in its infancy and largely unshaped. A 1910 piece by Joseph Avent, superintendent of Goldsboro, North Carolina, schools, noted that while a few cities had created superintendencies in the 1830s and 1840s, the position concentrated on supervision rather than administration as late as 1885: "But today, the business systems of the country being taken as models, it is generally recognized that there is great economy of educational resources in having this educational labor [supervision and administration] divided and then directed by a competent and responsible head" (Avent, 1910, p. 3). Avent describes how the superintendent must meet local conditions and cites the case of one who did not respond to the town's habit of speaking to everyone, known or not, and was therefore perceived as "stuck up" and sent packing after a short tenure. The superintendent must, above all, ensure "entirely harmonious" relations with the board. He must also select teachers and promote "new things." Avent does not specify what these might be, but he provides advice to the superintendent on the best way of convincing the board to adopt them.

The superintendent must also take into account the rights of the public that pays his salary and court them. "If a superintendent come into frequent close contact with the people, open-minded and open-hearted, knows them and is known of them, he will seldom retain the idea, if he shall ever have had it, that he is the sole repository of educational wisdom in that community. Most people are reasonable beings, but they are sociable before they are reasonable."

Nowhere in his description of the desirable traits and behaviors a good superintendent should display does Avent mention matters of pedagogy or philosophy of education as important to the conduct of the superintendency. The superintendent should, nevertheless, make frequent visits to classrooms to assist teachers.

An article by P.O. Cole does mention that the superintendent must inspire the teacher. And how might he accomplish this? "When the superintendent visits his schools he may, during his stay, take charge of one or two recitations and thus allow the teacher a few moments relief, while at the same time he is inspiring the pupils with new life and vigor for their work" (Cole, p. 7). Some articles argue that the superintendent should know more about teaching than the teacher; others argue that this is impossible and that the superintendent should defer to the teachers' judgments. These contradictions reflect another aspect of the superintendency at the time—there was no consensus on what the duties should be. Many articles of the time identify the premiere quality of the superintendent as what today would be called a "networker," someone endowed with large amounts of Howard Gardner's "interpersonal intelligence."

It may have been difficult for the superintendent to attend even to such things as inspiring teachers. The front pages of *ASBJ* featured full-page cartoons with some explanatory text at the bottom. That of May 1911 was labeled "Cut Him Loose" and showed a man labeled "school superintendent" chained to a post called "administrative details" while a young girl labeled "pupil" stands bundled up in the snow and is about to be set upon by a wolf labeled "neglect." Says *ASBJ*, "Too many super-intendents are so tied down by clerical and routine duties that they cannot devote their best efforts to the large problems of the schools." The November 1911 cartoon depicted a cart labeled "public school" being driven by a man named "school board." Of the two horses pulling the cart, the one labeled "professional administration" is muscular and lively, whereas the one called "business management" shows his ribs and strains from the ef-fort. The caption reads: "The efficiency of many school systems is suffering because the School Boards are neglecting the em-ployment of able business executives." Cartoons such as these would, presumably, stimulate school officials and board mem-bers to bring efficient business practices to education.

If superintendents were burdened with mundane duties and handicapped by the absence of an able business manager, some-thing that promised as much relief as "scientific management" appeared to pledge would surely have been welcome. If the superintendency was not yet in a formed state, that alone would have left it vulnerable to scientific management's influence.

As for the criticism of schools, Callahan implies that the schools were the target of special venom, but that may not have been the case. The onset of criticism and "scientific manage-ment was also the time of the muckrakers. Ida Tarbell's *History of the Standard Oil Company* had appeared in 1904, Upton Sin-clair's *The Octopus* in 1906. During this same period, Lincoln Steffens used his position as editor of *McCall's* to expose cor-ruption in government.

In a similar vein, Ella Frances Lynch fired a mean salvo against public education in a 1912 *Ladies Home Journal* essay. Identified as a former teacher by the magazine, the following paragraph is typical of her broadside:

> Can you imagine a more grossly stupid, a more genu-inely asinine system tenaciously persisted in to the fear-ful detriment of over seventeen million children and at a cost to you of over four-hundred-and-three dollars each year—a system that not only is absolutely ineffective in its results, but also actually harmful in that it throws every year ninety-three out of every one hundred chil-dren into the world of action absolutely unfitted for even

the simplest tasks in life? Can you wonder that we have so many inefficient men and women; that in so many families there are so many failures; that our boys and girls can make so little money that in the one case they are driven into the saloons from discouragement, and in the other into the brothels to save themselves from starvation? Yet that is exactly what the public-school system is today doing, and has been doing. (Lynch, 1912)

In one regard, Ms. Lynch sets the stage for modern critics by making statements about school standards and outcomes when she obviously has no data to warrant her claims. Attacks such as hers, by no means uncommon, could be taken as evidence for Callahan's claim.

On the other hand, E.C. Hartwell, superintendent of Petoskey, Michigan, schools, saw the brickbats as part of the general tendency to attack all social institutions. In an *ASBJ* piece called "Muckraking the Public School," Hartwell offered this comment:

The past decade has been the golden age for muckrakers. The desire to "expose" something has grown and flourished like the green bay tree. Floods of bilious ink have been poured forth on every institution in our national life. A deep pall of pessimism has been draped about nearly every feature of business and social activity. Accounts of bribery, boodle, graft, corruption, incompetence and malfeasance of all sorts have filled our press and periodicals. Even the children, grown cynical before they reach the high school, talk glibly of all the failings that human flesh is heir to. (Hartwell, 1912)

As an antidote to Lynch's venom, Hartwell invited readers to visit schools.

It cannot be determined from a single essay how representative Hartwell's sentiment was, but if it was widespread, then the schools were only one of many institutions under attack. Rather than distracting superintendents from a concern with scholarship and standards, the cult of efficiency may have been simply something that offered the promise of better ways of accomplishing their already many ongoing activities.

The *American School Board Journal* was one of the principal periodicals of the day, but hardly the only one and perhaps not the best one for determining the concerns of school administrators. If one looks away from *ASBJ* to *The School Review*, the principal journal of the time for secondary school educators, one again finds a number of articles concerning school efficiency testing, standards, and standardization. But the bulk of the articles continue to dwell on what to teach and how to teach it, the value or lack of value in particular instructional sequences, and the scholarly review of learned books. A profession with a clearer idea of its mission was not so readily co-opted by the fad of efficiency. (Callahan actually reaches a similar conclusion about this and the general influence of muckraking at the end of the book, but the single paragraph in which the conclusion appears seems an afterthought that does not illuminate the treatise from the beginning.)

Finally, Callahan appears to have misread or, perhaps, overlooked some work that contradicted his thesis. He is most derisive about Franklin Bobbitt and his contributions to the efficiency movement:

> The most unfortunate aspects of Bobbitt's system were his invitation to laymen, and especially businessmen, to interfere with the work of the schools; his oversimplified and mechanical conception of the nature of education and his almost complete lack of understanding of teaching as an art; his building up of the authority of the administrator on the one hand while limiting the freedom of the teacher on the other....(Callahan, 1962, p. 92)

This might have been true of Bobbitt in the 1913 treatise that is Callahan's reference, but by 1918, an entirely different tone suffuses Bobbitt's writing. In his 1918 tome, *The Curriculum*, Bobbitt does note the development of the mechanistic system Callahan lamented in his own book and also reaffirms his commitment to the application of science in education. Bobbitt contends that the application of science to schools had not been accomplished well by this mechanistic system. "Lest it be thought that all tendency to mechanization of the workers is to be found only in the field of material production, let us note a case upon the professional level: that of teachers." He then describes how in many schools teachers are highly specialized and perform only one aspect of the educational task, passing students along to another specialist when that aspect is completed. To see the larger picture of the whole child and the whole process is the role of the principal and superintendent. "The supervisory brain, so to speak, does the thinking for the whole organization; the teachers are but the hands and voices of this brain" (Bobbitt, 1918, p. 78).

Thus far, this is precisely what Callahan had lamented. But then Bobbitt totally rejects this system!

> This feudal theory tends at present to be strong wherever organization develops....The less the workers trouble their superiors by thinking and insisting upon being heard, the better for all.
>
> This feudal theory is being supplanted rather rapidly by a democratic theory....In the school field, it is not the superintendent or principal who takes the place of the general teacher...but it is the total group. It is not the manager who is to do the thinking that goes into the work; it is rather the entire associated group....Where all are made intelligent as to the group-labors, the sum of the knowledge of the specialists added to that of the generalists is greater than that of the generalists alone; and this aggregate is a far more effective directive agency. And as workers are changed from industrial serfs to freemen with minds and rights to think and with responsibility resting upon them for thought and suggestions, they are filled with a new spirit. Recognized as men, they become men; act like men; and the curve of their operative efficiency mounts rapidly upward. (Bobbitt, 1918, pp. 78–79)

Bobbitt by 1918 was contending that we should *not* apply Taylor's scientific management to education. Why, it doesn't even work in business and industry:

> Under the so-called "Taylor System" of scientific management, all the thinking is done by specialized officials in the "planning room."...Instructions are typewritten, and sent out to the workmen. The latter are not expected to do any thinking or judging or deciding; this is all done for them; they are only to obey orders.
>
> This system is looked upon by many factory managers as the most perfect that has yet been devised. It puts science in the saddle. Yet the system is not popular. Where it is tried, it is frequently abandoned. It usually breaks down, we are told, because most labors are so complicated that the planning-room cannot foresee all contingencies. (Bobbitt, p. 83)

Because of these unforeseen contingencies, the nonthinking workers stop work until new instructions arrive. Often these instructions don't work because the planners are too remote from the job. The science of scientific management is visible only to the planning room. The workers only see orders. This system cannot work. "The relative failure of the Taylor System seems to result from insufficient attempt to enlist the intelligence and initiative of the men." The Taylor System is a halfway step as a process of establishing higher standards. "Science rules in the planning-room; it must also rule in the consciousness of the workmen." If Bobbitt still held this view and were writing today, he might well conclude by saying, "We must empower teachers."

This type of economy-oriented standards movement receded with the onset of the Great Depression. The anti-efficiency views of educators such as Jesse Newlon and George Counts were influential, and, perhaps more important, many well-educated people were out of work. Still, the concern with finance, personnel, and unimportant aspects of instruction continued to occupy many superintendents, and from time to time other articles appeared trying to establish standards for schools by measuring their efficiency.

"The Low Productivity of the Education Industry" was the title of an influential article in *Fortune* magazine in 1958. The author, Daniel Seligman began by noting that it was hard to gauge productivity even in something so apparently fixed and controllable as the automotive industry. He posed the difficulty in these terms:

> In education, it would seem even harder to put a firm figure on the value of the output, for the value in this case depends decisively on quality, which is probably impossible to measure in objective terms. There is not even agreement as to whether the changes in American education over the past two decades—or the past *five* decades—represent an improvement or a deterioration of the educational product.

Seligman noted that the taking on of "less capable students" during this period may well have affected quality. Still, whatever it was that the schools were churning out, we would "want the schools to turn out students with the greatest possible efficiency," which for Seligman meant that we would want to optimize the number of students graduated and minimize the input of man-hours and capital.

By these sorts of measures, Seligman found the efficiency of the schools had declined: the number of "teacher-days" had increased by 250 percent since the turn of the century, whereas the number of pupils had grown only by 100 percent (number of "teacher-days" appears to be the number of days in a year a teacher taught multiplied by the number of teachers). Seligman acknowledged that student attendance was much higher in 1958 than in 1900. Factoring in improved attendance—which occasioned the decline of the truant officer—Seligman concluded that the schools' output had risen by 170 percent, still far less than the increase in teaching time. His arithmetic, presuming there were some actual calculations, is not included in the article.

The cost per pupil had also been rising, Seligman found. This was related in part to declining class size, which, he suspected but could not prove, had no bearing on achievement.

To solve these problems, Seligman turned, as many others have, principally to technology, although he also thought the use of teacher's aides to "relieve teachers of the many burdensome chores" they had would also help. He was particularly optimistic about television but thought that other audiovisual aids such as film, which had previously been used to offer "occasional dreary shows," could help. "Now any school with a projector can offer a superb course in high-school physics." A box next to the main text offered a profile of B.F. Skinner and his teaching machine. The teaching machine, the article hinted, might be the great technological breakthrough needed to improve standards and efficiency.

Along with the technological innovations, Seligman also echoed earlier calls for "scientific programming," which would reduce "the large numbers of classrooms and laboratories lying idle much of the day." He waxed enthusiastic about Space Utilization, Incorporated, which had pioneered such programming. But the area with the greatest potential for increasing productivity was "in the realm of school management. The schools have just begun to discover scientific management" (Seligman, 1958).

Seligman also made another interesting comment, but he ignored its importance, offering it only as a parenthetical remark. Discussing the increasing amount of money spent on the "plant" of education, he observed that it was larger than the plants of the steel or auto industries. "Moreover, the steel industry's new facilities have brought it a steadily rising output. The industry's productivity has been rising at an average of 3 or 4 percent a year....No comparable economies are visible in the education industry." And then the parentheses: "(Nor are they visible, of course, in most of the other service industries)."

In penning this parenthetical note, Seligman came close to realizing that he was trying to compare the incomparable. Service industries cannot be compared to manufacturing because service is always labor intensive. The costs of service industries have always risen faster than those of manufacturing, except, perhaps, when a resource becomes expensive, or, as is about to happen, technology replaces people. Had Seligman come to this realization fully, he might have compared education to something other than steel and autos.

The echo of scientific management continues today in attempts to measure the efficiency of schools in meeting standards by means of "education production functions," a type of analysis conducted by several economists, most notably Eric Hanushek at the University of Rochester. Hanushek began such analyses as early as 1972, but his best-known article among educators appeared in the May 1989 issue of *Educational Researcher,* in which he concluded that *"there is no strong or systematic relationship between school expenditures and student performance"* (Hanushek, 1989, p. 47).

Hanushek's logic is straightforward—and flawed. Hanushek looked for relations among a variety of variables and student achievement as measured by test scores in 197 studies. Not all of them focused on school expenditures per pupil. Only 65 of the studies directly examined per-pupil costs. This is important to note because those who have voiced support of Hanushek's claims, most notably former Secretary of Education William Bennett, have often claimed that the per-pupil cost analysis was based on 187 studies. Such a claim creates an impression that the base of data is much larger than it actually is.

Hanushek's analytical procedure was a relatively primitive vote-counting technique. He tallied the number of studies according to whether the results were statistically significant and whether the conclusion pointed toward money's making a difference or not. Of the 65 studies, only 16 had significant results. Thirteen of these were in the direction that money made a difference; three said it did not. Of the statistically insignificant results, 25 were in a positive direction, 13 negative; for 11, no determination of direction could be made.

It is hard, looking at these results, to understand Hanushek's conclusion. As independent consultant Keith Baker pointed out, Hanushek never explained what kind of decision rule he used to reach it (Baker, 1991, p. 629). If, as Baker did, one uses a 5 percent decision rule, the conclusion is quite different. Baker observed that when one conducts a large number of studies, some of them will reach a statistically significant level by chance. Baker's 5 percent rule says, "we expect 5 percent of the studies to be significant by chance. Does this accord with what we see?" In the case of the Hanushek data set, the answer is, "No." By the 5 percent rule, only three of the 65 studies would attain significance, but in fact 13 did.

Moreover, Hanushek concerned himself only with studies that found statistically significant results. However, the lack of statistical significance does not mean that there was no difference. Some studies found differences in the direction of money's making a difference; others found differences in the opposite direction. However, those in the direction of money as an agent of effectiveness far outnumbered those in the opposite direction. If we add in those studies where the directionality would be in the right direction—as would be done in a meta-analysis, for instance—the overwhelming majority of the studies do not support the conclusion that money doesn't matter. Hanushek's own data do not support his conclusions.

According to Baker, Bennett and Hanushek ignored the salience of the finding. They should have been concerned not that there was no relationship between money and achievement, but that there *was* and that it was positive. Baker argues persuasively that the proper relationship between money and level of achievement is negative (it is important to distinguish level of achievement from changes in achievement, as will be discussed below).

> Think about hospital costs and dead patients. We would not be surprised to find that patients who die cost more in medical care than those who are cured. Indeed, policy makers guarantee this outcome by making every effort to prolong life. We would not argue that a negative correlation between medical costs and cures indicates medical failure.
>
> A good school resembles a good hospital in that more resources are devoted to treating those who are the most difficult to deal with—the sickest patients or the least able students. (Baker, 1991, p. 629)

This leads to the logical flaw in Hanushek's arguments. Having claimed to find no relationship between level of achievement and expenditures, Hanushek then went on to argue that additional monies will have no effect on *gains* (change) in achievement: "School reform discussions that begin with the premise that constraints on expenditures are the most serious roadblock to *improved* student performance are, at best, misguided" (Hanushek, 1989, p. 50, italics added).

But Hanushek's data are silent on improvement; they speak only to the *level* of student achievement. Level of student achievement is affected, as many studies have shown, by many nonschool factors having to do with family and community variables. For instance, as noted in Chapter Two, 83 percent of the variance in state-level NAEP scores can be accounted for by using only four variables, all of which are nonschool variables. Baker, on the other hand, cites several studies indicating that gains in achievement are relatively independent of these variables. This makes a certain amount of sense. Who would expect that a slum school and a suburban school, given precisely the same amount of money, would achieve at the same level? On the other hand, if the levels were increased, we might well see gains in both schools. The Hanushek collection of studies does not address this issue.

Unfortunately, Hanushek's conclusion has now become an article of faith and impervious to data. When data are presented, they are used selectively and deceitfully. In his 1994 book, *Making Schools Work*, Hanushek claims in many places, as does the title of one chapter, that we are experiencing "Rising Expenditure, Falling Performance." Presenting NAEP science scores for 17-year-olds, he claims that "achievement on science exams, as shown in figure S-2, is depressingly representative of the performance pattern for the population as a whole and for its major subgroups" (Hanushek, 1994, p. xix).

But Hanushek's figure S-2 most decidedly is not representative. His figure S-2 depicts the NAEP science trends for 17-year-olds. It is, as observed in Chapter One, unique. It is the only one of the NAEP trends showing a decrease from its inception. NAEP science trends for other ages are improving, and those for reading and math are also stable or improving. The science trend stands alone. If one enlarges the universe of test scores beyond NAEP, one also sees that many achievement test scores, which are not shown or discussed anywhere in Hanushek's book, are at all-time highs.[1]

Even the appropriate use of "education production functions" does not in itself set some kind of standard. It is, rather, a way of looking at whether or not performance is rising commensurate with increases in various inputs, most particularly, those involving money. A production function showing rising inputs and stagnant or declining outputs raises a question about standards and efficiency but does not point directly to any action that can bring about the desired changes.

Beginning in the early 1980s, interest in establishing such standards seemed to grow exponentially with each passing year, although, as this is being written, the interest, at least at the federal level, appears to be coming to a sudden halt. The interest evolved gradually as interest in using minimum competency tests grew. In *Preparing Instructional Objectives* (1962), Robert Mager of UCLA put it this way:

> If we can specify the minimal acceptable performance for each objective, we will have a performance standard against which to test our instructional programs; we will have a means for determining whether our programs are successful in achieving our instructional intent. What we must try to do, then, is indicate in our statement of objectives what the acceptable performance will be, by adding words that describe the criterion of success.

This "minimal acceptable performance" became the slogan of the minimum competency testing movement, and people were wont to define such tests in terms of a score below which anyone would be deemed incompetent. People often spoke of the skills themselves as being "essential" for success in life. In Virginia, for instance, those who judged the proposed objectives for a high school minimum competency test were asked to rate them as "essential, very important or unimportant" to success in life. Those judged essential were placed on the test. As with many such programs, however, the Virginia program showed logical inconsistencies. If the skills were all essential, then performance, logically, should be perfect, or else the person would be incompetent. The actual cutoff score for these "essential" skills, however, was set at 60. This process, common in other states as well, was, in fact, quite consistent with Binet's contention that it mattered not what the tests were as long as there were enough of them—but that was not the philosophy that infused minimum competency tests. The standard setting for MCTs was thought of in terms of establishing a floor below which no one could fall. Or fall and still get a high school diploma.

The philosophy was fatuous, of course, as Gene V Glass,

then of the University of Colorado, pointed out as early as 1978. "The language of performance standards is pseudoquantification, a meaningless application of numbers to a question not prepared for quantitative analysis" (Glass, p. 238).

When it came to the standards of minimum competency tests, Glass was dismissive:

> For most skills and performances, one can reasonably imagine a continuum stretching from "absence of skill" to conspicuous excellence. But it does not follow that the ability to recognize absence of skill (e.g., this paraplegic can type zero words per minute at zero percent accuracy) means that one can recognize the highest level of skill below which a person will not be able to succeed (in life, at the next level of schooling, or in his chosen trade). What is the minimum level of skill required in this society to be a citizen, parent, carpenter, college professor, keypunch operator? Imagine someone would dare to specify the highest level of reading performance below which no one could succeed in life as a parent. Counter-examples could be supplied in abundance of persons whose performance is below the "minimal" level, yet who are regarded as successful parents....The attempt to base criterion scores on a concept of minimal competence fails for two reasons: 1) it has virtually no foundation in psychology; 2) when its arbitrariness is granted but judges nonetheless attempt to specify minimal competence, they disagree wildly. (pp. 250–251)

For the latter allegation, Glass produced a number of studies that attempted to set cutoff scores on a variety of tests for a variety of purposes and that showed judges render very different judgments. For instance, in judging the necessary knowledge for a physician recertification test, different judges set the cut score from 36 percent to 80 percent. Shades of Starch and Eliott!

Glass concluded that establishing absolute standards was impossible and called for a "comparative" approach to setting standards. "Increases in cognitive performance are generally regarded as good," he said, "decreases as bad." Glass thought that in setting standards, the concepts of "good" or "bad" should be replaced with "better" or "worse." Arbitrariness could not be avoided in these decisions, he said, but it would likely cause less disruption to measure current performance and then shoot for some specified improvement in the future rather than to set a cutoff score below which a person was not deemed "minimally competent....In education, one can recognize improvement and decay, but one cannot make cogent absolute judgments of good and bad."

Aside from capricious judgments, the use of minimum competency cutoff scores sometimes had the effect of reifying the concept of minimum competency. That is, people were seen as belonging in one of two categories, "competent" and "incompetent." This occurred sufficiently often to generate a satire in the leading, and usually severely serious, measurement periodical, *The Journal of Educational Measurement*. But the satire made an important point, illustrated in this quote:

> It was only when the need for a decision arose that we were forced to impose an artificial dichotomy on the distribution of beardedness scores. Prior to doing this, it had been obvious that there were as many degrees of beardedness as there were beards. After the dichotomy had been made, we found ourselves referring to people as if there were simply two kinds—bearded and un-bearded—forgetting the oversimplification which this involved. We began to ask ourselves: "I wonder to what category that person *really* belongs," as though bearded and non-bearded were pre-ordained categories and our task was merely to discover the truth. But beardedness, like height, beauty, competence, and most human characteristics, is a matter of degree, even if our use of language sometimes makes it appear otherwise. (Rowley, 1982, p. 89)

Glass's pronouncements hardly stopped anyone from making absolute judgments of good and bad. The idea of a floor below which no one should fall was too engaging an image for politicians and policymakers to be killed just because it didn't make any sense. As has happened so often in the history of American education, logic and facts took a subordinate place to politics and ideology.

During the period of minimum competency madness, say, 1975–85, some of our best psychometricians often found themselves writing material when they would much rather have left the pages blank. Lorrie Shepard of the University of Colorado, for instance, let herself be goaded into writing a chapter on setting performance standards and taking a stand of "constructive pessimism": "State officials required by law to implement a minimum competency testing program can hardly refuse to set passing scores on the grounds that it is bad psychology and insupportable psychometrically. Standards must be set, so what is the most defensible procedure?" (Shepard, 1980, p. 169). Of course, according to the Nuremberg Precedent, state officials not only *could* refuse, they were morally *bound* to refuse if they thought the results unconscionable. But most psychometricians and others having to cope with these tests did not see the MCTs as overwhelmingly evil, and a few who did were not willing to pay the price that refusal to obey the law would cost.

In the early 1980s, MCTs began to fade from the scene. They had, after all, caused minimal disruption. Few students were denied diplomas, and even that shame was usually a private matter: no one in the audience knew that the student on stage at graduation was obtaining a "certificate of attendance" rather than a diploma. The reticence of employers to use the diploma as some kind of "standard" or condition of employment also diminished the importance of not earning one.

Although a concern with minimal competency testing faded, it did not do so because citizens became convinced that schools were producing competent graduates. Indeed, by 1983 disenchantment was in the air. Stories—or rumors anyway—abounded about how the United States' competitiveness with Japan and Germany, two countries we had rescued after World War II, had waned. In 1977, a panel appointed by the College Board had reported on the SAT decline that had begun in 1963. Although the College Board and ETS insisted that the SAT did not measure school quality, the public and the media assumed it did, and both had become increasingly alarmed as the papers and television put each new dip on the front page or in prime-time news.

While a variety of writers had voiced alarm about the rush of technology since the turn of the century, the advent of computers—in particular, their shift from machines that occupied large rooms and needed people with arcane skills for their operation to devices that sat on anyone's desk and offered "user friendly" engagement—contributed to a sense that technology was becoming more important than ever. Lists of the fastest-growing jobs usually showed them to be those using the new technologies (the lists, often inaccurate, were usually cast in terms of rates; they seldom showed the fastest-growing jobs in terms of numbers, jobs that were mostly unskilled. Indeed, during this period the number of jobs requiring skilled labor was declining.[2]

The perceived onrush of technology was accompanied by a sense that schools were failing to groom our students to cope with it. *A Nation At Risk* (1983) played on this uneasiness by observing that

> Computers and computer-controlled equipment are pen-etrating every aspect of our lives—homes, factories and offices.
>
> One estimate indicates that by the turn of the cen-tury millions of jobs will involve laser technology and robotics.
>
> Technology is radically transforming a host of other occupations. They include health care, medical science, energy production, food processing, construction, and the building, repair, and maintenance of sophisticated scientific equipment.

A Nation At Risk played to other insecurities of the day as well. It listed 13 indicators of risk, the first being that American students do not do well in international comparisons. One of its "findings" was that "'minimum competency' examinations fall short of what is needed, as the 'minimum' tends to become the 'maximum,' thus lowering educational standards for all."

Risk carried an underlying assumption pertaining to tech-nology that people would need more education and higher skills to deal with it. This is not necessarily correct and certainly not true for many people, perhaps a majority. The initial phase of a new technology often, indeed, creates a new class of skilled users. We have already noted that in connection with computers themselves. After personal computers became popular, the first editions of word-processing, database, and spreadsheet appli-cations programs for them required logic, skills, and persever-ance to cope with the cloudy prose of user manuals.

By comparison, the applications packages of today are a snap. The use of the Internet offers an instance of a technology in transition from arcana to lay use. Similarly, point-and-shoot cameras produce images that almost equal the quality of their manually operated ancestors but require no knowledge of film speeds, shutter speeds, or f-stops and how those latter two char-acteristics affect what is in focus in a picture. In general, a devel-opment in technology does not necessarily require new and more difficult skills for large segments of the populace. There was, as well, no evidence that minimum competency tests had had any effect on lowering standards. It was certainly true that, for students who had difficulty with these tests, the MCTs caused the curriculum to narrow in the direction of the test. Some of those who observed such deflection argued that even this more narrowly focused education was more than the students were getting prior to the imposition of the test. In fact, a 1993 survey of course taking showed that enrollments in "nonacademic" courses in high school had peaked in 1961 at 43 percent and by the time of *Risk*, had fallen back to about 35 percent. In addition, achievement test scores had started rising before most MCTs were in place and continued to climb during the duration of the fad.

Still, by combining the concern for functioning in a technological society, the concern for competing with other nations, and the concern for moving beyond minima, *Risk* went a long way toward changing the nation's educational focus. Its initial recommendation had to do with curricular content and how much of it students should study, but its second recommendation was labeled "Standards and Expectations." It read, "We recommend that schools, colleges, and universities adopt more rigorous and measurable standards, and higher expectations, for academic performance and student conduct, and that four year colleges and universities raise their requirements for admission...." As noted earlier, the call of *Risk* was largely for "more," not "different."

A Nation At Risk also proved to be a powerful antidote to the common interpretation of two earlier reports: *Equality of Educational Opportunity* (1966) by James Coleman (et al.) and *Inequality: A Reassessment of the Effect of Family and Schooling in America* (1972) by Christopher Jencks (et al.). These reports had analyzed a number of variables that contributed to school success and had concluded that when family and community characteristics were taken into account, schools accounted for little of the variance in achievement among different groups. "It's all family" became the stereotypical—and erroneous—response to Coleman's and Jencks's work. Coleman himself argued that the results meant that massive amounts of money needed to be spent on high-poverty schools. *A Nation At Risk* restored, in people's minds anyway, the idea that schools are important and that changes in them will do good things not only for the individuals who get a better education but also for the nation as a whole.

If timing is everything, *A Nation At Risk* could not have appeared at a better moment. The same short season saw the independent publication of John Goodlad's *A Place Called School,* Ernest Boyer's *High School,* and Ted Sizer's *Horace's Compromise.* Whereas *Risk* could be seen as a federally sponsored study external to educators, Goodlad, Boyer, and Sizer were well-known members of the educational community, and all were now challenging the status quo.

In addition, one response to the schools-don't-matter reports of Coleman and Jencks was to search for schools that did seem to matter. The resulting "effective schools research" spearheaded by reformers such as Ronald Edmonds and Lawrence Lezotte had become a popular bandwagon. At the time that *Risk* appeared, there was only one critical review of this popular movement. Two others would appear in June 1983, showing that the evidence on which the movement was based was weak, that the movement relied more on ideology and evidence than research, that the language of the movement was fuzzy, and that, as Larry Cuban would say, "No one knows how to grow an effective school." Practitioners of effective-schools rhetoric largely ignored the critics, and the model continued to attract some adherents.

As noted in earlier chapters, there was also ferment in the assessment community. Criterion-referenced tests had become a popular alternative to norm-referenced tests, although, as Chapter Two demonstrates, most criterion-referenced tests had no criterion attached to them. In his article "Improving Educational Standards in American Schools," historian Daniel Resnick of Carnegie Mellon University and his wife, pyschologist Lauren Resnick of the University of Pittsburgh, called attention to the fact that in other countries assessments were related to curricula and in this way served to maintain standards. There is nothing in the Resnicks' article to suggest that they have in mind the ambitious authentic assessments of complex performances now in vogue, but they do argue that "we need examination systems that are tied to the curriculum, for which teachers can legitimately prepare students, and for which students can study" (November 1983, p. 180).

Also in this confluence of events, at the time that *Risk* appeared, cognitive psychology was emerging from its cocoon in which it seemed an arcane science with a strange vocabulary understandable only by the few practitioners of the art. Some aspects of cognitive psychology now began to be seen as applicable to and revolutionary for classroom practice. University of Pittsburgh cognitive psychologists Robert Glaser (the first to use the phrase "criterion-referenced test," although not the first to formulate the concept) and Lauren Resnick were two such cognitive researchers who also had an intense interest in assessment.

Finally, the psychology of using tests to compare states had shifted almost 180 degrees since the development of NAEP in the 1960s. As discussed in Chapter Two, in the 1960s, state-by-state or district-by-district comparisons were anathema. As late as 1978, Rhode Island Senator Claiborne Pell had asked a testing conference audience how many of them favored a national test. Three of the 300 attendees showed a positive response. "You'll change your minds," Pell grumbled ominously. Although the testing community still had no need or desire for state or national tests, now governors, spearheaded by education-reform-minded southern governors, such as James Hunt of North Carolina, Lamar Alexander of Tennessee, Charles Robb and Gerald Baliles of Virginia, and Richard Riley of South Carolina, demonstrated a new spirit of competition, not only with one another but also with the rest of the nation. Southern governors were anxious to attract industry both from other states and other nations, and they developed strategic plans for doing so. Robb's Governor's Commission on Virginia's Future often looked at how Virginia fared in competition with other states on educational as well as strictly economic indicators. Other states had similar commissions. The futurists who addressed the Virginia group revealed that such traditional industrial lures as the presence of water or even cheap labor no longer held the attraction they once did. New incentives, such as good schools and a well-trained workforce, had assumed more importance.

As late as 1970, most states did not have a state testing program, but by the time of *Risk,* almost all did. Some used both locally developed assessments and commercial achievement tests, but neither of these categories would permit comparisons across all states. Given the new desire for comparative data, the search began for such indicators. While NAEP was posited as one useful candidate, its history prohibited it from being fully satisfactory. NAEP was still enjoined from reporting at the state or district level, and, as its developers had planned, NAEP was still a measure of what students did and did not know, not how well they stacked up on what they *should* know.

Two later events completed the stage setting for the emergence of a program to establish national standards along with national assessments built around these standards. The first event was a decision by the National Council of Teachers of Mathematics (NCTM). Responding to the various critiques of American education, NCTM decided to develop national standards for mathematics. NCTM published its curriculum standards in 1989. In that same year, the National Governors' Association, headed by then-Arkansas Governor Bill Clinton, met at an "education summit" in Charlottesville, Virginia, with President George Bush and White House staffers. The summit produced the first-ever set of national educational goals. They numbered six:

In the year 2000,

1. All children in America will start school ready to learn.
2. The high school graduation rate will increase to at least 90 percent.
3. American students will leave grades four, eight, and twelve having demonstrated competency in challenging subject matter including English, mathematics, science, history, and geography; and every school in America will ensure that all students learn to use their minds well, so they may be prepared for responsible citizenship, further learning, and productive employment in our modern economy.
4. U.S. students will be the first in the world in science and mathematics.
5. Every adult American will be literate and possess the knowledge and skills necessary to compete in a global economy and exercise the rights and responsibilities of citizenship.
6. Every school in America will be free of drugs and violence and will offer a safe, disciplined environment conducive to learning.

Even a cursory reading of these goals uncovers about equal parts apple pie, motherhood, and nonsense. Behind them lies a fair amount of cynicism, since the Bush administration was not prepared to put up any capital to help schools meet the goals. To critics, the goals looked like a good way of pretending to do something about education without spending any money.

In any case, with the onset of national goals, talk of standards was everywhere. Fairfax County, Virginia, school superintendent Robert R. Spillane captured the prevailing mood well when he said that the lack of standards in U.S. schools

is education's dirty little secret....What most of the public has now learned, and many have called their representatives in Congress about, is that the abilities of front-

line workforce in many competitor countries are substantially higher than they are in the United States, that
these countries are educating *everybody* to higher levels
than we are, and that one of the main differences between us and them is standards: they have them and we
don't. (Spillane, 1993, p. 36)

Robert Rothman expressed a similar sentiment. A reporter
for *Education Week*, Rothman took a year's leave to work with
the Center for Research in Evaluation, Standards, and Student
Testing (CRESST) at UCLA and is currently on another year's
leave with the New Standards Project at the University of Pittsburgh. Both centers are at the heart of standards-setting activities. In his 1995 book, *Measuring Up*, Rothman asks:

What is the best way to change what happens in the
classroom to bring about high levels of learning for all?
That is still a matter of heated debate. But there is near-
universal agreement that the first step is setting standards and creating assessments to measure them.

The agreement is hardly as "near-universal" as Rothman as-
serts, but given the circles he has traveled in the last two years,
one can certainly understand why he might think so.[3] Spillane's
and Rothman's comments could well be applied to reactions to
the National Education Goals: once the goals were in place, the
obvious question became, "How do we know if we've met them?"

To answer this question, Congress created the National
Council on Educational Standards and Testing, a group whose
acronym, NCEST, seldom failed to provoke a chuckle. According to NCEST, it "was created to advise on the desirability and
feasibility of national standards and tests and recommend long-
term policies, structures, and mechanisms for setting voluntary
education standards and planning an appropriate [use] of tests."

In a technically independent but functionally related way
(in that many of the same players were involved), Pittsburgh's
Resnick and Marc Tucker of the Center on Education and the
Economy (CEE) proposed to develop a system of assessments
to measure performance on "high but attainable" standards. The
proposal emerged out of the CEE's report *America's Choice:
High Skills or Low Wages* (given the trends in job creation, as
documented by Richard Barnett in 1993 and Jeremy Rifkin in
1995, a more appropriate title would have been "High Skills
and Low Wages"). *America's Choice* had called for establishing

standards and assessments at various ages, culminating in a "certificate of initial mastery" at about age 16.

The scope of this proposal is enormous, and a number of participants have exhibited a certain amount of naïveté about its feasibility. For instance, Michael Cohen, who currently splits his time between the CEE and the U.S. Department of Education, where he is an adviser to Secretary of Education Richard Riley, once spoke about how the project would develop "high but attainable" standards. I reminded him that the minimum competency tests of the 1970s had established what we could call "low but attainable" standards—and that some children had failed to attain even these. "But that was different," Cohen said. "Then, you just took the regular curriculum and added something extra to it. We're going to change everything. We're going to change what's taught and how it's taught and how it's assessed."

Over in the halls of government, after much debate, NCEST came down on the side of national—but not federal—standards and a system of national tests to go along with them. On opportunity to learn (OTL) standards, NCEST wrangled and waffled. Jonathan Kozol's *Savage Inequalities* had made the case that resources among different schools were so disparate that simply holding students in impoverished schools to the same standards as those in affluent schools would be merely another cruelty visited upon the poor students. Some means of monitoring the education delivered to the students and what the students brought to the educational setting was needed. Those who opposed OTL standards saw them as fertile ground for federal meddling in state activities. This fear, recall, had surrounded the creation of NAEP. In addition, beginning with the Reagan administration, the country had experienced more than a decade when at least the executive branch of the federal government looked to extricate itself from much of its previous role in education.

In the end, NCEST proposed "school delivery standards developed by the states collectively from which each state could select the criteria that it finds useful for the purpose of assessing a school's capacity and performance." Thus, NCEST came down firmly favoring OTL standards—which it called school delivery standards—but left it to the states to choose among them.

This stopping short of the water allowed NCEST *not* to confront the Herculean task of developing OTL standards or even of specifying what they ought to look like. Andrew Porter of the University of Wisconsin cast his eye on the field and found himself somewhat blinded by what he saw:

The sheer number of candidates for school performance standards raises the question of criteria for deciding what to include. Obviously, the first criterion should be importance, but importance for what? If the goal is to ensure every student a reasonable opportunity to learn what is required by the demanding new student assessments, then standards should reflect good predictors of such performance. Exercising this criterion should place heavy emphasis upon the research literature.

Porter asserted that OTL standards should look first at what content was actually covered in the classroom. Immediately, though, he had to admit that "covering the content" was not sufficient unless accompanied by "effective pedagogy." "Unfortunately," he wrote, "there is less agreement on what constitutes good pedagogical strategies than there is on content."

Porter then turned sanguine but vague: "Nevertheless, there is some agreement, including for example, a need for instruction to emphasize active student learning, where students take responsibility for constructing knowledge through writing, discussion, lab work, manipulatives, and computer simulation." I think that the agreement is less than Porter states and that the research base for the agreement is weaker than he contends. Accepting Porter's assessment for the moment, however, it is obvious that standards based on such effective pedagogical strategies would cost most schools their accreditation.

Recall that in *A Place Called School*, John Goodlad found that the most common school activity was teacher talk. Deborah Meier, former principal of the widely acclaimed Central Park East High School in New York City, has asserted that most discussions among students and between students and teachers are not really meaningful (nor, she contends, are most of those among teachers and principals [Meier, 1993]). Who would be the judge about the quality of discussions? How would we tell if students were "taking responsibility for constructing meaning?"

Even in terms of content, enormous problems abound. As Porter himself noted, the widely acclaimed NCTM standards cannot be used as they stand. "They are not at all prescriptive; instruction can vary considerably and still meet the standards. Operationalizing the zone of acceptable practice will require judgment and not be easy." This is masterful understatement using fine-sounding but distracting phrases, such as the "zone of acceptable practice." What on earth is that? It is the kind of concept invented on university campuses by those who are remote from schoolrooms, an affliction that impairs so many of the current notions about school reform.

To accept Porter's recommendations, one would have to accept a level of failure too painful for most to deal with. One would also commit to solving a measurement problem so immense that it has no solution in the foreseeable future.

When Governor Clinton became President Clinton, not too many changes were seen in Bush's education agenda, America 2000. The Clinton administration added two additional goals and created NESIC—the National Education Standards and Improvement Council—to "certify" that the "voluntary" standards submitted to them are up to snuff. NESIC is too new to have accomplished anything yet, but it has at least one unique quality: it unites Left and Right into a common hatred of its existence. At this writing, it might well be the most short-lived of recent government creations.

Goals 2000, as Clinton renamed Bush's program, is itself seen by the Right as a means toward a national curriculum and a national test and, in the worst instances, "official knowledge." "*Any reform that is acceptable to the educational establishment, and that can gain a majority in a legislature, federal or state, is bound to be worse than nothing,*" wrote Irving Kristol in explicating Kristol's first law of educational reform (April 18, 1994). Bruno Manno, a former assistant secretary of education under Bush and a fellow at the conservative Hudson Institute, saw it this way: "Brace yourself, America. The Clinton Administration's Goals 2000 Educate America Act is now law....As with any gift from Uncle Sam, the long-term results will be more Washington-knows-best red tape and directives imposing rules and regulations on your schools, communities, and states" (1994). Others, such as Ernest Boyer, saw the revolution without necessarily lamenting it: "Within a decade we have gone from the preoccupation of local control to national standards. There is no turning back" (Celis, 1994). Boyer's position might well have been negated by recent events. At the 1995 Council of Chief State School Officers Assessment Conference, the opinion was widespread that national standards were dead, although state-level efforts were still quite strong.

Are Higher Standards Necessary? Will National Standards Make a Difference?

The answers to these questions are yes and no, respectively.

Actually, national standards might make a difference, but it will be in the opposite direction than the one their proponents hope.

That most children could learn more than they currently learn is obvious to almost anyone who has had children in schools recently. Many students take a grade-point tumble during their first semester in college, even when the colleges are not the historically selective ones. One of my daughter's teachers in a suburban school used to threaten students by saying, "It won't be this easy in college!" Why should it be "this easy" in school? As a school-district director of research, I conducted follow-up surveys of high school graduates and asked, "If you could do it over, what one aspect of your life in school would you do differently?" Even though this was asked in a school district that sends about 90 percent of its students to college, the overwhelming number-one answer was some variant of "I would take things more serious and work harder." We could increase the articulation between high school and college without inducing the kind of student burnout seen in Japan, a proposal that calls to mind the workings of the Committee of Ten a century earlier.

There are, moreover, far too many horror stories of how students and teachers alike treat school like a game, a game where students can never admit their ignorance or acknowledge that they are having problems, two things both admissible and obvious in, say, learning to dance or play a new athletic game. I recall one instance when my daughter told me of a task that her high school English teacher had given her. I quickly mentioned several ways in which I thought the project could be made richer and more creative. At one point she said, "Oh, Daddy, it's only an *assignment*." Not something on which to waste precious energy, in other words. Her attitude is hardly unique. It will be changed by higher standards as represented by the New Standards Project.

If the tests are not authentic, neither is a lot of the instruction. One research study noted that in science lab settings, about half of the time the teacher being observed provided instructions to students that inevitably led them down a single path to the right answer. The other half of the time the teacher simply provided the answer. This is no way to learn science. Interestingly, the researchers who were watching this and similar teachers did not in the end say, "Boy, is this a lousy set of teachers." They said, "Boy, is this a lousy system." They noted that these teachers had to process 150 students a day, that they had enormous amounts of material to "cover," and that they felt obligated to do so. The researchers were sympathetic to the constraints the teachers faced. Although it was not a phrase of the time, they were in essence saying the school needed to be "restructured."

It is not at all clear, though, that the route to higher standards and restructuring passes through national content and performance standards and "voluntary" national assessments to determine how well students are meeting those standards. I think the whole operation will collapse of its own weight. But even if it gets airborne, I think it will only increase the "savage inequalities" now seen.

"The Second Bracey Report on the Condition of Public Education" summarized Kozol's book, which is about cities, and then discussed the nearly invisible rural underclass for whom the *conditions are worse*. The report cited stories of school districts in Michigan and Indiana that used to send their obsolete textbooks to Third World nations but who were now sending them to impoverished rural districts in Alabama and Mississippi, where one local superintendent described them as "godsends." Desks and chairs, also in short supply, were sent as well. The report also included a story broadcast on National Public Radio declaring that some science textbooks in Alabama firmly predicted that man might one day walk on the moon.

Once, when I repeated these stories at a meeting, I was assailed afterward by irate Alabamians who declared that these conditions did not exist. The science textbooks in Alabama were current, they contended. This led me to track down the author of the statement and thence to a brief written by Alabama Circuit Court Judge Eugene W. Reese. The brief indicates that, indeed, things were not as bad as I had described them. They were worse. The brief describes schools where students went without classrooms, without textbooks, without even drinkable water (made undrinkable in some places by the amounts of chemicals that had leached in, in other places by the amount of chlorine added to neutralize such chemicals). It speaks of students in oppressively hot classrooms or classrooms where the din from nearby vocational classes drowned out the instruction. It describes a school whose tiny athletic field was squishy with sewage leaking from the tank underneath it, schools where shelves collapsed and books were chewed up from termites, and so on, for 125 pages.

I hasten to point out that Alabama is not the target of the

litany above. Poverty is. Alabama simply is among those states with the highest poverty rates, and, in its case, the ill effects of poverty are augmented by a legacy of racial discrimination. But what, I would ask of anyone on the New Standards Project, will higher standards mean to children living and going to school under such conditions? Nothing, I submit.

On the other hand, in more affluent districts, the standards will at least be examined. A committee might be formed to review them and report to other teachers and the administration or board of education. A superintendent or school board might decide that adopting the standards will improve instruction in the district or at least have the politically expedient and good public relations value of showing that the district is keeping up with the latest developments. Because the standards will purportedly reflect the best ideas of the most forward-thinking, wisest curriculum people, there should be at least some ideas that these districts will find worth absorbing. The result, then, will be that the standards will influence the "cognitive haves" and be ignored by the "cognitive have-nots." This distance between the "aristocracy of worth and genius"—currently called "the cognitive elite"—and the rest of the population will grow.

Stanford's Larry Cuban made the same argument in somewhat more abstract terms in an *Education Week* article, concluding that national standards would leave unaffected the 40 percent of American schools that most need improvement.

"The Fourth Bracey Report on the Condition of Public Education" contained data revealing that, even in mathematics, where American students are such putative dolts, more than 70 percent of them were right up there with the top three countries, Taiwan, Korea, and Hungary. Poor students, on the other hand, did not score as high as even the lowest country, Jordan, or lowest state, Mississippi, which tied for last place. National standards will only increase the size of this chasm.

As this book is being written, the standards movement has lost some impetus. "Running out of Steam" was the title of the lead article in a 72-page special section of the April 12, 1995, issue of *Education Week*. It summarized the goal of the standards movement in this way:

> From the richest to the poorest, from the learning disabled to the gifted, students throughout the United States are taught from a common, demanding body of knowledge. They outperform all others on international as-

sessments. They graduate from high school and make a seamless transition into college or the workplace, where they demonstrate world-class skills, creativity, and academic prowess. (Diegmuller, 1995, p. SR4)

If *Education Week*'s characterization of the standards movement is accurate, it is not hard to see why the steam is failing. The scenario described above is but another example of the perennial millennialist thinking that afflicts education reformers. Against the millenarians of education stands the culture at large. For the last decade, educational reformers have been emphasizing the culture-transforming nature of education, ignoring the culture-conserving aspect of schooling favored by the culture as a whole. Nowhere is the conflict more clearly seen than in the rebellion against outcomes-based education, described in Chapter Four.

Chapter Four

The Evolution of Outcomes

In Chapter Three, we saw physician-turned-researcher J.M. Rice virtually run out of a superintendents' meeting in Indianapolis because he dared to measure educational effectiveness with a student outcome in 1897. It was not long, though, before attitudes changed dramatically. Some educators saw a revolution that would elevate education from a mere vocation to a profession: "The old method has been education within the sheltering walls of the cloister in which an occasional peephole has been cut, to satisfy the parent and silence the taxpayer. The new method proposes education in the open under the clear and penetrating rays of the search-light." Thus wrote Leonard Ayres of the Russell Sage Foundation in 1912. The searchlight was the scientific method:

> The new attitude of educators toward education means that we have ceased exalting the machinery and have commenced to examine the product. We have awakened to a startled realization that in education, as in other forms of organized activity, applied science may avail in improving even those processes that have rested secure in the sanction of generations of acceptance.
>
> The transformation now taking place in education means that it is our privilege to be part of a movement that is working changes comparable to those that are now remaking almost every form of industrial activity. (Ayres, 1912, p. 301)

Ayres then recounted the reaction to Rice's experiment and how the changed attitudes were reflected in educators' activities:

Fifteen years ago the school superintendents of America, assembled in convention in Indianapolis, discussed the problems then foremost in educational thought and action. At that meeting, a distinguished educator—the pioneer and pathfinder among the scientific students of education in America—presented the results of his investigations of spelling in the school systems of nineteen cities. These results showed that, taken all in all, the children who had spent forty minutes a day for eight years in studying spelling did not spell any better than the children in the schools of other cities where they devoted only ten minutes per day to the study.

The presentation of these data threw the assemblage into consternation, dismay, and indignant protest. But the resulting storm of vigorously voiced opposition was directed, not against the methods and results of the investigation, but against the investigator who had pretended to measure the results of teaching spelling by testing the ability of the children to spell.

In terms of scathing denunciation the educators there present, and the pedagogical experts, who reported the deliberations of the meeting in the educational press, characterized as silly, dangerous, and from every viewpoint reprehensible the attempt to test the efficiency of the teacher by finding out what the pupils could do. With striking unanimity they voiced the conviction that any attempt to evaluate the teaching of spelling in terms of the ability of the pupils to spell was essentially impossible and based on a profound misconception of the function of education.

By 1912, all that had changed, Ayres observed, noting the attitude of a recent convention:

Last week, in the city of St. Louis, that same association of school superintendents, again assembled in convention, devoted forty-eight addresses and discussions to tests and measurements of educational efficiency. The basal proposition underlying this entire mass of discussion was that the effectiveness of the school, the methods, and the teachers must be measured in terms of the results secured.

In *Education and the Cult of Efficiency* (1962), Raymond Callahan of Washington University charges Ayres with being one of the foremost efficiency experts, obsessed with efficiency. In these passages, however, Ayres appears only to champion the hope, so common at the time, that science, applied to the affairs of mankind, could render a better society. Elsewhere, six years later, he repeats his concern with science as it pertains to education:

> The scientific method is at base analytic scrutiny, exact measurement, careful recording, and judgment on the basis of observed fact. Science in education is not a body of information, but a method, and its object is to find out and to learn how. Courses of study are being adapted to the needs of children; teaching effort and supervisory control are becoming more efficient. The center of interest in education has become the child, rather than the teacher, and efforts to improve the quality of instruction begin by finding out what the children can do, rather than by discussing the methods by which the teacher proceeds. (*NSSE 17th Yearbook*, p. 14)

Later on, Ayres writes that while testing has become accepted in America, "the methods of [educational measurement] of today are still crude and imperfect must be admitted by even the most enthusiastic supporters of the movement. They deal most effectively with only the simple mechanical skills, and even here they are still far from perfect." Ayres seems confident that if perfection is not attained in the future, the situation will still certainly be much improved.

The basis for looking at education in terms of outcomes might be said to have started in 1892 with the Committee of Ten. At one point in its report, the Committee posits an implicit notion that the results of education can be measured:

> If twice as much time is given in a school to Latin as is given to mathematics, the attainments of the pupils in Latin ought to be twice as great as they are in mathematics. Again, if in a secondary school Latin is steadily pursued for four years with four or five hours a week devoted to it, that subject will be worth more to the pupil than the sum of a half dozen other subjects, each of which has one sixth of the time allotted to Latin. (quoted in Raubinger et al., 1969, p. 62)

Another committee, formed in 1895 to study college entrance requirements, went even further in asserting equivalence among equally studied subjects. In an 1896 *School Review* article, the committee's chair, A.F. Nightingale, superintendent of schools in Chicago, noted an earlier article by a certain Professor Tarr: "Professor Tarr in the *Educational Review* for June, writes: 'The theory of the college course is an admission that Physics or Chemistry or Geology as college studies are equal in rank to the study of Greek, or German, or Calculus." Tarr claimed this was not true in high school because science was so poorly taught. Nightingale objected: "The theory of the high school course is that these sciences are equal in work with German and Greek and Solid Geometry" (Nightingale, 1896, p. 421).

The statement from the Committee of Ten reflects the dominant "faculty psychology" of the day. Nightingale's statement also reflects this, along with the then-recent recognition of the empirical sciences, which had previously been considered inferior subjects of study. In either case, it was a short distance from this subject-oriented approach to the Carnegie Unit that appeared in 1909. By laying out a time-based outcome, the Carnegie Unit permitted a certain standardization of both high school courses and college entrance requirements. The College Entrance Examination Board (CEEB) adopted the Carnegie Unit the year it was first promulgated. Colleges and high schools rapidly followed suit. In 1905, Andrew Carnegie had given the Carnegie Foundation for the Advancement of Teaching $10 million to use as pensions for retiring college professors. At the time, neither high school nor college had a fixed definition. The foundation defined both, then declared that the colleges had to meet the foundation's definition in order to receive any funds. The colleges, in turn, put pressure on the secondary schools.

The Carnegie Foundation defined a high school as a four-year preparatory institution not connected with a college. It proposed that 14 Carnegie Units constitute a minimal high school course of study. It reasoned that the better high schools offered a four-year program of 16 units. Allowing for review and other possible encroachments on time, a 14-unit requirement seemed "fair." To call itself a college, an institution had to have at least six professors devoting full time to the work of the college, had to have a four-year course in liberal arts and sciences, and had to require for admission no less than what the foundation specified as a minimal high school preparation: four years and 14 units (Tompkins and Gaumnitz, 1954).

Although the Carnegie Unit drew some criticism from the beginning, objections grew after 1940. In that year, at least one book on high school administration complained that the Carnegie Unit impeded innovative curriculum efforts "to effect a satisfactory and desirable integration of experiences, which often calls for disruption of conventional subject matter boundaries."

By 1954, Department of Health, Education, and Welfare researchers Ellsworth Tompkins and Walter Gaumnitz had assembled a list of problems that various commentators had found in the Carnegie Unit:

1. It lends prestige to those subjects acceptable to college in terms of entrance Units, and discriminates against other subjects excellent in their own right but as yet unacceptable for Unit measure.
2. It considers of equal magnitude all subjects for which classes meet an equal number of minutes per semester....Five periods of English is equal to five periods of mathematics, etc.
3. It tends to make inflexible the daily and weekly time schedules of the school, for the Carnegie Unit nourishes the idea that a class should meet one period a day five times a week.
4. It restricts the development of a more functional curriculum based upon students' abilities, interests, and life needs, because it has been difficult for the high school to obtain units of credit acceptable to the colleges in certain more functional subjects.
5. It measures quantitatively experiences in different subjects and in different schools and counts them as similar in outcome.
6. It ranks pupils in graduating class despite the fact that few of them ever have exactly the same program of studies and despite the fact that seldom are all the years in school counted in the ranking of the pupil.
7. It measures a high school education (and diploma) in terms of time served and credits earned by the pupil. (Tompkins and Gaumnitz, 1954)

In short, said Tompkins and Gaumnitz, "the trouble with the Carnegie Unit, therefore, is that it interferes with good education."

They held out hope for change but indicated that "the development of satisfactory tests and suitable norms to indicate pupil progress toward major educational objectives is by no means easy, and it cannot be assumed that such tests are likely to be accepted by parents, pupils, and community without questions, even when their development is farther along than now."

Except for problem number four, which appears to reflect the Prosserian notion of life-adjustment education discussed in Chapter One, all of the listed problems were there from the beginning, though they were not all seen. The nation's zeitgeist was one into which the Carnegie Unit slipped smoothly, seeming to provide a "scientific" unit of analysis. The unit brought a nice apparent uniformity to school outcomes and was administratively easy to use and manipulate. It was, in a word, efficient.

"Cleanliness is next to godliness," is an old American aphorism. As we have seen, during the 1920s and 1930s, efficiency attained such a status as well. Writing in the 1930s, sociologist Robert Lynd observed that

> The 1920s were years of educational "efficiency" in American public education and of yardstick making by which to measure this efficiency, and Middletown was rendered especially conscious of these tendencies by its pride in the rapidly growing State Teachers College in its midst. Education was becoming "scientific" with a vengeance; "measurement" was in the saddle in all departments, from teaching to administration; and administration ceased to be the business of veteran teachers and became a series of specialties, its offices increasingly filled by specially trained persons....
>
> Middletown's school system, in step with those of other cities, has been becoming thoroughly "modernized" and "efficient" in its administrative techniques—to the dismay of some of the city's able teachers as they have watched the administrative horse gallop off with the educational cart. Some teachers regarded it as characteristic of the trend toward administrative dominance that in one recent year eight administrators and no teachers had their expenses paid to the National Education Association convention. (Lynd, 1937, pp. 205–206)

Raymond Callahan has referred to this trend as "An American Tragedy." He documents how a rising tide of criticism of the schools caused school superintendents to turn to ways of appeasing the critics. Most of the "outcomes" that they turned to measure with their new scientific apparati, though, concerned money. No one seems to have reported test scores. Middletown, in spite of pride in its new institution of higher education, kept no records of what proportion of each graduating class attended that college or other colleges and universities. It generated charts and bulletins such as "How Much Do Our Schools Cost the Taxpayer?" Lynd's skepticism about what was going on can be seen in his use of quotation marks.

Despite claims to the contrary over the years, in the present and, no doubt, into the future, America has never supported its public schools well and has always looked for signs that the money it does put forward is well-spent. Skepticism was rife about such expenditures at the turn of the century, when the selectivity of secondary education collided with the egalitarian impulse.

The spirit of criticism was captured in a series of articles in the *Ladies Home Journal* during the summer of 1912. It did not help that the most scathing of these was written by a former teacher, Ella Frances Lynch, whose broadside was quoted in Chapter Three.

To deal with this type of criticism—or to forestall it—administrators adopted scientific management as promulgated by Frederick Taylor and the army of efficiency experts that soon followed him. The spirit of these actions was captured in a speech by Frank Spaulding, a superintendent who had prospered in Newton, Massachusetts, known at the time as a devourer of superintendents. Said Spaulding:

> As we recall the familiar stock examples of scientific management that came to us from the material industries—such as the making of pig iron, the laying of bricks, and the cutting of metals—as we recall the multitude of stop watch observations and experiments, the innumerable, accurate measurements and comparisons of processes and results, out of which after many years these examples have grown, we may be pardoned if we felt a momentary doubt of the applicability to the educational industry of any management worthy to be characterized as scientific. (1913)

Spaulding conceded that "the ultimate and real products of a school system—those products that are registered in the minds and hearts of the children that go out from the schools—are immeasurable, and hence incomparable." Nor did he know of a single measure of the efficiency of a school, but there were some that could be made of "products or results." Among these he listed the following:

I refer to such results as the percentage of children of each year of age in the school district that the school enrolls; the average number of days attendance secured annually from each child; the average length of time required for each child to do a given definite unit of work; the percentage of children of each age who are allowed to complete their schools, with the average educational equipment of each; the percentage of children who are inspired to continue their education in higher school; and the quality of the education that the school affords.

Spaulding admitted that quality was difficult to measure, but he did try, although it is not completely clear how. He may have used grades and something he referred to as "points passed or earned" to declare that school number 9 in Newton was superior to school number 11 by 17 percent. What did his measures accomplish? They allowed him to look at the "conditions and means, the expenditures of time, effort, and money, in the several schools that yield such varying results, to the end that every school may adopt those plans that are proving most effective." For instance, school number 9 enrolled only 126 students, while school number 11 enrolled 817. Spaulding's calculations then revealed that school number 9 had a per-pupil cost of $131 per year, whereas school number 11 spent $431 on each child each year. Clearly, school number 9 was doing something right.

Spaulding also asked, "Which is more valuable, a course in Latin or a course in machine shop?" He thought academic discussion of the topic was futile, the answer unresolvable. But one could evaluate the two in terms of money. Spaulding then took the further step of equating educational value with dollar value, using something he called a "pupil-recitation" (modern readers should think "cost" each time they see the word "value"):

5.9 pupil-recitations in Greek are of the same value as 23.8 pupil-recitations in French; that 12 pupil-recitations in science are equivalent in value to 19.2 pupil-recitations in English; and that it takes 41.7 pupil-recitations in vocal music to equal the value of 13.9 pupil-recitations in art...

...thus confronted, do we feel like denying the equivalency of these values—we cannot deny our responsibility for fixing them as they are? This is a wholesome feeling, if it leads to a wiser assignment of values in future. Greater wisdom in these assignments will come, not by reference to any supposedly fixed and inherent values in these subjects themselves, but from a study of local conditions and needs. I know nothing about the absolute value of a recitation in Greek as compared with a recitation in French or in English. I am convinced, however, by the very concrete and quite local considerations, that when the obligations of the present year expire, we shall purchase no more Greek instruction at the rate of 5.9 pupil-recitations for a dollar. The price must go down, or we shall invest in something else.

Looking at his costs over time, Spaulding determined that increases in the number of recitations per instructor and increases in the number of pupils per recitation class operated against higher costs, while increases in teacher salaries and the number of recitations per week per pupil operated to drive costs up. The implications were obvious: increase the number of classes per teacher and the number of students per class. Cut teachers' salaries and the number of recitations given.

Finally, Spaulding concluded that it was silly to hire a business manager to oversee the expenditures of a district and a superintendent to take care of education issues. "They are inseparable; the frequent, I may say the prevalent, effort to distinguish the problems of the school into financial or business on the one hand, and educational on the other, results in two groups of problems barren of significance."

Spaulding may have been the quintessential superintendent of the new type. He was scarcely alone. In 1914, Horace Brittain noted the following:

> Recently there has been a tendency to increase the salaries of school superintendents and supervisors in large cities, and considerable competition has arisen between cities to secure the services of men and women who have distinguished themselves for efficient administration. Recently a large western city sent out a committee to investigate personally the records of prominent superintendents. As a result a man was chosen who had distinguished himself most along the line of efficiency engineering and unit cost accounting in education. As time goes on, such incidents will become frequent and a distinct profession of educational engineers—if such a word may be used for non-physical construction—will emerge. (Brittain, 1919, p. 14)

About the same time, Franklin Bobbitt, a professor at New York University, urged the same approach for principals to use with teachers. Bobbitt found that some classes of eighth-grade students did addition "at the rate of thirty-five combinations per minute" while others managed 105 combinations per minute. Such findings could be used to establish standards in schools to improve their efficiency. Educators, claimed Bobbitt,

> had come to see that it is possible to set up definite standards for the various educational products. The ability to add at a speed of 65 combinations per minute, with an accuracy of 94 percent is as definite a specification as can be set up for any aspect of the work of the steel plant. (Bobbitt, 1912, p. 7)

Bobbitt claimed that most teachers could not tell him how many combinations students could do in a minute; nor did the principals know. Bobbitt described scales not unlike a standardized test that could be used for the purpose. These scales would greatly benefit teachers: "Having these definite tasks laid upon her, she can know at all times whether she is accomplishing the things expected of her or not. She can herself know whether she is a good teacher, a medium teacher, or a poor teacher." Of course, principals could tell who the efficient and inefficient teachers were, and such scales would provide "incontestable evidence of inefficiency" that would make it easier to get rid of inefficient teachers.

At times, the talk among educators had a distinctly contemporary ring. Consider this from Stanford's Elwood Cubberley:

> Our schools are, in a sense, factories in which the raw products (children) are to be shaped and fashioned into products to meet the various demands of life. The specifications for manufacturing come from the demands of the twentieth century civilization, and it is the business of schools to build its pupils to the specifications laid down. This demands good tools, specialized machinery, continuous measurement of production to see if it is according to specifications, the elimination of waste in manufacture, and a large variety in the output.

The "continuous measurement of production to see if it is according to specifications," though, was nothing like the kinds of performance outcomes being suggested today. Usually, the obsession with counting things, with efficiency, and with emulating industry extended to the use of the school "plant." Spaulding was principally concerned with cost accounting, Bobbitt with simple mechanical problems. Bobbitt claimed that once the simple countings had been achieved there would be "time enough" to develop ways to measure the more difficult, intangible outcomes of education. He never attempted such measurement himself.

Callahan refers to the results of Bobbitt-like countings as "The Descent into Trivia" (p. 241) and cites no less a person than the U.S. Commissioner of Education, William J. Cooper, as leading the way down. In his 1933 book, *Economy in Education*, Cooper stated that

> one superintendent in Kansas had reported that through co-operative buying, "he was able to save over 40 [percent] on paper fasteners, 25 [percent] on thumbtacks, 20 [percent] on theme paper, 30 [percent] on colored pencils, and 50 [percent] on hectograph paper." In another instance one school board had discovered that "it paid 50 cents a ton more for coal" than some other boards. He then gave a series of suggestions for economizing. "Frequently schools purchase ink by the quart, paying a good price for it and still more for its transportation. If one makes ink from ink powder he will usually have an article which is good enough for school work." Money could also be saved on lumber for manual training classes by purchasing "odd lengths and ungraded lumber" which could be bought for "[one third] the price of first-class material." On the matter of school paper he noted "there is always some waste. A sheet may be larger than needed. The best remedy for this is to supply two sizes, one the regular $8^{1}/_{2}$ by 11", the other $8^{1}/_{2}$ by $5^{1}/_{2}$. If the superintendent will study his paper and its uses he will be able to eliminate odd sizes and buy more standard sizes. Toilet paper is frequently a source of waste. I have seen school toilets in which the ceiling and walls were literally coated with paper which had been dipped in water and thrown." As for paper towels, "considerable saving can generally be made both in the amount paid for them and in the number used. Payne, after a rather carefully controlled experiment, reports that a roll of towelling saved 38 [percent] over individually folded towels."

Apparently nothing was too small to measure and save

money on the cost. As noted earlier, Callahan's hypothesis that the "carefully controlled experiments" on such things as the cost of paper towels was the result of superintendents' accepting the verdicts of Taylorized scientific management. The outcome was that a profession that should have been at the forefront of determining the aims of education became instead mere managers, attending to administrative trivia, or as a slang term put it some years ago, administrivia.

The other "outcome" of education was not so readily countable: the disciplined mind. As noted in Chapter One, at the time of the development of the Carnegie Unit, and for another 30-odd years educational practice was based on a psychology of faculties. These faculties, virtually analogous to physical faculties, could be developed and strengthened through practice. Latin, Greek, and mathematics were held to be the best exercises to develop the mental faculties. Although one might impress an audience by speaking Latin (and apparently many speakers did), the study of Latin was largely a means, not an end. The natural sciences had to labor long and hard themselves to attain such stature.

The goal of developing a disciplined mind was therefore predicated on what psychologists now call generalizability or transfer of training. Education, especially secondary education, was thus thrown into quite a state when experiments by Thorndike and others appeared to refute the notion of transfer. If Latin doesn't assist in other areas, why expend four years of effort on it in school? In any case, the decline of faculty psychology caused educators and psychologists to explore new areas of outcomes for education.

Two other trends of the time helped give impetus to the search for educational outcomes other than the disciplined mind. One was simply the democratization of the secondary school. It might be said that until well into the twentieth century, educators practiced a form of ability grouping. Most people were in the "not-in-school" group. This allowed secondary schools to concentrate on the collegiate curriculum, even though not many of the already highly selected graduates went to college. As secondary education became more universal, many educators conceded that not all children would be able to learn as well as the select few that had earlier attended. Lewis Terman, developer of the Stanford-Binet IQ test, opined that it took an IQ of 110 to handle the traditional high school curriculum. Apparently Prosser used Terman's estimate in 1945 when he proposed life-adjustment education for the 60 percent of those who would not go to college or prosper in vocational programs.

The second trend that diverted the search for outcomes away from faculties was the rise of behaviorist psychology as the dominant brand of psychological theorizing. Both the atheoretical behaviorism of those such as B.F. Skinner at Harvard and the grandiose theoretical behaviorism of those such as Clark Hull at Yale reigned so sovereign that for a time they forced those who would refer to an interior mental state with the word "cognitive" to do so out of public view.

Earlier we saw that assessment became profoundly affected by the rise of behaviorism through the concern with "behavioral objectives." If, as the behaviorists asserted, we can directly observe only behavior, and if that behavior alone is sufficient to the domain of the psychologist, then the "disciplined mind" is a will-o'-the-wisp that should not contend for our attention. (We should also recall that not only had faculty psychology apparently been discredited but also educational research and theory were heavily influenced by developments in psychology rather than in sociology or anthropology; the history of educational research would likely be far different had either of these latter two disciplines formed its basis.)

Within this behavioral tradition arose an interest in defining the objectives of education in behavioral terms. During the 1948 convention of the American Psychological Association, an informal meeting of testing professionals decided that it would be useful to have a "theoretical framework" that would facilitate communication between assessment specialists and also "stimulate research on the relations between examining and education." A somewhat large and informal committee headed by Benjamin Bloom of the University of Chicago set about to construct just such a framework. The committee soon decided that three such frameworks were required: cognitive, affective, and psychomotor. The group decided that each of these frameworks should be constructed so as to reveal the natural relationships among the educational goals to be described. That is, each framework should be a taxonomy.

The taxonomies were conceived as neutral descriptions in the same way that the Dewey decimal system classifies all books without conveying any differential values for any of them. The committees also deliberately assumed that the structure of schools would remain in its then-current form. The hope of the taxonomers was that the descriptions would "facilitate the exchange of information about curricular developments and evaluation devices. Such interchanges are frequently disappointing now because all too frequently what appears to be common ground between schools disappears on closer examination of the descriptive terms being used" (Bloom et al., 1956).

Bloom chaired the subcommittee on the cognitive domain, while David Krathwohl of Syracuse University headed up the group working in the affective area. These two taxonomies, especially the cognitive, have had enormous currency, although they have often been misinterpreted. Two versions of the psychomotor domain were published but largely ignored. The presence of the taxonomies, though, and the popularity of the cognitive framework helped orient educators more toward looking at outcomes of education in terms of well-defined behaviors.

Also out of the behaviorist tradition came the events described in Chapter Two as the minimum competency testing movement. The first instance of such a test to be so called occurred in Denver in 1958, a specific reaction to complaints of businessmen that students couldn't read basic material, couldn't make change, etc. However, the development in Denver remained limited to that venue until the early 1970s. In 1972, the Oregon Board of Education decreed that in addition to passing courses, students would have to demonstrate competency in certain areas, these areas being left mostly up to localities. Interest in minimum competency testing quickly spread to other states. By 1977, William Spady, then of the National Institute of Education, was able to refer to a new trend called Competency Based Education (CBE) as "a bandwagon in search of a definition." Commenting on the state of affairs in Oregon, Spady wrote:

> Underlying the Oregon action were two years of public hearings that explored the alleged inability of prevailing school curricula, practices, and standards to assure that youngsters completing twelve years of formal education could survive e*conomically and socially as independent young adults.* Implicit in the Oregon discussion was a challenge to the validity of using time and course credits as bases for certifying student accomplishment and the relevance of current curricula to the life-role demands youngsters would face after leaving school. Similar concerns have, of course, been voiced in most other states. (Spady, 1977, p. 9; italics added)

This is a radical departure from many other notions of the

goals of education. There is no mention of a disciplined mind. Indeed, there is no mention of mind. It is very much a life-adjustment approach to education, but whereas Prosser derived his pedagogy from the needs of students, Spady (and many others since) took his from the needs of society, the "life-role demands" that youngsters would face as they strove to "survive economically and socially as independent young adults." Instead of tailoring education to students' needs, students would be fitted to society's needs.

To be sure, not all educators saw this as a desirable focus for education. Some 50 years earlier, in *Democracy and Education*, Dewey had voiced a diametrically opposed view:

> In directing the activities of the young, society determines its own future in determining that of the young. Since the young at any given time will at some later date compose the society of that period, the latter's nature will largely turn upon the direction that children's activities were given at an earlier period. (Dewey, 1916, p. 41)

For Dewey, education *was* life, was an end in itself no matter how many instrumentalities it might also acquire. What students did in schools should take place under democratic processes, and the activities should be carried out for their intrinsic worth.

Later, about the same time that Spady was formulating his basic principles of competency based education, Henry Levin of Stanford University was reflecting a Dewey-like stance, calling competency based education a "social efficiency" view of the purposes of education. Levin cited an earlier piece by Harvard sociologist Alex Inekeles describing social efficiency as the view that

> In general, the objective of socialization is to produce competent people, as competence is defined in any given society. It aims to develop a person who can take care of himself, support others, conceive and raise children, hunt boar or grow vegetables, vote, fill out an application form, drive an auto…(Levin, 1978, p. 310)

This worried Levin.

> For if the social order for which we are preparing youth is intrinsically corrupt and undesirable, why should we prepare youth for that eventuality? Studies of the workplace, for example, have found that a large proportion

of jobs are boring, provide no intrinsic meaning, and are injurious to both the human body and spirit...should we judge schools on the basis of the ability of their students to tolerate boredom, accept intrinsically meaningless work tasks, and accede to a corporate order that relegates them to fragmented and repetitive work activities in behalf of social control and profitability? Certainly the logic of the social efficiency view does not question the legitimacy of the social order and its historical basis. (Levin, 1978, p. 311)

Dewey and Levin notwithstanding, the notion that educational outcomes should be defined in terms of competencies has proven a popular one. And just what *was* competency based education? According to Spady, it was as follows:

a data-based, adaptive, performance-oriented set of integrated processes that facilitate, measure, record and certify within the context of flexible time parameters the demonstration of known, explicitly stated, and agreed upon learning outcomes that reflect successful functioning in life roles.

That was a mouthful, as Spady recognized. Treating each segment of the definition in detail, he concluded that

the definition of a competency used here renders the concept of *life-roles* and their attendant activities as the prime movers in framing outcome goals, designing curricula, providing instruction, and measuring student performance. This approach, therefore, defines *competencies*, as indicators of successful performance in life-role activities (be they citizen, driver, family member, intimate friend, recreational participant, or life long learner).

Skills such as reading and computation and states such as high motivation are *enablers*. They are not outcomes. "Capacities" such as sensitivity, awareness, and the appreciation of beauty are *enrichers*, not outcomes.

The "flexible time parameters" put Spady squarely in the corner of those who, like Block and Bloom, had earlier developed and advocated the concept of mastery learning (ML). In traditional schools, time is held constant and learning varies. Under conditions of mastery learning, learning is held constant and time varies (in theory, anyway; the reality to date has proven rather more complicated). Spady writes:

> Essentially, both ML and CBE emphasize the primacy of the outcome goal as the fundamental concern of the educational enterprise and treat time and opportunity as elements that serve those goals. This means, of course, that CBE calls into question the traditional organization into semesters or quarters, into courses, and into a process that uses comparisons among students, rather than a standard, to assign grades. (Spady, 1977, p. 11)

Spady acknowledged that the technology of assessing life-role activities was only in its infancy and that systems concerned with the quality of data acceptable for determining competency "will have to pay a steep price in time and personnel resources required for the task." Spady omitted a steep price in money, as well. No one at the time could have guessed how steep the price would later be in political backlash.

To the extent that school systems used attendance or course completions or grades as criteria, they were not competency based. They were more certification-based, relying on seat-time to define the traditional Carnegie Units as outcomes.

In the years since CBE was first formulated, its nature has changed little, aside from the change in name to Outcomes Based Education (OBE) and a continuing elaboration of the basic ideas. Spady defines an outcome as

> learning results that we want students to demonstrate at the end of significant learning experiences. They are not values, beliefs, attitudes or psychological states of mind. Instead, outcomes are what learners can actually do with what they know and have learned—they are the tangible application of what has been learned. This means that outcomes are actions and performances that embody and reflect learner competence in using content, information, ideas, and tools successfully. Having learners do important things with what they know is a major step beyond knowing itself. (Spady, 1994, p. 2)

Spady sees four levels of outcomes. In increasing size and scope, they are those that are used for classroom reform, those used for program alignment, those used for external accountability, and those used for system transformation. This last is a "future focused, tightly grounded system around a comprehensive framework of key life dimensions." It focuses on meeting life challenges and generally requires long-lasting demonstrations with an emphasis on authentic learning. Transformational outcomes "encourage a total rethinking of appropriate instructional methods and useful learning and demonstration contexts for students. Passive listening and traditional seatwork give way to active and challenging environments" (Spady, 1994, p. 97).

A statement that calls for "total rethinking of instructional methods" will likely be looked at askance by a number of folk. It is certainly this kind of writing that has, in part, but only in part, gotten Spady in trouble with the Christian and the secular Right (a controversy discussed later in this chapter). Actually, much of Spady's writing in this vein sounds very much like some of the more enthusiastic Progressives cited in Chapter One, with behaviorism grafted on.

Outcomes Based Education, née Competency Based Education, did not, of course, spring full-blown from the head of Spady or anyone else. As noted, its progenitor was mastery learning, which influenced it a great deal. Mastery learning itself seems to find its ancestry in a 1963 article by Harvard University psychologist John B. Carroll. Carroll's "model" (it was not enough of a formalism to be called one) was encapsulated in a single verbal formula, verbal because proper means of quantification were not available at the time:

Degree of learning = f (time actually spent/time needed)

Reading aloud, we would say, "Degree of learning is a function of time actually spent divided by the time needed." Time needed, in turn, depended on aptitude for learning specific tasks and would vary within an individual from setting to setting, a conception not unlike that which infuses much "authentic assessment" today. Time needed was further influenced by the student's ability to understand instruction—something Carroll felt was independent of his construct of aptitude—and of quality of instruction. Carroll was at pains to point out that time spent could not be equated with elapsed time. It referred, rather, to the amount of time the student actually spent engaged in the learning task, and this, in turn, was influenced by the amount of time the student was willing to spend on the task, a willingness that Carroll termed "perseverance."

The denominator in the equation existed only because schools, for a variety of reasons, did not provide enough time for some students to achieve the learning task set for them and because students need widely different amounts of time to learn the same material.

As a model, Carroll's conception came to very little. Most educators and psychologists today would find it very naïve and simplistic. However, as a source of inspiration in a particular direction, it had enormous influence. It called attention to learning as a function of time in a way that other models previously had not. It is common today for school critics to say that traditional schools hold time constant and let achievement vary. What we should do, say the critics—and also proponents of OBE—is hold learning constant and let time vary. But when Carroll first presented this notion 30 years earlier, it was a radical departure.

In Carroll's conception, aptitude is conceived in terms of rate of learning. Children vary greatly in this rate, but all can learn to the same *level.* Some just need more time. This conception is strong in Spady's most recent book (1994) on OBE, and to me, too, it seems remarkably naïve. But that is getting ahead of the story.

Others who read Carroll's article found it intriguing, and a few, such as James H. Block and Benjamin Bloom at the University of Chicago, labored to elaborate it into a working system. Of Carroll's model, Bloom wrote that if students are normally distributed in terms of aptitude and if we give all of them the *same* instruction, then achievement will be highly correlated with aptitude, and the results of achievement will also be normally distributed. But if "the kinds and quality of instruction and learning time allowed are made appropriate to the characteristics and needs of *each* learner, the *majority* of students will achieve mastery. The correlation between aptitude and achievement should approach zero" (Bloom, 1971, p. 50).

Elsewhere in the same essay (p. 49), Bloom wrote "that 'individual differences' between learners exist is indisputable. What is disputable is that these variations play a role in student learning and must be reflected in our learning and achievement criteria. The fact that they do play a role in student learning and are reflected in the standards and criteria is due to our present policies and practices rather than to the necessities of the case."

Such a happy state of affairs as Bloom posited must have excited him and the others working in the field a great deal. First, mastery learning held the promise of breaking the strangle hold of the normal curve. This would be no mean accomplishment, and the possibility was something of an obsession with Bloom. Elsewhere he and colleagues later wrote:

There is nothing sacred about the normal curve. It is the distribution most appropriate to chance and random activity. Education is a purposeful activity, and we seek to have the students learn what we teach. If we are effective in our instruction, the distribution of achievement should be very different from the normal curve. In fact, we may even insist that our educational efforts have been *unsuccessful* to the extent that the distribution of achievement approximates the normal distribution.

Second, in addition to quashing the normal curve, mastery learning offered a rebuttal to James Coleman whose findings had emphasized the potency of family and community variables in achievement. Referencing Coleman and a half dozen other reports, Bloom allowed that

while this potential [of schools] may be very great, it is clear that the reality of school effects has been far from this potential....What is maintained is that the schools are *potentially* able to make very great differences in the careers and lives of their students....Theoretically, almost all the students can learn to a relatively high level anything the schools have to teach. (Bloom, 1971, p. 48)

Since the mid 1960s, many educators had been striving to reduce the achievement gaps between whites and various ethnic groups, especially blacks, and Bloom's prospect offered a reason for optimism.

Actually, Coleman had said that schools made great differences. He *assumed* the existence of schools and then failed to find large differences *among* schools, not that schooling itself had no influence. The effect of school per se received a small empirical test when schools in Prince Edward County, Virginia, closed rather than submit to racial integration. Tests on students not attending schools showed them well below previous levels of achievement.

Six years later, Bloom remained fired with the prospects of mastery learning that he had seen in 1970. Now, however, he thought even more emphatically that mastery learning could be not only a way of realizing the potential impact of schools but also a means of reducing vastly, if not eliminating entirely, the learning gap between rich and poor, between whites and minorities:

One implication of the theory is that *equality of learn-*

ing outcomes can be a goal of education rather than *equality of opportunity.* Such a goal suggests that teachers must find ways of giving each child the help and encouragement he needs when he needs it rather than ensuring equality of treatment of all children. It means that the teachers and the instructional material and procedures should emphasize acceptable levels of learning for all children rather than be satisfied that each has been "treated" fairly and equally. (Bloom, 1976, p. 215)

Bloom became widely known for his assertion that 90 percent of all students could learn what the school asks of them. In his 1976 treatise, he asserted that perhaps 1 to 3 percent of students would learn much faster than the other students. For these, "no effort should be made to retard their drive and incentives to learning in order to keep them in step with other students." At the other end of the spectrum, another 1 to 3 percent would be much slower. But even they could make "effective learning progress" with enough time, attention, and resources. Bloom, not being a classroom teacher, did not realize that he was laying down a political minefield for teachers; nor did he recognize the size of the task he was setting for them.

Bloom's longstanding work in educational objectives and his interest in mastery learning dovetailed with another aspect of his research that came to be known as "the two sigma problem." Researchers conventionally use the lower case of the Greek letter sigma to designate the standard deviation of a distribution of numbers. Some of Bloom's students claimed that their studies of tutoring had found that one-on-one tutoring would elevate scores by two standard deviations, two sigmas. Such a gain has enormous practical implications. In a normal distribution of test scores, for instance, a shift of two sigmas could mean a shift from the 50th percentile to the 98th, or from the 16th percentile to the 84th. Of course, no system can afford one-on-one tutoring for many students; therefore, the search was on for instructional techniques that would approximate the effectiveness of tutoring.

In a 1984 article, Bloom claimed that mastery learning by itself could produce one-sigma effects. If this were true, it alone would be the equivalent of moving students from the 50th percentile to the 84th, a consequence of some consequence. Blacks and whites differ on many tests by about one sigma. A technique that could wipe out that differential would be of considerable import indeed. Overall, a one-sigma increase in school outcomes would mean an enormous gain in school learning for everyone.

Claims such as this led Johns Hopkins University educational researcher Robert Slavin to conduct a "Best Evidence Synthesis" (BES) of the research on mastery learning. A BES is similar to a meta-analysis, a technique for combining many different studies into a single metric. In most meta-analyses, investigators simply throw all available studies into the hopper, producing for each one something called an "effect size," an indication of how potent a particular educational innovation or treatment has been (or has not been). Effect sizes for individual studies can be combined and averaged, just as different lengths can be. The average effect size allows some determination about the practical impact of an innovation in a way that the traditional statistical tests of significance do not.

As noted, a BES is similar to meta-analysis, but in a BES, the investigator establishes criteria for admitting studies into the analysis, while most meta-analyses simply sift the literature and take all studies found. One of Slavin's criteria for including studies of mastery learning was that the studies had to last at least four weeks. Slavin felt this was necessary to eliminate studies producing only ephemeral effects. This criterion excluded a large number of studies.

Overall, Slavin found that

> the '2-sigma' challenge proposed by Bloom is probably unrealistic, certainly within the context of group-based mastery learning. Bloom's claim that mastery learning can improve achievement by more than 1 sigma is based on brief, small, artificial studies that provided additional instructional time to the experimental classes. In longer term and larger studies with experimenter-made measures, effects of group-based mastery learning are much closer to $1/4$ sigma, and in studies with standardized measures there is no indication of any positive effect at all.

The distinction between experimenter-made and standardized measures is problematical. Slavin feels that the experimenter-built tests might be "biased" in favor of the treatment. To this author, though, it only makes sense to measure the outcomes with instruments built around the instruction. Standardized tests may well be instruments that are too blunt and insensitive to detect changes. In any case, however, the results are nowhere near as large as claimed or hoped for.

Slavin does not dismiss mastery learning as a failure. Its theoretical underpinnings are too potent for that:

> The disappointing findings of the studies discussed in this review counsel not a retreat from this area of research but rather a redoubling and redirection of efforts to understand how the compelling theories underlying mastery learning can achieve their potential in practical application.

Slavin also raised the issue of whether mastery learning was a "Robin Hood" approach to instruction. One of his findings was that mastery learning studies seemed to produce changes in low-achieving groups but not in high-achieving groups. Did the high achievers have to stop learning while the low achievers caught up? This issue has been raised repeatedly in connection with mastery learning.

Bloom, for his part, rejected the notion of fast and slow learners. At one point, Bloom said that when he first entered the field of educational research, "the prevailing construct was *there are good learners and there are poor learners.* Later this was amended to *there are faster learners and there are slower learners.* By the end of the 1970s, though, Bloom had concluded that "*most students become very similar with regard to learning ability, rate of learning, and motivation for further learning—when provided with favorable learning conditions*" (emphases in the original). Suffice it to say that the provision of such "favorable learning conditions" has not occurred on any scale. In reality, the situation vis-à-vis Robin Hood effects is complex (Bloom, 1976, Introduction).

In some compensatory programs, such as Reading Recovery and Success for All, the answer seems to be no, there is no need for those already learning to wait for the slow learners to play catch-up. In these programs, children having difficulty learning to read are given, among other things, one-to-one tutoring sessions outside of the regular classroom. Both programs have been adjudged successes by most observers, but we should note that the tutoring of nonreaders has not produced anything like the two-sigma gains claimed by Bloom for tutoring, or even the one-sigma gains for mastery learning. In Reading Recovery, for instance, the goal of the program is to have the slow readers reading up to the level of the average child in the classroom. In many urban settings, this is still well below "grade level" and in any case is not reached for all children. In theory, the federal

Chapter I programs for disadvantaged students should have out-comes similar to those of Reading Recovery and Success for All.

It is clear, however, that mastery learning fully implemented and OBE à la Spady will not result in all children's learning to the same levels. If anything, these two processes will *increase* the differentials between fast and slow learners. Consider this passage from Spady:

> Even in fairly traditional versions of Mastery Learning model, teachers are encouraged to avoid this potential "waiting" [catch-up] problem by having faster learners engage in challenging extension and enrichment activi-ties once they have accomplished their basic work. Stu-dents pursue related content and concepts in-depth through stimulating projects and exercises while their classmates spend time mastering the initial material. This strategy gives focused attention to faster learners and continually provides them with opportunities to extend their learning without having to "wait" for slower learn-ers to catch up. It is not, however, the same as employ-ing an authentic continuous progress model that would allow them to move forward in the curriculum at their own pace whenever ready. (Spady, 1994, p. 167)

Although one might wonder if this is a realistic description of learning in the classroom, it is not too much of a stretch to see in this paragraph that the faster learners are being given "in-depth," "stimulating" material that will increase their advantage over the slower learners. The underlying assumption is that the "basic" material with which the slow learners are struggling is more important than the "extensions" provided to the fast learn-ers, but in reality it is likely the reverse.

We should also consider the possibility that "providing extra time" for slow learners does them no favor. The notion that additional time does provide an advantage reflects an all-too-common "adulto-centric" point of view. We adults will "give" the child extra time. But if a child is having difficulty with a topic, he might well perceive himself trapped in an unpleasant situation. The last thing he might want is the "gift" of additional time. The child might well wish to leave the scene. Requiring a child to spend additional time on material with which he is having trouble may be boring and painful to the child and cruel on the part of educators. This is a prospect that, apparently, no one has been willing to consider as yet. In addition, no research has shown that it is better to master fewer objectives well than to acquire some knowledge of more objectives (although in many settings it is clear that teachers, following the tyranny of scope-and-sequence, are trying to cover too much material, and that the resulting shallow knowledge probably works to the detriment of understanding).

If these kinds of differentials appear in traditional mastery classes, what would happen if we did implement a true "continuous progress model" where instruction is optimized for all students and all "move forward at their own pace whenever ready?" Clearly, such a program would greatly magnify the differences between fast and slow learners. One can *imagine* a program tailored to each child's "learning style," if learning styles exist, and to each child's stronger intelligences (using a multiple intelligence approach such as that of Harvard's Howard Gardner) as a means of reducing these differentials, but one can certainly do little more than imagine it. It seems wholly unrealistic for an actual school setting.

THE BACKLASH COMETH

In their book *Research on Educational Innovations* (1993), Arthur Ellis and Jeffrey Fouts of Seattle Pacific University take one chapter to examine the evidence for the efficacy of OBE. They find the approach reasonable in the extreme. "After all," they say, "who could find fault with an attempt to clarify the outcomes we seek?" As they used to say about monumental mistakes in *Mad* magazine, "Hoo boy!" Critiques started modestly, but the smoldering indictments erupted rapidly into a firestorm of criticism. The November 1993 issue of *Citizen*, the newsletter of the conservative Christian group, Focus on the Family, put William Spady on its cover with the question, "Can You Trust Him With Your Schools?" To *Citizen*, the answer was clearly, emphatically no. The headline for the March 1994 editorial in *Educational Leadership*, published by the Association for Supervision and Curriculum Development, asked, "Is Outcome-Based Education Dead?" The September 1994 *School Administrator*, a publication of the American Association of School Administrators, carried the word "outcomes" scrawled graffiti-like across the cover and below it the phrase "*The Dirtiest Word in School Reform.*" What happened?

This soon after the events, it is hard to see through the smoke of battle and how it all got started, but the first salvos appear to have been fired as objections to some outcomes prepared for the state program in Pennsylvania. It is not hard to see why objections occurred. The "outcomes" in Pennsylvania and elsewhere strayed far from the definition provided by Spady and other behaviorally oriented researchers (although Spady, along with Bloom, were allocated most of the blame by the objectors). Some outcomes entered the affective realm; some gave the impression that students would learn "state sanctioned attitudes." Such statements clanged loudly against some people's religious beliefs, world views, suspicions, and even paranoia.

In Pennsylvania, for instance, "outcomes" included such statements as "All students make sound environmental decisions in their personal and civic lives" and "All students understand and appreciate their worth as unique and capable individuals and exhibit self-esteem." These are hardly what Spady had in mind as "outcomes" or what Bloom or David Krathwohl considered as parts of the cognitive or affective domains. Recall that for Spady, outcomes must be stated in demonstrable terms, must be something that can be seen. The taxonomers were more liberal in their definitions, but they, too, tried to restrict themselves to observables.

Ironically, Spady's defense of his program in terms of specified behaviors itself backfired and opened up another line of attack. An unsigned article in the August 23, 1993, *New American* carried the headline "Outcome-Based Education: Skinnerian Conditioning in the Classroom." At one point, the article cites Spady's definition of an outcome then adds the following, which captures well the tone, mood, and strategy of many critics of OBE:

> Certainly nothing very sinister sounding there [in the definition of OBE], right? In fact, it sounds commonsensical, even ordinary. After all, isn't that basically what we shoot for in the traditional educational setting? We set our goals (or "outcomes") and then direct our curriculum to achieving those goals.
>
> Unfortunately, like everything else associated with OBE, Spady's definition is intentionally deceptive.
>
> In fact, the first thing one learns when getting acquainted with OBE is that everything about it is deceitful and deceptive. Words take on meanings entirely divorced from those traditionally associated with them. Orwell's "Newspeak" is alive and flourishing in OBE programs....

According to Ann Herzer, "Outcome-Based Education is essentially a more advanced version of Professor Benjamin Bloom's Mastery Learning, which is pure Skinnerian, behaviorist, stimulus-response conditioning and indoctrination."

Herzer is identified in the article only as a teacher trained in mastery learning.

Then, as final proof of OBE's odiousness, the article quotes Spady acknowledging OBE's ancestry through the just discredited mastery learning. As a matter of fact, mastery learning and OBE are quite distinct. Bloom, after he had laid out the goals of mastery learning, concentrated on the kind of activities that might lead to mastery. He was quite neutral with regard to *what* was being mastered. For OBE, on the other hand, the "what" is the primary focus.

Elsewhere, the article quotes Bloom as saying that "the purpose of education and schools is to change the thoughts, feelings, and actions of students." Bloom did say this. Out of context, this *might* have some diabolical tinge to it in the minds of some people, but it occurs in *All Our Children Learning*, in a passage where Bloom is talking about education as growth—"growth," which implies the kinds of changes noted. Most of the book is another optimistic but, for most people, mundane explication of how mastery learning can solve some of the social and educational problems outlined earlier in this chapter.

Several other quotes in the attacking article indicate the emphasis that OBE advocates put on change, including a quote from Carl Rogers, characterized as "another demigod in the pantheon of psychology," stating that "the goal of education must be to develop individuals who are open to change." As a clinician, Rogers would have encountered mostly people whose psychological difficulties stemmed, at least in part, from rigidity, from an inability to change their neurotic behavior. For him, cure required change. To those opposing OBE, change looks sinister. According to the article, the OBE promulgators, it seems:

have an incredible fixation with "change" and it is quite clear from their writings that the change they have in mind is not the change desired by the American public. All surveys show the overwhelming majority of Americans calling for a return to "basics," in education: the three R's plus traditional values and discipline. The educationist elite, however, will have none of that.

In fact, it probably wouldn't hurt for the champions of OBE and other novel programs to go back and reread Eric Hoffer's *The Ordeal of Change*.

The article then raises such typical targets of the Right as the federal government in general and the U.S. Department of Education in particular, and the Carnegie Foundation for the Advancement of Teaching. The article looks askance at former President George Bush, the 1989 Education Summit between Bush and the governors, the New American Schools Development Corporation (NASDC), and two of NASDC's funded development programs, the Modern Red School House and Roots and Wings.

"But it does not stop there," says the article. "After all, we are now a 'global community,' and if centralizing educational control at the national level is a good thing, then a world OBE plan must be even better. And, yes, it is well under way." Among the conspirators are UNESCO, UNICEF, the United Nations Development Program, the World Bank, and other UN "globocrats."

"The totalitarian implications of this system should be obvious and should be cause for public outrage and a massive public outcry that will shake from office the political powers responsible for this abominable plan." Recalling a 1938 essay that accused Franklin Roosevelt's New Deal of being "the American people's first experience with the dialectic according to Marx and Lenin," the article concludes that "OBE is one of the latest American experiences with the Marxian dialectic." It closes with a chilling quote from George Orwell's *Nineteen Eighty-Four* depicting the kind of totalitarian world that will develop if children are educated under the precepts of OBE.

Readers who think this article is unrepresentative of OBE criticisms should disabuse themselves of that notion. This is a typical piece save for the fact that, as an essay, it coheres better than most. The thinking is quite similar to that in articles written about the various "patriotic" militias after the federal building in Oklahoma City was bombed in April 1995. Indeed, one article about a Michigan militia credited its origins to the fight against OBE.

The attack on the Modern Red School House, one of 11 projects funded by NASDC, carries no small amount of irony, as that developmental effort is spearheaded by the likes of former Secretary of Education William Bennett and conservative school critic, Denis Doyle of the Hudson Institute. To see the religious Right skewering the secular Right is something of a novelty.

Bennett and his chief lieutenant in the Department of Education, Chester E. Finn, Jr., were, in fact, among the most vocal people chastising educators for concentrating on inputs and processes rather than outcomes.

Bennett now claims that the proponents of OBE have taken the term but changed its meaning. He still defends OBE when it is represented by cognitive outcomes such as those measured by Advanced Placement (AP) examinations:

> The real concern is when those in the education establishment use OBE to (1) do away with objective measurable criteria (like standardized tests); (2) do away with the traditional subject-based curriculum in favor of an emphasis on things like general skills, attitudes, and behaviors; and (3) advance their own radical social agenda. Increasingly OBE is applied to the realm of behavior and social attitudes—becoming, in effect, a Trojan Horse for social engineering, an elementary and secondary school version of the kinds of "politically correct" thinking that has infected our colleges and universities. (Bennett, 1994 pp. 1–2)

As if *all* education and schooling were not "social engineering."

Bennett's remarks appear as one of nine articles on OBE and mastery learning in the February 1994 issue of *Educational Excellence Network News and Views*, a monthly compilation of articles and op-ed pieces. The network was cofounded by former Assistant Secretaries of Education Chester Finn and Diane Ravitch, and it serves the conservative community through publication and distribution by the Hudson Institute. The nine articles do include a straightforward primer on OBE from the Education Commission of the States, but the rest are negative and indicate how hard the political Right has tried to distance itself from OBE. The nine pieces also include a reprint of Slavin's Best Evidence Synthesis of mastery learning research, followed by a disclaimer from Slavin stating, in part, that "use of my review as evidence against OBE is totally irresponsible and inappropriate."

It was not only OBE's invasion of private space and its totalitarian character that unleashed critics. Phyllis Schlafly, founder of the conservative Eagle Forum, argued that OBE converted the "three R's" to the "three D's: Deliberately Dumbed Down." If you establish an outcome that every child will slam-dunk a basketball, clearly for many children the basket will have to be lowered.

Schlafly also scored what she interpreted (and misinterpreted) as OBE's "feel good" emphasis, its emphasis on attitudes, its anti-phonics commitment (!?), its lack of accountability, its unaccept-able ambiguity, its unproven merits, and its invasion of pupil privacy. Schlafly envisaged computer files that included attitudi-nal, behavioral, and medical data and that might well be avail-able to employers, something that would violate not only the Hatch Act but also most state privacy laws (Schlafly, 1994).

Perhaps the most visible critic of OBE to date has been Peg Luksik, a Pennsylvania homemaker and sometime gubernatorial candidate, whose videotape "Who Controls the Children?" force-fully presents the conspiracy interpretation of OBE. Luksik be-gins by discussing Pennsylvania's now-defunct Educational Quality Assessment (EQA). Part of EQA, which primarily tested traditional curriculum areas, did ask students about "locus of control." Locus-of-control questions determine whether people see themselves in control of their destiny or see destiny con-trolled by external events. Luksik claims that questions about locus of control were scored "right" and "wrong" and that the right answer in such questions was what she calls "go with the flow"—to impose no internal locus of control (self-control). If the "right" answer is not to be in control of yourself, that opens for Luksik the question given in the title of the tape. Who *does* control the children?

In the tape, she describes how she was told that different states had different goals, which they were free to develop. She claims, however, that as she went from state to state examining state goals for education, she found them all to be the same. Lurking behind this uniformity is the federal government con-trolling the purse strings and consciousness.

Although her immediate target was Pennsylvania's OBE pro-gram, OBE per se plays only a small role in the videotape. It is both the catalyst and signifier of something else, control. A larger role is ascribed to the computer and to the quest of both states and the federal government to wrest control of the children away from families. At one point, having spoken of how the EQA allowed control from the state down to the district level, she says that "with the computer, control goes down to the indi-vidual child. They *will* conform, or they will not move forward." Thus, while Thomas Jefferson saw education as a means of pro-tecting us from state control, Luksik and many OBE opponents view OBE as the *vehicle* of state control.

What the children must conform to, says Luksik, are the

state-established outcomes, which have more to do with attitudes and values than with basic skills. While state and federal governments clearly hunger for power, so does big business. At one point on the tape, she holds up the second SCANS report, *Learning a Living,* and notes ominously that this report originates not with the U.S. Secretary of Education (which would be bad enough), but with the U.S. Secretary of Labor: "It is being driven by big, big, big industries who need the proper workers of tomorrow." Luksik notes that the SCANS report never refers to children as children but always as "human resource material" and "human capital."[1]

Control is Luksik's obsession. She attacks values clarification not because it is inherently evil but because the person in charge of the process controls the "universe of choices." She presents as an instance of values clarification the classic lifeboat situation in which a student must choose whom to toss overboard. She then observes that "the children can't say no, can't develop a plan to save all the people in the boat. I [the state] control the universe of choices."

Holding up for view something called "The Bettendorf Survey," she implies that OBE will lead to such things as children's seeing this nation as having been stolen from Native Americans and to condoning homosexuality. One question on the survey apparently asks, "If you could eliminate an entire race, would you?" and "Which one?"

Luksik dismisses as ultimately a lie the contentions of the states and the federal government that the outcomes will be locally controlled. Luksik claims that OBE is enormously expensive (something Spady acknowledged when it was still called competency based education), hence districts cannot afford it. Given that districts cannot afford to construct OBE at the district level, Luksik maintains, the state will provide "technical assistance," as will the feds. She draws an analogy, telling the audience the states tell the localities they can use local decision making to reach the goals in any way they want. But given the need for federal and state "technical assistance," this is like her telling the audience they can build any plane they want, as long as they end up with a Cessna. Such analogies are not, in fact, far from comments made by Lauren Resnick of the New Standards Project that the Project will establish the standards and states can choose how they will meet them.

Even innovations that most educators would view as wonderful but improbable for a variety of reasons are presented as enhancing the state's control of students to the detriment of the family's. Luksik says, somewhat ominously, that the Pennsylvania plan calls for "an IEP for every child" (IEP stands for Individual Education Plan, something required for special education students currently). Educators would certainly champion this as the acme of individualized instruction, but they also see it as improbable in real school settings: teachers cannot tailor their instruction to this degree in a typical setting of 25 children per class. But if the goal of the program is state control, not education, then an IEP is a device to give the state maximum leverage in molding the child.

All in all, the tape is a wonderful amalgam of common sense, accurate statements, inaccurate statements, unstated implications, innuendos, and well-organized paranoid delusions.

Although Spady has attempted reconciliation with some leaders of the Christian Right, an accord is not possible for some groups because OBE violates fundamental tenets. For instance, some groups hold that the transfer of knowledge from teacher to pupil is direct and that the function of the teacher is to effect such transfer. Putting the responsibility for learning on the learner, as OBE does, is deemed inappropriate.

Some words that educational reformers take as neutral send many on the religious Right into paroxysms of fear and loathing. How many times has the phrase "competition in the global economy" been uttered in the last decade? Millions, maybe even billions. It is often voiced as part of a concern, or accusation, that schools are failing to prepare students for the future. No doubt most educators and reformers felt (and feel) they are doing the right thing to try to create schools that will prepare students to compete in the global economy. But to some on the Right, the very word "global" conjures up one-worlders, "globocrats," a new world order, a loss of American sovereignty, rule by socialism in which individual differences are suppressed, and control of America by the United Nations and the Trilateral Commission. As noted earlier, this mentality is quite similar to that displayed by various private militiamen interviewed shortly after the April 1995 bombing of the federal building in Oklahoma City.[2]

Some of us who watched the incoming Clinton administration expected few changes in George Bush's America 2000 education agenda. As noted, when it comes to education, critics on the Right and on the Left mostly agree that a crisis in education exists. In addition, Clinton had been governor of an impoverished state that needed improving. More importantly, he had headed up the National Governors' Association when it held a joint "education summit" with President Bush in 1989. For all these reasons, many educators anticipated continuity from the Bush to the Clinton administrations.

In parts of the Right, however, that very continuity was suspect. "Is it really possible to defeat one party and yet maintain the educational program of that party?" asked one large document in its introduction (Patrick, 1994). The answer was no. The continuity meant that neither Bush nor Clinton were in control of the agenda. This document, titled *Research Manual: America 2000/Goals 2000—Moving the Nation Educationally to a "New World Order,"* traces the source to a UNICEF-UNESCO conference in Thailand and offers a 700-plus page manual on how to understand the conspiracy and the devious roles of NASDC, the Organization for Cooperation and Development (made up of 19 developed nations), the Committee for Economic Development, and other organizations—even implicating, again, William Bennett along with Empower America, the Rand Corporation,[3] John Chubb, Chester E. Finn, Jr., Chris Whittle, and others. The flavor of the tome can be appreciated by citing a couple of definitions from the glossary of "Education Jargon":

> **Cooperative Learning:** A group of 2 to 5 students with varied abilities within a single class who develop feelings of responsibility for achieving group goals. Those involved usually earn a group grade. Declared to be a solution to educational problems regarding self-esteem, improved racial relations and mitigating adverse effects to tracking and remediation, as well as promoting a "sink-or-swim-together" mentality and a feeling of personal responsibility for pursuing and accomplishing group goals. There are several purposes: the elimination of competitiveness and individualism while promoting cooperation, prescribed social skills, social problem solving, responsibility for achieving group success instead of personal success and a means of assuring all children will learn. It lowers academic standards by forcing the higher achieving student to bear the burden of success for others. It is a form of socialism or collectivism in its truest and highest form. (p. 677)

> **Outcome Based Education:** The restructuring plan of the nation, aimed at the demolition of all traditional edu-

cation. Its goal is reducing the child to a human resource that's to be developed to meet the needs of the economy and the New World Order. It mandates that all students must meet the state and national outcomes—prescribed learning objectives which focus on both cognitive and affective goals. The broad outcomes have little to do with academics, but concentrate on beliefs, feelings, values, attitudes, and behavior. The ultimate aim or goal is the development of the politically correct attitude of all children regarding the environment, multicultural diversity—including acceptance of homosexuality as a lifestyle and elimination of heterosexualism, responsible sexuality—safe sex and birth control rather than self control, the feminist agenda and the elimination of nationalism and the acceptance of the New World Order. (p. 679)

This latter definition is rather more encompassing than the one put forward by Spady or those of other OBE advocates.

The OBE proponents—and many other reformers who, while not precisely on the OBE bandwagon, argued for reforms that clearly fit an OBE approach—were, to put it mildly, nonplussed by the attacks from the Right. Like Fouts and Ellis, cited in the opening paragraph of this chapter, these reformers could scarcely think of anything more reasonable than specifying what one wanted students to know and be good at, then measuring to see if they knew and were good at what had been specified.

Robert Marzano of the Mid-Continent Educational Laboratory in Aurora, Colorado, and principal developer of a cognitively oriented program called Tactics for Thinking recounted his feelings in late 1993 as he prepared to meet with what he called "an auditorium filled with angry community members":

[I knew] Tactics for Thinking was not designed to woo their children away from Christianity to a religion called "New Age." Based on straightforward principles of cognitive psychology, the program had nothing to do with an anti-Christian religion, especially one I had never heard of. "All this will be cleared up," I told myself, "once I explain the research and theory on which the program is based. Besides, I'm a Christian myself; I even spent four years of my life in a monastery."

After the meeting, Marzano was, well, chastened:

Only in retrospect can I see how naïve I was.

I came to two important conclusions that night: (1) nothing I could do or say would convince these people that I and my program were not part of this New Age religion, and (2) something was going on beneath the surface. The second conclusion bothered me the most. Their questions all seemed to address a conspiracy that I was supposed to be a part of. (Marzano, 1993, p. 6)

Marzano made more of an attempt to understand the Christian Right than they made to understand him. In perusing the literature of the Right, Marzano constructed a list of 52 people and organizations that had been labeled "New Age." The group included not only the usual suspects but also the Amway Corporation, Blue Cross/Blue Shield, Lions International, the Mormon Church, Mother Teresa and Pope John XXIII, the Muppets, NASA, and Russian leaders Mikhail Gorbachev and Boris Yeltsin. The list bore the same traits of paranoia and inclusiveness as seen in the definitions of cooperative learning and outcomes-based education (see pp. 213–214). Indeed, Marzano reports that he "discovered a massive literature base that used a similar line of reasoning and sometimes identical tone and content."

Independent of the religious and secular Right's objections, the fate of OBE is not clear. For one thing, there is considerable question as to whether many of the most desired "outcomes" can be translated into purely behavioral form. Some cognitive psychologists have argued that perhaps the most important cognitive development as children mature is "metacognition," which refers to the monitoring of cognition, or thinking about thinking. This, obviously, is not a directly observable behavior.

There is, moreover, some evidence that important outcomes, even if measurable, may require years to observe. For instance, one study by Darrin Lehman of the University of British Columbia and Richard Lempert and Richard Nisbet of the University of Michigan considered different kinds of reasoning skills in first- and third-year graduate students in chemistry, law, medicine, and psychology. Both cross-sectional studies of different students and longitudinal studies of the same students were conducted, with similar outcomes. Students in medicine and psychology showed substantial increases in their statistical and methodological reasoning skills when given real-life problems in these areas that they would not have encountered in the courses of study. Law and chemistry students, whose fields do not involve such reasoning during the first two years of graduate school, showed much smaller gains. When given problems in conditional reasoning, on the other hand, medical students and psychology students again showed significant gains, but so did students in law school, where conditional reasoning is a critically important skill. Again, chemistry students showed no gain.

Such studies, of course, call into question the much earlier, shorter, more artificial studies of E.L. Thorndike that appeared to refute the notion of transfer or the development of "the disciplined mind." But these newer studies have received minimal attention to date.

The fate of OBE is also in question because many education practitioners are not used to thinking in such terms, and it is not clear that they will want to change or even see such a change as desirable. There is a question among some educators about whether education is reducible to outcomes that can be observed. The quote from Elliot Eisner in Chapter Three indicates this type of mentality: "Education is about learning how to deal with uncertainty. It is about learning how to savor the quality of the journey."

Or consider this quote from Israel Scheffler, cited by John Goodlad:

> [Education is] the formation of habits of judgment and the development of character, the elevation of standards, the facilitation of understanding, the development of taste and discrimination, the stimulation of curiosity and wondering, the fostering of style and a sense of beauty, the growth of a thirst for new ideas and visions of the yet unknown. (1992, p. 3)

One wonders to what extent these notions can be rendered into behaviorally observable terms. Everything that exists, exists in some amount said Thorndike. To this mentality, Eisner had said some years ago, "Some things cannot be measured, they can only be rendered." The debate about quantification is not likely to end soon.

Epilogue

Where Do We Go from Here?

*You must examine your authority for what it is,
and abandon that part of it which is official,
board-appointed and dead. Then you must
accept the natural authority you have as an
adult, belonging to a community of adults which
includes the kid's parents and relatives, all of
whom expect the kid to get a "good education"—
by which they mean he becomes literate and
equal, not that he becomes a non-reading intellectual. Your assumption must be that everyone
can do it, and that you teach* one person at a
time *how to do it if he needs to know. Then you
are a teacher, instead of a manager; not before.*

—James Herndon,
How to Survive in Your Native Land (1971)

*When I think back on all the crap
I learned in high school,
It's a wonder I can think at all.*

—Paul Simon,
"Kodachrome,™" (1973)

Commencing about a century ago, the public schools have come under almost perennial inspection. The tools have changed from impressionistic data to "hard" test scores and other observables, but the watchers have been always active. What does one make of the perpetual scrutiny of American schools? Why, as with no other institution of the nation, save possibly the government itself currently, are the schools constantly probed, poked, provoked, and scolded? In thinking of an answer, consider this:

When I first moved into the administration building of Cherry Creek, Colorado, Schools in August 1986, there was a green sheet of paper on the bulletin board just outside my office. The paper displayed two lists: one itemized the worst problems of schools in the 1940s, the other the most pervasive problems schools faced in the 1980s. The 1940s list contained such horrors as talking in class, chewing gum, making noise, running in the halls, getting out of place in line, wearing improper clothing, and not putting paper in wastebaskets. The catalog for the 1980s presented drug abuse, alcohol abuse, pregnancy, suicide, rape, robbery, and assault.

I probably thought I was lucky to be working in a place like Cherry Creek, where these problems were certainly muted. Had I but given the list a bit more thought, it might have occurred to me that these problems weren't the *most prevalent* problems in any Colorado district.

Such a thought did occur to Barry O'Neill of Yale University (O'Neill, 1994). When he observed the lists on a bulletin board, he decided to trace their origins. In his search, O'Neill discovered that they had been embraced by public figures of all political stripes: William Bennett, Rush Limbaugh, Phyllis Schlafly, Ross Perot, George Will, Anna Quindlen, Herb Caen, and Carl Rowan, among the notables. The lists had turned up in *Time* and on CBS television news. Their origins had been ascribed to CBS news, *CQ Researcher*, and the Heritage Foundation. Everyone knew the lists were true.

As it turned out, though, a single individual, one T. Cullen Davis of Fort Worth, Texas, had concocted the lists. As part of his conversion to born-again Christianity, Davis had undertaken a crusade against the public schools. What methods did Davis use to construct these lists? He explained to O'Neill: "How did I know what the offenses in the schools were in 1940? I was there. How do I know what they are now? I read the paper."

The point of the story of the lists is not that they were created virtually out of whole cloth, which they were. The point is that the lists, the origin of which no one had tried to trace before, were widely believed by virtually everyone. Why? O'Neill asked. Why? I ask.

O'Neill gave his answer in terms of the tradition of Puritan jeremiads. In these sermons, the preacher would remind the members of the congregation of their covenant with God, attribute the current afflictions to retribution for breaking this covenant, and conclude with a warning to renew the covenant. In terms of a modern covenant with the schools, O'Neill offered this analysis:

Americans today regard their country as the richest, freest, and fairest, with the best social system, but cannot square this with the social problems of America's young....The school lists are a collective moan of anxiety over the gap between ideals and reality. When Puritans or modern Americans enumerate their faults, they are declaring their dedication to their ideals, reassuring each other that at least their goals remain high. (p. 49)

I think O'Neill is at least partly right. But there is a vindictiveness in enumerating the schools' faults that partakes of something else. As we saw in Chapter One, whenever America has faced tough social problems, it has turned to its schools as the solution, but it has never put adequate resources at the schools' disposal. No matter how it is calculated, the costs of K–12 education in the United States never rank us better than average among developed nations, although many have claimed otherwise (with either no data or a highly selective set). And even that ranking is misleading. Fewer of the dollars in American school budgets reach the classroom than in other countries because American schools provide services that other countries either do not provide at all or provide only in reduced amounts. Among the 19 nations of the Organization for Economic Cooperation and Development (OECD), the United States is the only one where more than half of school employees are not teachers (OECD, 1993, p. 100). This is not a function of William Bennett's famous "administrative blob," which in most places does not exist; it is bus drivers, counselors, etc. Faced with huge problems and inadequate resources, the schools cannot, of themselves, solve the problems.

If there is an institution in this nation guilty of original sin in the eyes of the critics, it is the public school. In 1880, when few people were in school, Shakespearean scholar Richard Grant White noted the millions of dollars that were being spent on public schools and asked this:

What is the result? According to independent and competent evidence from all quarters, the mass of pupils in these public schools are unable to read intelligently, to spell correctly, to write legibly, to describe understandingly the geography of their own country, or to do anything that reasonably well-educated children should do with ease. They cannot write a simple letter; they cannot do readily and with quick comprehension a simple "sum" in practical arithmetic; they cannot tell the meaning of any but the commonest of the words that they read and spell so ill. (Gross and Chandler, 1964, p. 229)

White claimed that census figures showed that the longer a community had had public schools, the greater its rates of crime, immorality, and insanity. Ever since White's commentary, no matter what objective indicators of quality said about how well the schools performed, that performance has not been good enough for the critic—and it will not, I suspect, ever be good enough.

The generally high expectations critics have for American schools (and the misguided nostalgia for the way they used to be) are exacerbated by the fact that it is intellectuals, often intellectuals remote from actual school life, who typically undertake to pass judgment on the schools' performance. We saw in Chapter Two that E.L. Thorndike wanted nothing of the messiness of a real school. That attitude has been pervasive among many researchers and policy analysts. It is only recently that academe has deigned to decline Thorndike's disposition and has begun to look at teachers and students as they are found inhabiting actual schools.

That schools are studied largely by intellectuals poses a problem. As noted in Chapter One, schools have never been hotbeds of intellectual activity, although their attention to intellectual matters has increased over the years. I can't imagine the *New York Times* could replicate today its scandalous 1943 survey of college freshmen. Still, in part because of our dedication to equity, high schools are not the selective institutions they were a century ago. This likely makes them boring to many people who later become university professors. Ironically, teachers and administrators (and, later, college faculty) have assiduously steered those with real intellectual gifts toward a professorship as the lone legitimate career; these teachers and administrators are then castigated for their failings when their pupils actually become professors.

In addition, almost all adults have unrealistic expectations for youth. "Why can't they be like we were?" went the refrain of a 1960 song in *Bye, Bye Birdie!*—"Perfect in every way. Oh, what's the matter with kids today?" It's a perennial question. Only occasionally does someone think to recall Will Rogers's comment that "The schools are not as good as they used to be and never were."

Moreover, it is a common human foible that we cannot understand how things that are easy for us can be so difficult for others. Thus, when the professoriate takes to evaluate the schools, it lays on them a double whammy: in addition to the usual adult deprecation of youth, the academy's residents cannot understand why the schools can't render everyone intellectually brilliant. It is members of the university community who are asked, by and large, to form the reform commissions; it is they who write the policy papers. But this group has not been supportive of American schools for many years, while managing to say little of a critical nature about their own institutions of higher education.

None of the above should be taken to mean that the schools are blameless for a situation in which they are regularly criticized. As previously noted, I believe Raymond Callahan's thesis about the cult of efficiency in schools is mostly correct, insofar as school administrators became obsessed with it. (Of its otherwise preventing a flowering of scholarship among administrators, I am much less certain.) One outcome of this concern with efficiency was an enthusiastic adoption (by administrators, not by teachers) of "efficient" tests. As Norman Frederiksen has written, efficient tests drive out inefficient tests. Multiple-choice tests are very efficient, and they effectively drove out alternatives for a long time. But, as we found Frederiksen saying in Chapter Two, "Most of the important problems one faces in real life are ill structured, as are all the really important social, political, and scientific problems in the world today." But this ill-structured nature of problems and of people's ability to cope with and solve them are the very things that multiple-choice questions *cannot possibly* test, as Frederiksen showed.

If many schools have become more intellectually sterile today—not a firm conclusion, by any means—it is not because of a commitment to universal secondary education but because of a commitment to a kind of efficiency, at least in tests, that *precludes* rich intellectual life. At the 1995 assessment conference of the Council of Chief State School officers, it was clear that, in many states and districts, multiple-choice tests are back—with a vengeance. I think the premature abandonment of the various assessment forms that generally go under the rubric of "authentic" will be a tragic mistake if, indeed, it happens. The technology of multiple-choice tests has been extant for three quarters of a century. Other, more complex assessments should not be abandoned simply because we failed to develop them to the same state of maturity in less than a decade.

The importance of authenticity, in instruction even more than in assessment, as a goal of the public schools cannot be overemphasized, even as we must acknowledge it is not part of students' or teachers' daily experience most of the time. Deborah Meier, able to bring some of this authenticity to the poorest part of New York City as principal of Central Park East Secondary School, describes the problem as it plays out in too many schools. She avers that one cannot be coach or expert if one is also judge or executioner, a dual role too many educators actually play:

> As my son explained to me one day when I was trying to convince him to ask his teacher to explain something to him, "Mom, you don't understand. The last person in the world who I'd let know what I don't understand is my teacher." Schooling becomes a vast game in which teachers try to trick students into revealing their ignorance while students try to trick teachers into thinking they are not ignorant. (Meier, 1993, pp. 605–606)

The reader might wish to reflect on the pathology contained in Meier's son's comment. Meier goes on to lay out some general principles of authenticity (although she does not use that term):

> Human beings by nature are social, interactive learners. We check out our ideas, argue with authors, bounce issues back and forth, ask friends to read our early drafts, talk together after seeing a movie, pass on books we have loved, attend meetings and argue out our ideas, share stories and gossip that extends our understandings of ourselves and others. Talk lies at the heart of our lives. This kind of exchange is never allowed in school, nor modeled there—not between children, nor between adults. Monthly faculty meetings are no better imitations of true discussion than the average so-called classroom discussion....No one among the powerful policymakers wonders, as they imagine the perfect curriculum, what it means to teach a subject year after year, based on

someone else's design. We organize schools as though the ideal were an institution impervious to human touch. (p. 606)[1]

We saw in Chapter One how the attempt in the 1960s to design "teacher-proof" materials produced disastrous results. Indeed, the attempt to fit people into such situations leads to teachers acting in what long-time teacher James Herndon called "idiot roles" in schools, roles that stand in stark contrast to life outside the school house walls:

Yet, released from school to their private lives, teachers are marvelous gardeners, they work on ocean liners as engineers, they act in plays, win bets, go to the movies, build their own houses, they are opera fans, expert fishermen, champion skeet shooters, grand golfers, organ players, oratorio singers, hunters, mechanics…all just as if they were smart people. Of course, it is more difficult to build a house or sing Bach than it is to teach kids to read. Of course, if they operated in their lives outside of [school] the same way they do in it, their houses would fall down, their ships sink, their flowers die, their cars blow up. (Herndon, 1971, p. 106)[2]

One can see what happens when teachers can get out of their "idiot roles" in school and act as real people. One sees then that the intense involvement of teachers is an important aspect—perhaps the most important aspect—of intense involvement by students. At the Key School, a magnet school of the Indianapolis Public School District, teachers, in part, teach "pods." Pods are mini "courses" in which the teacher teaches material that interests her outside of school. The presumption is that what turns teachers on turns the kids on, too. It works. I once went on a field trip with a group of Key School students who had been studying a pod about Victorian architecture. We visited and explored Victorian houses in Indianapolis. The contrast of this experience with the typical field trip could not have been more stark. The students did not have to be rounded up constantly; they paid attention, noticed various features in the houses and generally seemed to be serious and involved with the material. For her part, the teacher talked to them as she might have to anyone else who was interested in her avocation.

The impact of a teacher's involvement was demonstrated in a more emphatic way one day when I was visiting a school in

Colorado. In the teachers' lounge, one mathematics teacher recounted how an earlier school in which he had worked had hired a new science teacher who, for some reason, broke the contract at the last minute, forcing other teachers hurriedly to cover various science areas. This teacher, not a science teacher, was assigned to teach physics, a subject he had never taught. He recalled his anxiety at teaching this alien subject and trying to stay at least even, if not ahead of, the students. Some eight years later, he said, a young man entered his classroom and told him he had been in that physics class and was just completing a doctorate in physics. The teacher admitted that the student must be doing this in spite of his awful initiation into the field. No, said the young man, *because* of it. "You showed me how you go about solving problems when you don't know what the answer is." Of course, we don't know if the other members of the class felt the same way.

Meier notes that nothing makes a class more restive than the spectacle of a teacher fumbling for the right answer. But this fumbling may well be part of playing the idiot role: a "right" answer is not necessarily the same thing as a *real* answer. The latter can only come from a *real* problem. How often does a student get to see a teacher coping with a genuine problem?

Thus it is the case that schools can stand some considerable improvement, certainly. This is not the same as school bashing, just as certainly. Trying to explain to a reporter that I was not a "defender" of schools, I said I thought I could walk into any school in the country and quickly find something to improve. She said, "I know. I feel the same way about newspapers." We likely all feel that way about where we work.

But the reader of this book may have noticed that many of the preceding comments refer to the perceptions of "the critics." That is because those perceptions are not shared by the public at large—at least not for *their* schools. The perpetual criticism of the schools has convinced the public that there is, indeed, a crisis in education. It just isn't in their schools. In the 1995 Phi Delta Kappa/Gallup poll, only 20 percent of the public gave the nation's schools an A or a B grade. Yet, when asked to judge the school that their eldest child attended, 65 percent gave their schools those high grades (Elam and Rose, 1995). This is a consistent finding, year after year.

How do we explain this finding? It is not hard. A survey by the American Association of School Administrators shows overwhelmingly that people depend first on television and then on newspapers to obtain their information about the nation's schools. These sources have been consistently negative about the condition of the schools (Bracey, 1994b). But when gathering information about the local schools, people turn to local sources, including school officials, who are regarded as credible.

As I have shown repeatedly elsewhere, the condition of American public education is much better than portrayed in the media (Bracey, 1991, 1992, 1993, 1994a, 1994b, 1995). The crisis constructed by the critics and reported in the media is very much, to use the title of a recent book by David Berliner and Bruce Biddle, *The Manufactured Crisis*.

We have seen that, over the last century, American schools have moved from being highly selective at the secondary level to being universal. They have moved as well from vaguely defined products such as the "disciplined mind" to observable outcomes and a concern for standards.[3]

Will standards and attention to observable outcomes help schools become more authentic institutions? At this point, it is hard to say. The various professional organizations have expended a great deal of effort to develop standards for their curriculum areas. At the moment, though, difficulties exist in moving these standards from the organizations through the classroom door. One is simply the sheer quantity of paper that the various standards occupy. Any teacher is likely to be intimidated by their very size, especially if he or she has to deal with more than one curriculum area.

In addition, those who have attacked outcomes-based education have also managed to taint the standards movement. There was, until recently, wide support for standards. "People think their kids should know more," said Emily Wurtz, a member of Senator Jeff Bingaman's staff. But, she continued, after Lynne Cheney attacked the history standards in the *Wall Street Journal*, opponents of various standard-setting activities were emboldened to attack the standards (Wurtz, 1995). Ironically, some of these critics have managed to plant the notion that, despite the emphasis on high standards, the standards movement will, in fact, contribute to the "dumbing down" of the curriculum. Educators might say that all children can learn, but the man in the street carries a bell curve in his head.

Moreover, while people may want their children to "know more" in general, they are not knowledgeable about the standards movement and, if the 1994 survey by Public Agenda is correct, they are more concerned about "the basics":

> The problem that education reformers face in their drive to replace multiple-choice tests with more "authentic" forms of assessment is not that people object to the idea. The problem is that this particular recommendation seems somewhat tangential to people's chief concerns about the schools. It is as if people are saying, "Well, that's all well and good, but what about the guns, the drugs, the truancy, and the students who can't add, spell, or find France on a map? (Public Agenda, 1994, p. 19)

Richard Grant White would feel right at home. Public Agenda's conclusions are echoed by reports from focus groups, according to Cathy Belter of the National Parent Teachers Association and Susan Traiman of the Business Roundtable (Belter, 1995; Traiman, 1995).[4]

The area of standards is one where the education community has moved ahead of the public at large and, it appears, has lost that public in the process. Public Agenda reports that "people don't understand why the reforms are considered better, and people haven't been all that impressed with the teaching reforms they have seen in the past....people seemed to fear that teaching 'fads' were replacing time-honored ways of doing things" (Public Agenda, p. 20). As noted earlier, educators have been using such phrases as "transformational outcomes-based education" and emphasizing the need for change, even revolutionary change, in how people learn. The public, though, has been more concerned with the culture-conserving function of schools. Its response has been, essentially, "Not with my kid, you don't."

There is considerable irony here. I noted in Chapter One that people have a misguided nostalgia for how things used to be in schools. And educational innovations have been nothing if not driven by fad over the years. New methods appear to be "time-honored" only after people are no longer experiencing them. That they should appear as such is curious. Criticism of public schools rose to its contemporary levels shortly after World War II, which means that even aging baby boomers have lived in an era of critics' chronic carping about the schools—50 years of complaints, comrades. Given this, it is remarkable that parents have as good an opinion of schools as they do.

It is true, though, that we educators have not done a good

job of telling people why we consider the reforms to be better. In addition to actual disinformation spread about outcomes and standards, there is a real lack of information about some reforms. Virtually no parent, it appears, understands the use of inventive or invented spelling. Of course, this reform has nothing to do with the various professional standards, but the standards have suffered guilt by association. Indeed, the 1995 Phi Delta Kappa/Gallup survey of the public's attitudes toward education finds that few parents have actually read much about standards. In this vacuum, disinformation can thrive, and standards can suffer what has been called "death by anecdote." If inventive spelling is what the reforms are all about, we don't want any, thank you.

Even given my skepticism about the ultimate impact of standards, this is not an anti-standards treatise. Standards can be useful simply to establish the ultimate level of the topic. The Little League coach needs to know about the level of play in the major leagues, even as he does not expect his charges to perform at that level. We always need to be familiar with the professional level of any performance area. I simply think that there are too many technical problems with many of the standards projects to make them feasible. And I worry that teachers will not see them as their own. Teaching might be a uniquely "wheel-inventing" occupation: every person has to reinvent the wheel in order to make it his or her wheel.

In addition, the people developing standards lack the clout to make the standards matter where they are needed most. I recently had a conversation with Ira Glass, a Chicago-based National Public Radio reporter who has spent the last two years observing in and reporting on Chicago schools. Given that former Secretary of Education William Bennett once called Chicago's public schools the nation's worst, I asked Glass, "Is there any hope?" His answer was yes, but only if class size can be substantially reduced. A lot of the kids who are there, he said, really aren't *there*. With small enough classes, he thought, teachers might be able to think of ways to reach some of these kids. But reducing class size to any significant degree (say, to the levels of Project STAR in Tennessee, a definitive demonstration that small classes are effective) takes money—a lot of money. This nation does not have a history of bestowing money on schools located in poor areas, and at this moment it certainly does not appear to have the sentiment or will to do so. Unfortunately, the people developing standards are not in a position to change this.

The fact is that many of our most pressing educational issues will not be solved through standards and assessments. When I took data from the Second International Assessment of Educational Progress and merged it with the 1992 National Assessment results, I found that while Taiwan and Korea had the highest scores as nations, Asian students in American schools outscored them and white students tied Hungary for third place. Thus, if "world-class" status is defined by the highest-scoring nations in these international comparisons, more than 70 percent of our students (the proportion of K–12 population constituted by white and Asian students) are world-class (Bracey, 1994a, p. 116). Standards likely will improve the performance of these groups. But that is not the problem.

The problem is that black, Hispanic, and disadvantaged urban students all scored below the lowest country, Jordan, and lowest state, Mississippi. I report the data by ethnicity because that is the way that the National Assessment and NCES reported it, but there is much other evidence to support the contention that the real culprit in these numbers is money, or, more precisely, lack of money (Bracey, 1992 and 1994a, p. 117). A funding system based on property taxes absolutely precludes any meaningful provision of equity in funding. I don't think standards will mean anything to these low-scoring groups, for they have more immediate and more pressing problems to deal with. Teachers faced with obsolete or missing textbooks, unworkable plumbing, undrinkable water, and hungry students probably can't appreciate the standard-setting efforts of the NCTM.

Smaller classes would improve achievement without any regard to changes in standards. So would making better use of cognitive psychology, collaborative learning, technology, and any number of things that I mention in *Transforming American Schools* (1994). Some of these suggestions are discussed at greater length in *The Manufactured Crisis* (1995), which also contains suggestions for a number of other ways to improve American education.

The notion that standards are crucial to school improvement becomes even weaker when one considers that principal rationales for developing them were based on false assumptions. If we had standards, went one line of argument, our students would be as good as those in other nations and the country could compete in the global economy. The acquisition of higher levels of learning, went another, would enable the students to get good jobs. But as we have seen, the schools are *not* significantly linked to competitiveness, and the jobs are not there. At this writing, two giant banks have agreed to merge, and one outcome of the merger is the loss of 12,000 jobs. If the trend toward the elimination of work continues—as it surely will—schools will need to focus on what people do with their non-work time. The school-to-leisure transition looms as the important one, not the school-to-work transition. Study after study has found the American economy to be the most competitive and the American worker to be the most productive. It is already the case that it is when these workers leave their jobs that they become Joe Sixpacks, consuming hours of mindless television. Schools need to do something about *that*.

As assessments developed, American educators shifted from vague descriptions of school outcomes to explicit ones. At the same time, over the last 40 years, there has been a mounting concern with equal educational opportunity. Initially this concern was with equality of inputs. In the last 20 years or so, the concern has shifted to outcomes. As long as the emphasis was on inputs and as long as the outcomes were poorly described, Americans could ignore the fact that the signal quality of American education is the difference in quality in different localities—e.g., slums versus suburbs. *Money* magazine managed to get past the usual stereotypes in a study of suburban and private schools, which had this to say about choosing private schools over public ones: "Here's the bottom line: You're probably wasting your hard-earned money" (Topolnicki, 1994, p. 112). On the other hand, both Jonathan Kozol and I have documented "savage inequalities" among schools (Kozol, 1991; Bracey, 1992).

With people now focusing on outcomes—clear and precise outcomes—it would seem that we have reached a defining moment when we cannot ignore those inequalities. We must see that they collide with our egalitarian ethic. Will we acknowledge these injustices? More important, will we then do something about them? I am not sanguine.

The power of psychological denial is enormous. John Kenneth Galbraith contends that we simply will not see the "functional underclass" because we need it and because we are the contented class. But even discontents do not always give rise to appropriate actions, as Bruno Bettelheim pointed out some years ago in relation to the Holocaust (Bettelheim, 1960). Currently we can see this phenomenon operating in the United States. If the mythical rational man from Mars were to visit this nation, surely he would be surprised to see one group of citizens,

tobacco growers, permitted—even subsidized!—to grow a product that kills another group of citizens. But most earthlings don't
seem to lose any sleep over it. When it comes to dealing with
the problems of inequalities in American schools, I'm not certain we're up to passing that final examination.

Notes and References

Prologue

NOTES

1. Having come across the article "The End of Jobs" (Barnett, 1993) and the book *The End of Work* (Jeremy Rifkin, 1995), I was inspired to write an essay, "America's Choice: High Skills and No Wages."

2. There is no NAEP reporting category for "disadvantaged rural." Were there one, I would predict that group would score lower still.

3. People interested in seeing the data that prove the critics wrong are referred to "The Bracey Report on the Condition of Public Education," which has appeared every October since 1991 in *Phi Delta Kappan* magazine; to my earlier book, *Transforming America's Schools*, published by the American Association of School Administrators (AASA) in 1994; to David Berliner's *The Manufactured Crisis*, published by Addison-Wesley in 1995; or to Joseph Schneider's and Paul Houston's *Exploding the Myths*, also published by AASA.

REFERENCES

America's Choice: High Skills or Low Wages! Rochester, NY: National Center on Education and the Economy, 1990.

Bracey, Gerald W. "What If Education Broke Out All Over?" *Education Week* (March 28, 1994): 44.

Galbraith, John Kenneth. *The Culture of Contentment*. Boston: Houghton Mifflin, 1992.

Gardner, Howard W. *Frames of Mind*. New York: Basic Books, 1983.

Gardner, John. *Excellence: Can We Be Equal and Excellent Too?* New York: Harper & Row, 1961.

Ishizaka, Kazuo. "Japanese Education—The Myths and the Realities." In *Different Visions of the Future of Education*. Ottawa: Canadian Teachers Foundation, 1994.

Mandel, Michael J. "Will Schools Ever Get Better?" *Business Week* (April 17, 1995): 64–68.

National Center for Education Statistics. *Education in States and Nations*. Washington, DC: U.S. Department of Education, 1993.

Spady, William. *Outcomes Based Education: Critical Issues and Answers*. Arlington, VA: American Association of School Administrators, 1994.

Tucker, Marc, and Ray Marshall. *Thinking for a Living*. Rochester, NY: National Center on Education and the Economy, 1992.

Workforce 2000. Indianapolis: Hudson Institute, 1988.

Chapter One

NOTES

1. In *The Bell Curve*, Richard Herrnstein and Charles Murray show that well into this century, most chief executive officers held no more than a high school diploma. Today most have advanced degrees.

2. And radically different from my schooling in the 1950s, for that matter. My children learned biology in terms of evolution, ecology, DNA, etc. In both high school and college, I memorized phyla.

3. The Greek *skoli*, from which the word *school* comes, means holiday or feast day.

4. Paul Whiteman was a popular band leader at the time.

5. I was in Europe at the time and had been traveling since October 1973, mostly in Asia and Africa, but had no trouble keeping up with events. When Nixon stepped down, I listened to live radio coverage in my Copenhagen apartment and noticed many lights were on around the neighborhood, even though it was 2:00 a.m. in Denmark. When television returned to the air in the morning, the videotaped speech aired immediately.

6. There apparently was no final document beyond this draft. Although it was unsigned, Glenn Campbell at Stanford University's Hoover Institute has confirmed to other researchers its authenticity. Campbell chaired the group that wrote the memorandum.

7. Much of this material, down to the quote from *A Nation At Risk*, was obtained in conversations with commission staff member Milton Goldberg, writer James Harvey, and commission members Emeral Crosby and Jay Sommer during early 1995.

8. As codified in the Goals 2000: Educate America Act, signed into law on March 31, 1994.

9. See Prologue Note 3.

REFERENCES

Aikin, Wilfred. *The Story of the Eight-Year Study*. New York: Harper and Brothers, 1942.

America's Choice: High Skills or Low Wages! Rochester, NY: National Center on Education and the Economy, 1990.

Baker, Russell. "Beset by Mediocrity," *New York Times* (April 30, 1983): A23.

Bell, Terrel. *The Thirteenth Man.* New York: Free Press, 1988.

Bestor, Arthur. *Educational Wastelands: The Retreat from Learning in Public Schools.* Champaign, IL: University of Illinois Press, 1953.

Bracey, Gerald W. "Education's Data-Proof Ideologues," *Education Week* (January 25, 1995): 44.

Buckley, William F., Jr. "The Obvious Solution: Tuition Tax Credits," *Washington Post* (May 3, 1983): A19.

Cohen, Richard. "Them," *Washington Post* (May 12, 1983): B1.

Cremin, Lawrence J. *Popular Education and Its Discontents.* New York: Harper & Row, 1989.

————. *The Transformation of the School: Progressivism in American Education.* New York: Alfred A. Knopf, 1961.

Ebel, Robert L. "The Case for Minimum Competency Testing," *Phi Delta Kappan* (April 1978): 546–548.

Featherstone, Joseph. "How Children Learn," *New Republic* (September 2, 1967).

————. "Schools For Children: What's Happening in British Classrooms?" *New Republic* (August 19, 1967).

————. "Teaching Children to Think," *New Republic* (September 9, 1967).

Feinberg, Lawrence, J. "Panel Urges Measures to Halt Decline of Education in America," *Washington Post* (April 27, 1983): A1.

"For Better Schools" (editorial), *Washington Post* (May 3, 1983): A18.

Fuller, Harry J. "The Emperor's New Clothes or Primus Dementat," *Scientific Monthly* (January 1951): 32–41.

Gardner, Howard W. *Frames of Mind.* New York: Basic Books, 1983.

Gerstner, Louis V., Jr., Roger D. Semerad, Denis Philip Doyle, and William B. Johnston. *Reinventing Education.* New York: Dutton, 1994.

Goodman, Ellen. "Grading Time," *Washington Post* (May 10, 1983): A19.

Gross, Carl H., and Charles C. Chandler, eds. *The History of American Education through Readings.* Boston: D.C. Heath and Company, 1964.

Hall, G. Stanley. "The Ideal School As Based On Child Study," *Journal of Proceedings and Addresses* (1901): 474–488.

Hofstadter, Richard. *Anti-Intellectualism in American Life.* New York: Alfred A. Knopf, 1962.

Hoover, H.D. Personal communication, February 1995.

Intress, Ruth. "In College, One in Four Plays Catch-up," *Richmond Times Dispatch* (September 24, 1994): B-1.

Kaestle, Karl. *Literacy in America: Reading and Readers from 1880 to 1980.* New Haven, CT: Yale University Press, 1991.

Kerr, Clark. "Is Education All That Guilty?" *Education Week* (February 27, 1991).

Kilpatrick, James J. "At Bottom, Americans Just Don't Give a Damn," *Washington Post* (May 3, 1983): A19.

Knight, Edgar W. *Fifty Years of American Education, 1900–1950.* New York: Ronald Press, 1952.

Kraft, Joseph. "A Suggestion for Conservatives: Come Off It," *Washington Post* (May 3, 1983): A19.

Krauthammer, Charles. "Save the Border Collie," *Washington Post* (July 15, 1994): A21.

Mann, Judy. "School Alarm," *Washington Post* (April 29, 1983): C1.

Myrdal, Gunnar. *Objectivity in Social Research.* New York: Pantheon Books, 1969.

Nasar, Sylvia. "The American Economy: Back on Top," *New York Times* (February 27, 1994) sec. 3: 1.

Newman, Arthur J., ed. *In Defense of the American Public School.* Berkeley, CA: Shenkman Publishing, 1978.

Perkinson, Henry J. *The Imperfect Panacea.* 3d ed. New York: McGraw-Hill, 1991.

Progressive Education Association. *Adventures in American Education Series.* New York: Harper and Brothers, 1942.

Raubinger, Frederick M., Harold G. Rowe, Donald L. Piper, and Charles K. West. *The Development of Secondary Education.* Toronto: Collier-Macmillan, 1969.

Ravitch, Diane. *The Troubled Crusade.* New York: Basic Books, 1983.

Rickover, Hyman G. *Education and Freedom.* New York: E.P. Dutton, 1959.

Schaefer, Robert J. *The School As a Center of Inquiry.* New York: Harper & Row, 1967.

Shanker, Albert. "Competing for Customers," *New York Times* (June 27, 1993a) sec. 4: 7.

———. "World Class Standards," *New York Times* (July 4, 1993b) sec. 4: 7.

———. "The Wrong Message," *New York Times* (July 11, 1993c) sec. 4: 7.

Shepard, Lorrie A. "Psychometricians' Beliefs About Learning Influence Testing," *Educational Researcher* (October 1991): 2–9.

Silberman, Charles. *Crisis in the Classroom*. New York: Random House, 1970.

Spillane, Robert. "Student Achievement Standards," *Education Week* (June 2, 1993): 36.

Spring, Joel. *The Sorting Machine: National Educational Policy Since 1945*. New York: David McKay, 1976.

Tanner, Daniel. "A Nation 'Truly' At Risk," *Phi Delta Kappan* (December 1993): 288–297.

Tyler, Ralph. *Perspectives on American Education: Reflections on the Past, Challenges for the Future*. Chicago: Science Research Associates, 1976.

Walberg, Herbert J. "Changing IQ and Family Context," *Educational Technology* (June 1976).

Whittington, Dale. "What Have Our 17-year-olds Known in the Past?" *American Educational Research Journal* (Winter 1992): 776–788.

Will, George F. "Bad Report Card," *Washington Post* (May 1, 1983): B7.

Wilson, Sloan. "It's Time to Close Our Circus," *Life* (March 24, 1958): 36–37.

Wirtz, Willard, et al. *On Further Examination: Report of the Advisory Panel on the Scholastic Aptitude Test Score Decline*. New York: The College Entrance Examination Board, 1977.

Woodring, Paul. "A Second Open Letter to Teachers," *Phi Delta Kappan* (April 1978): 515–517.

Wurtzel, Alan. "Getting from School to Work," *Washington Post* (December 7, 1993): A25.

Zajonc, Robert. "Family Configuration and Intelligence," *Science* (April 1976): 227–236.

Chapter Two

NOTES

1. For a history of IQ measurements, the reader is referred to Stephen J. Gould's *The Mismeasure of Man*.

2. For a history of the Scholastic Aptitude Test (SAT), the reader is referred to David Owen's *None of the Above* and James Crouse and Dale Trusheim's *The Case Against the SAT*. A more approving history can be found in *Life with the SAT*, by George Hanford, former president of the College Entrance Examination Board.

3. One informal study noted that a raw score that produced a rank at the 50th percentile in the first grade led to only the 37th percentile

in the second grade. On the other hand, the score equivalent to the 50th percentile in the seventh grade led to a rank of 47 in the eighth grade.

4. These are the technical rules by which the levels were established. The p-values—proportion of students getting the items right—of the items for groups at different levels: The p-values within the target group had to be at least .65. The p-values in the group below the target group had to be less than .50. The difference in the p-values in the two groups had to be at least .30. The p-values had to be based on samples of at least 100 students.

5. Such an imposition occurs in the Rasch one-parameter model of item response theory.

REFERENCES

Alexander, Lamar, and Thomas James. *The Nation's Report Card: Improving the Assessment of Student Achievement.* Cambridge, MA: National Academy of Education, 1987.

Ayres, Leonard, P. "History and Present Status of Educational Measurements." In *Seventeenth NSSE Yearbook.* Bloomington, IL: National Society for the Study of Education, 1918.

Baker, Eva L. "Can Educational Research Inform Educational Practice? Yes!" *Phi Delta Kappan* (March 1984): 453–455.

Berliner, David. "The 100-Year Journey of Educational Psychology." In Thomas K. Fagan and Gary R. VandenBos, eds. *Exploring Applied Psychology: Origins and Critical Analyses.* Washington, DC: American Psychological Association, 1993.

Buros, Oscar. "Editors' Comments on Testing: Fifty Years in Testing," *Educational Researcher* (July/August 1977): 9–15; also in *Eighth Mental Measurements Yearbook* (1978): 1972–1983.

Caldwell, A., and S. Courtis. *Then and Now in Education: 1845–1923.* Yonkers-On-Hudson, NY: World Book Company, 1924.

Cronbach, Lee J. "Five Decades of Public Controversy Over Mental Testing," *American Psychologist* (January 1975): 1–14.

"The Debate at the White House Conference," *Phi Delta Kappan* (September 1965): 17–18.

Educational Achievement Stands: NAGB's Approach Yields Misleading Interpretations. Washington, DC: General Accounting Office, GAO/PEMD-93-12, 1993.

Eisner, Elliot W. "Can Education Research Inform Educational Practice?" *Phi Delta Kappan* (March 1984): 447–452.

Forsyth, Robert A. "Do NAEP Scales Yield Valid Criterion-Referenced Interpretations?" *Educational Measurement: Issues and Practice* (Fall 1991): 3–9.

Frederiksen, Norman. "The Real Test Bias," *American Psychologist* 39 (1984): 193–202.

Glaser, Robert. "A Criterion-Referenced Test." In W. James Popham, *Criterion Referenced Measurement: An Introduction.* Englewood Cliffs, NJ: Educational Technology Press, 1971.

————. "Criterion-Referenced Tests: Part I. Origins," *Educational Measurement: Issues and Practice* (Winter 1994a): 9–12.

————. "Criterion-Referenced Tests: Part II. Unfinished Business," *Educational Measurement: Issues and Practice* (Winter, 1994b): 27–30.

————. "Instructional Technology and the Measurement of Learning Outcomes: Some Questions," *American Psychologist* (1963): 519–521.

Glass, Gene V. "Standards and Criteria," *Journal of Educational Measurement* (Fall 1978): 237–261.

Greenbaum, William. *Measuring Educational Progress.* New York: McGraw-Hill, 1977.

Hand, Harold C. "The Camel's Nose," *Phi Delta Kappan* (September 1965): 8–12.

Hanson F. Allan. *Testing, Testing: Social Consequences of the Examined Life.* Berkeley, CA: University of California Press, 1993.

Hazlett, James A. "A History of the National Assessment of Educational Progress, 1963–1973." Unpublished doctoral dissertation (1974).

Herrnstein, Richard, and Charles Murray. *The Bell Curve.* New York: Free Press, 1994.

Jacobs, Walter Ballou. "The Dangers of Examinations," *The School Review* (September 1896): 675–681.

Jaeger, Richard M. "General Issues in Reporting of NAEP Trial State Data." Unpublished paper (October 1991).

Koretz, Daniel. "State Comparisons Using NAEP: Large Costs, Disappointing Benefits," *Educational Researcher* (April 1991): 19–21.

Lapointe, Archie. "Profiling American Students' Strengths and Weaknesses in Science Achievement." In S.K. Kajumdar, L.M. Rosenfeld, P.A. Rubba, E.W. Miller, and R.F. Schmalz, eds. *Science Education in the United States: Issues, Crises, and Priorities.* Philadelphia: The Pennsylvania Academy of Science, 1991.

Linn, Robert F. "Criterion-Referenced Measurement: A Valuable Perspective Clouded by Surplus Meaning," *Educational Measurement: Issues and Practice* (Winter 1994): 12–15.

Mager, Robert F. *Preparing Instructional Objectives.* 2d ed. Belmont, CA: Fearon, 1975.

Mullis, Ina, and Lynn B. Jenkins. *The Science Report Card: Elements of Risk and Recovery.* Princeton, NJ: Educational Testing Service, 1988.

Popham, W. James. *Criterion-Referenced Measurement.* Englewood Cliffs, NJ: Prentice-Hall, 1975.

―――――. "The Instructional Consequences of Criterion-Referenced Measurement," *Educational Measurement: Issues and Practice* (Winter 1994): 15–18.

―――――. "Muddle-Minded Emotionalism," *Phi Delta Kappan* (May 1987): 687–688.

Popham, W. James, and Theodore R. Husek. "Implications of Criterion-Referenced Measurement," *Journal of Educational Measurement* (Spring 1969): 1–9.

Robinson, Glen, and David Brandon. *State Level NAEP Scores: Should They Be Used to Compare and Rank State Educational Quality?* Arlington, VA: Educational Research Service, 1994.

Ruch, Giles M. *The Objective or New-Type Examination.* New York: Scott, Foresman & Co., 1929.

Shanker, Albert. "The End of the Traditional Model of Schooling: A Proposal for Using Incentives to Restructure Our Public Schools," *Phi Delta Kappan* (February 1990): 345–357.

Stufflebeam, Daniel L., Richard M. Jaeger, and Michael Scriven. *Summative Evaluation of the National Assessment Governing Board's Inaugural Effort to Set Achievement Levels on the National Assessment of Educational Progress.* Kalamazoo, MI: The Evaluation Center of Western Michigan University, 1991.

Terman, L.M. "The Psychological Determinist; or Democracy and the IQ," *Journal of Educational Research* (1922): 57–62.

Thorndike, E.L. "The Nature, Purposes, and General Methods of Measurements of Educational Products." In *Seventeenth NSSE Yearbook.* Bloomington, IL: National Society for the Study of Education, 1918.

Thorndike, E.L., E.O. Bregman, M.V. Cobb, and Ella Woodyard. *The Measurement of Intelligence.* Collected papers published as *Classics in Psychology.* New York: The Arno Press, 1973.

Trow, William Clark. Foreword to W. James Popham, *Criterion-Referenced Measurement: An Introduction.* Englewood Cliffs, NJ: Educational Technology Press, 1991.

Tyler, Ralph. "Assessing the Progress of Education," *Phi Delta Kappan* (September 1965): 13–16.

Wiggins, Grant. *Assessing Student Performance.* San Francisco: Jossey-Bass, 1993.

Yerkes, Robert M. "Testing the Human Mind," *Atlantic Monthly* (1923): 358–370.

Chapter Three

NOTES

1. At a Brookings Institution luncheon symposium for the release of Hanushek's book, he reiterated the claim that in the last 20 years expenditures for schools had doubled and test scores had been flat. I held up a chart that showed test scores declining in the 1960s and 1970s, then reversing and rising to record levels. "They aren't flat," I said. Hanushek and symposium chair, Chester E. Finn, Jr., cast me a glance, then continued as if the chart did not exist. Shortly thereafter, I penned a piece called "The Right's Data-Proof Ideologues" that was published in the Commentary section of the January 25, 1995, issue of *Education Week*.

2. For instance, the top 10 fastest-growing jobs from 1990 to 2005, as projected by the Bureau of Labor Statistics, account for 3,162,00 jobs. Most of these jobs require some skills, though not necessarily those related to high technology. Many of them are for some type of medical assistant, reflecting the fact that the nation is aging. On the other hand, retail sales—the top occupation—accounts for 4,465,000 jobs. Only two of the top 10 jobs in terms of numbers are skilled: nurses and managers. The decline of skilled labor was discussed first by Richard Barnett in "The End of Jobs" (*Harper's*, September 1993) and most recently and extensively by Jeremy Rifkin in *The End of Work* (New York: Putnam, 1995).

3. More accurately, one could say that Rothman is mostly right but that the support for the standards in many places is only money-deep.

REFERENCES

American Heritage Dictionary. New York: Houghton Mifflin, 1992.

Avent, Joseph. "The Practice of the Superintendent," *American School Board Journal* (June 1910): 3.

Baker, Keith. "Yes, Throw Money at the Schools," *Phi Delta Kappan* (April 1991): 628–631.

Bobbitt, Franklin. *The Curriculum.* Cambridge, MA: The Riverside Press, 1918.

————. "High School Costs," *The School Review* (October 1915): 505–511.

————. "Supervision of City Schools." In *Twelfth NSSE Yearbook*. Bloomington, IL: National Society for the Study of Education, 1913.

Bracey, Gerald, W. "The Fourth Bracey Report on the Condition of Public Education," *Phi Delta Kappan* (October 1994): 115–127.

Callahan, Raymond E. *Education and the Cult of Efficiency.* Chicago: University of Chicago Press, 1962.

Celis, William O. III. "New Education Legislation Defines Federal Role in Nation's Classrooms," *New York Times* (March 30, 1994): 1.

Cole, P.O. "The Ideal Superintendent," *American School Board Journal* (May 1910): 7.

Cuban, Larry. "Effective Schools: A Friendly but Cautionary Note," *Phi Delta Kappan* (June 1983): 695–696.

———. "A National Curriculum and Tests: Charting the Direct and Indirect Consequences," *Education Week* (July 14, 1993): 25.

Edson, Andrew W. "School Surveys and School Inquiries," *American School Board Journal* (May 1914): 11.

Eisner, Elliot W. "Do American Students Need Standards?" Macie K. Southall Distinguished Lecture, Vanderbilt University, November 1992b.

———. "The Federal Reform of Schools: Looking for the Magic Bullet," *Phi Delta Kappan* (May 1992a): 722–723.

Fishel, H.W. "The Girl—How Educate Her?" *American School Board Journal* (February 1906): 21.

Glass, Gene V. "Standards and Criteria," *Journal of Educational Measurement* (Fall 1978): 237–261.

Gruenberg, Benjamin. "Some Economic Obstacles to Educational Progress," *The American Teacher* (September 1912): 90–91.

Hanushek, Eric A. "The Impact of Differential School Expenditures of School Performance," *Educational Researcher* (May 1989): 45–51.

———. *Making Schools Work*. Washington, DC: Brookings Institution, 1994.

Hartwell, E.C. "Muckraking the Public School," *American School Board Journal* (December 1912): 9.

Hazlett, James A. "A History of the National Assessment of Educational Progress, 1963–1973." Unpublished doctoral dissertation, 1974.

Ishizaka, Kazuo. "Japanese Education—The Myths and the Realities." In *Different Visions of the Future of Education*. Ottawa: Canadian Teachers Federation, 1994.

Journal of Education (July 3, 1919): 8–9. Unsigned commentary by "A Friend of the Editor."

Kristol, Irving. "Inevitable Outcome of 'Outcomes,'" *Wall Street Journal* (April 18, 1994).

Lynch, Ella Frances. "Is Our Public School System a Failure?" *Ladies Home Journal* (1912).

Mager, Robert. *Preparing Instructional Objectives*. Palo Alto, CA: Feardon Press, 1962.

Manno, Bruno V. "Goals 2000: Washington Knows Best," *Educational Excellence Network News and Views* (May 1994): 57–58.

National Commission on Excellence in Education. *A Nation At Risk.* Washington, DC: U.S. Department of Education, 1983.

Pirsig, Robert. *Zen and the Art of Motorcycle Maintenance.* New York: Morrow, 1974.

Ralphe, John H., and James Fennessy. "Science or Reform: Some Questions about the Effective Schools Model," *Phi Delta Kappan* (June 1983): 689–694.

Ravitch, Diane. *National Standards in American Education.* Washington, DC: Brookings Institution, 1995.

Resnick, Daniel P., and Laurie B. Resnick. "Improving Educational Standards in American Schools," *Phi Delta Kappan* (November 1993): 178–181.

Rothman, Robert. *Measuring Up.* San Francisco: Jossey-Bass, 1995.

Rowley, Glenn. "Historical Antecedents of the Standard Setting Debate: An Inside Account of the Minimal Beardedness Controversy," *Journal of Educational Measurement* (Summer 1982): 87–96.

Scott, Fred Newton. "Efficiency for Efficiency's Sake," *The School Review* (September 1914): 34–42.

Sears, Jesse. *The School Survey.* Boston: Houghton Mifflin, 1925.

Seligman, Daniel. "The Low Productivity of the Education Industry," *Fortune* (October 1958): 135.

Shepard, Lorrie A. "Setting Performance Standards." In Ronald A. Berk, ed. *A Guide to Criterion-Referenced Test Construction.* Baltimore: The Johns Hopkins University Press, 1980.

Spillane, Robert R. "Student Achievement Standards," *Education Week* (June 2, 1993): 36.

Starch, Daniel, and Edward C. Elliott. "Reliability of the Grading of High-School Work in English," *The School Review* (September 1912): 442–458.

Wiggins, Grant P. *Assessing Student Performance.* San Francisco: Jossey-Bass, 1993.

Wirtz, Willard, and Archie Lapointe. *Measuring the Quality of Education: A Report on Assessing Educational Progress,* Washington, DC: Wirtz & Lapointe, 1982.

Chapter Four

NOTES

1. Frankly speaking, although I do not subscribe to the conspiracy theories of Peg Luksik and her peers, I have considerable reservations about the role of business in education. I have written an article, "Schools Should Not Prepare Students for Work," arguing that such preparation is the job of business and industry and that they shouldn't be allowed to shirk it. The article repeats some of the arguments made in Chapter Three that most work is without intrinsic interest and that preparation for such work consists of teaching children to endure boredom. It is no accident that while anecdotes abound about employers' complaints that students lack basic skills, survey after survey actually finds that they do, indeed, worry most about attitudes. The situation was well captured in a "Frank and Ernest" cartoon in which a personnel officer tells Frank and Ernest, "What we want is someone who is smart enough to pass our aptitude tests and dumb enough to work for what we pay." That is a nasty and unavoidable fact of life, but schools have no business being a partner in preparing children for it.

2. Even now, having perused much literature of the Right, I feel obliged to mention that I am not making this up or presenting only unrepresentative views. Although apparently not a religious act, the Oklahoma City bombing indicates the depths to which the paranoid can descend in this country. Recall that both Pat Robertson and Jerry Falwell have declared "war" against the larger culture.

3. The Rand Corporation invented Planning by Objective (PBO), which the document apparently has confused with PPBO, the Program Planning and Budgeting Office of the U.S. Department of Education. PPBO is identified in the document as the ancestor of OBE.

REFERENCES

Ayres, Leonard P. "Measuring Educational Processes Through Educational Results," *The School Review* (May 1912): 300–309.

Bennett, William. "Remarks," *Educational Excellence Network News and Views* (February 1994): 1–2.

Bloom, Benjamin. *All Our Children Learning.* New York: McGraw-Hill, 1982.

—————. *Human Characteristics and School Learning.* New York: McGraw-Hill, 1976.

—————. In James H. Block, ed. *Mastery Learning: Theory and Practice.* New York: Holt, Rinehart and Winston, 1971.

Bloom, Benjamin H., M.D. Engelhart, Edward J. Furst, Walker H. Hill, and David R. Krathwohl. *Taxonomy of Educational Objectives: Cognitive and Affective Domains.* New York: David McKay, 1956.

Bobbitt, Franklin. "The Supervision of City Schools." In *Twelfth NSSE Yearbook*. Bloomington, IL: National Society for the Study of Education, 1913.

Brittain, Horace. "The Financial Relations of Boards of Education to Municipal Governments," *American School Board Journal* (March, 1919): 4.

Carroll, John B. "A Model of School Learning," *Teachers College Record* (May, 1963): 723–733.

Cooper, William J. *Economy in Education.* Palo Alto, CA: Stanford University Press, 1933.

Cubberly, Elwood P. *Public School Administration in the United States.* Boston: Houghton Mifflin, 1919.

Dewey, John. *Democracy and Education.* New York: Macmillan, 1916.

Ellis, Arthur, and Jeffrey Fouts. *Research on Educational Innovations.* Princeton, NJ: Eye on Education, 1993.

Goodlad, John. *Toward Education Communities.* Seattle: University of Washington, 1992.

Lehman, Darrin, Richard Lempert, and Richard Nisbet. "The Effects of Graduate Training on Reasoning," *American Psychologist* (June 1988): 431–443.

Levin, Henry. "Educational Performance Standards: Image or Substance," *Journal of Educational Measurement* (Winter 1978): 309–319.

Lynd, Robert. *Middletown in Transition.* New York: Harcourt Brace and World, 1937.

Marzano, J. Robert. "When Two Worldviews Collide," *Educational Leadership* (December/January 1994).

Nightingale, A.F. "Report of the Chairman," *The School Review* (September 1896): 416–423.

Patrick, James R. *Research Manual: America 2000/Goals 2000—Moving the Nation Educationally to a "New World Order."* Moline, IL: Citizens for Academic Excellence, 1994.

Raubinger, Frederick M., Harold G. Rowe, Donald L. Piper, and Charles K. West. *The Development of Secondary Education.* London: The Macmillan Company, 1969.

Scott, Fred Newton. "Efficiency for Efficiency's Sake," *The School Review* (September 1914).

Schlafly, Phyllis. "My Seven Objections to Student Outcomes," *The School Administrator* (September 1994): 26–27.

Slavin, Robert. "Mastery Learning Reconsidered: A Best-Evidence Synthesis," *Review of Educational Research* (Summer 1987): 175–213.

Spady, William. "Competency Based Education: A Bandwagon in Search of a Definition," *Educational Researcher* (January 1977): 9–14.

————. *Outcomes Based Education: Critical Issues and Answers.* Arlington, VA: American Association of School Administrators, 1994.

Spaulding, Frank. *National Education Association Proceedings,* 1913.

Tompkins, Ellsworth, and Walter Gaumnitz. "The Carnegie Unit: Its Origin, Status and Trends." Washington, DC: U.S. Department of Health, Education and Welfare Bulletin No. 7 (1954): 4–19. Reprinted in Raubinger et al., *The Development of Secondary Education.* Toronto: Collier-Macmillan, 1969.

Epilogue

NOTES

1. If one wishes to see the effects of such authenticity and some of its outcomes in teachers and students alike, one can do worse than to watch Fred Wiseman's film, *High School II*, a valentine to Deborah Meier and her Central Park East Secondary School. Wiseman's portrayal, which originally aired on the Public Broadcasting System, is all the more remarkable given that Wiseman is not only America's premier documentary film maker but also a man who is usually critical, even caustic, in his cinematic treatment of American institutions. Twenty-five years earlier, Wiseman had painted a suburban Philadelphia school with such colors that the movie, *High School*, was banned by court injunction within a 75-mile radius of the city.

2. For what it is worth, I think Jim Herndon's treatise is the best book ever written about schools. Jim had been teaching low-ability middle school students for 13 years at the time of publication and continued for another 15 years. Independent of its wisdom in talking about schools, the book is exquisitely written and guaranteed to evoke strong emotions. If you get through it without laughing out loud, check your pulse: you might be dead. It should have garnered a Pulitzer prize.

3. It would probably be a good undertaking to try to reconceptualize the notion of the "disciplined mind" in more contemporary terms. Similarly, attention should be paid to what observable behaviors might reflect the qualities described by Israel Sheffler in Chapter Four.

4. To judge from the frequency with which I hear anecdotes, I believe I may be the only person in the nation who has never encountered a high school graduate who can't make change. Or, perhaps the presence of this creature might turn out to be similar to the construction of "the lists."

REFERENCES

Belter, Cathy. Presentation to the Alliance for Curriculum Reform, August 24, 1995.

Berliner, David C., and Bruce J. Biddle. *The Manufactured Crisis: Myths, Fraud, and the Attack on America's Public Schools*. New York: Addison-Wesley, 1995.

Bettelheim, Bruno. "The Ignored Lesson of Anne Frank," *Harper's* (November 1960).

Bracey, Gerald W. "The Fifth Bracey Report on the Condition of Public Education," *Phi Delta Kappan* (October 1995): 147–155.

—————. "The Fourth Bracey Report on the Condition of Public Education," *Phi Delta Kappan* (October 1994a): 115–127.

—————. "The Media's Myth of School Failure," *Educational Leadership* (September 1994b): 80–84.

—————. "The Second Bracey Report on the Condition of Public Education," *Phi Delta Kappan* (October 1992): 104–117.

—————. "The Third Bracey Report on the Condition of Public Education," *Phi Delta Kappan* (October 1993): 104–117.

—————. *Transforming America's Schools: an R for Getting Past Blame*. Arlington, VA: American Association of School Administrators, 1994.

—————. "Why Can't They Be Like We Were?" *Phi Delta Kappan* (October 1991): 104–117.

Education at a Glance. Paris: Organization for Economic Cooperation and Development, 1993.

Elam, Stanley M., and Lowell C. Rose. "The Twenty-Seventh Annual Phi Delta Kappa/Gallup Poll Survey of the Public's Attitudes Towards the Public Schools," *Phi Delta Kappan* (September 1995): 41–56.

First Things First. New York: Public Agenda, 1994.

Herndon, James. *How to Survive in Your Native Land*. New York: Simon & Schuster, 1971.

Kozol, Jonathan. *Savage Inequalities*. New York: Crown, 1991.

Meier, Deborah. "Reinventing Teaching," *Teachers College Review* (Summer 1993): 594–605.

O'Neill, Barry. "Anatomy of a Hoax," *New York Times Magazine* (March 6, 1994): 46–49.

Topolnicki, Denise. "Why Private Schools Are Rarely Worth the Money," *Money* (October 1994): 98–112.

Traiman, Susan. Presentation to the Alliance for Curriculum Reform, August 24, 1995.

White, Richard Grant. "The Public School Failure," *North American Review* (December 1880): 537–550. Reprinted in Carl H. Gross and Charles C. Chandler, eds. *The History of Education Through Readings.* Boston: D.C. Heath and Company, 1964.

Abbreviations

AASA:	American Association of School Administrators
ACT:	American College Testing
AERA:	American Educational Research Association
AFT:	American Federation of Teachers
AIT:	Agency for Instructional Technology
AP:	Advanced Placement
APA:	American Psychological Association
ASBJ:	American School Board Journal
ASCD:	Association for Supervision and Curriculum Development
BES:	Best Evidence Synthesis
CBE:	Council for Basic Education; also, competency-based education
CCSSO:	Council of Chief State School Officers
CEE:	Center on Education and the Economy
CEEB:	College Entrance Examination Board
CLASS:	Center on Learning, Assessment, and School Structure
CPI:	Consumer Price Index
CRESST:	Center for Research in Evaluation, Standards, and Student Testing
CRT:	criterion-referenced tests
CSSO:	Chief State School Officer(s)
CU:	Carnegie Unit
ECAPE:	Exploratory Committee on the Assessment of Progress in Education
ECS:	Education Commission of the States
EQA:	Educational Quality Assessment
ESEA:	Elementary and Secondary Education Act
ETS:	Educational Testing Service
FSM:	Free Speech Movement
"g" factor:	general factor
GAO:	General Accounting Office
GATT:	General Agreement on Tariffs and Trade
GED:	general equivalency diploma
GNP:	Gross National Product
GRE:	Graduate Record Examination
IAEP:	International Assessment of Educational Progress
IEP:	Individual Education Plan
The Iowas:	ITBS, ITED (see below)
IQ:	intelligence quotient
ITBS:	Iowa Tests of Basic Skills
ITED:	Iowa Tests of Educational Development

Law of WYTIWYG:	What You Test Is What You Get
MCT:	minimum competency test
ML:	Mastery Learning
NAEP:	National Assessment of Educational Progress
NAESP:	National Association of Elementary School Principals
NAGB:	National Assessment Governing Board
NASDC:	New American Schools Development Corporation
NASSP:	National Association of Secondary School Principals
NCES:	National Center for Education Statistics
NCEST:	National Council on Educational Standards and Testing
NCME:	National Council for Measurement in Education
NCTM:	National Council of Teachers of Mathematics
NDEA:	National Defense Education Act
NEA:	National Education Association
NESIC:	National Education Standards and Improvement Council
NGA:	National Governors' Association
NRT:	norm-referenced test
NSF:	National Science Foundation
NSSE:	National Society for the Study of Education
OBE:	outcomes-based education
OECD:	Organization for Economic Cooperation and Development
OPEC:	Organization of Petroleum Exporting Countries
OTL:	opportunity to learn
"p" value:	proportion of students getting the item right on a test
PBO:	Planning by Objective
PDK:	Phi Delta Kappa
PEA:	Progressive Education Association
PPBO:	Program Planning and Budgeting Office
PSSC:	Physical Science Study Committee
SAT	Scholastic Aptitude Test; after 1993, Scholastic Assessment Test
SCANS	Secretary's Commission on Achieving Necessary Skills
SRA:	Science Research Associates
SREB:	Southern Regional Education Board
TQM:	Total Quality Management